POPE JOHN PAUL II
AND
THE CATHOLIC
RESTORATION

POPE JOHN PAUL II
AND
THE CATHOLIC
RESTORATION

Paul Johnson

SERVANT BOOKS
Ann Arbor, Michigan

Cover photo by Karsh of Ottowa (*Camera Press*)

Trade paperback edition published by
Servant Books, Box 8617, Ann Arbor, Michigan 48107.

ISBN 0-89283-183-9

Printed in the United States of America

1 2 3 4 5 6 7 8 9 10 88 87 86 85 84

The hardcover edition was published by
St. Martin's Press, New York.

This book is dedicated to
my friends and colleagues at
the American Enterprise Institute
for Public Policy Research,
in grateful recollection

'And I will restore to you the years that
the locust hath eaten'

The Book of Joel 2.25

Contents

Part One

THE MAKING OF A POPE

I

The Forge

THE ROMAN CATHOLIC CHURCH is a divine autocracy. Its direction is centred in the personality of its sovereign pontiff, the Bishop of Rome, whose teaching from his episcopal chair (*ex cathedra*) has traditionally been regarded by Catholics as divinely inspired, and so infallible, when touching on faith and morals.[1] This belief was formulated as dogma at the First Vatican Council (1869-70), and reaffirmed by the Second Vatican Council (1962-5) in its Dogmatic Constitution *Lumen Gentium* (1964). It states that the bishops of the church form an order analogous to the apostolic college of St Peter and the other apostles, in which the primacy of the Roman Pontiff, as St Peter's successor, remains intact.[2]

The health of the church and the character of its pontiffs are thus constitutionally linked. Catholics believe that the College of Cardinals, in electing each pope, is guided by the Holy Spirit, so that Divine Providence participates in their collective decision. There is a general belief, too, that Providence watches closely over the childhood and career of a man destined to be pope, shaping them to its inscrutable purposes. Just as the early years of a future canonized saint are illuminated by the roseate light of foreknowledge in his hagiography, so the *curriculum vitae* of a pope is selectively edited and adorned, by friends, relatives, teachers and associates. Acts of piety are stressed, virtues heightened, the trivial or insignificant transformed into portents and foreshadowings. Gradually the bare bones of biographical narrative take on the incrustations of imaginative piety. The historian must sift through this material, not indeed in any cynical spirit, but with respectful sobriety.

All the same, in looking at the life of Karol Wojtyla, Pope John

Paul II, it is difficult to dismiss entirely the notion of a providential destiny. As pope, he has repeatedly referred to Auschwitz as 'the Golgotha of the modern world', the stage chosen by history for the representative enactment, in our age, of the Christian drama of suffering and redemption. There, the consequences of enormous sin were made manifest in this world; and there, the human heart was able, from time to time, to raise itself above that scene of unprecedented wickedness, and turn unspeakable horror into spiritual beauty. The analogy of Golgotha applies with equal force and on a larger scale to Poland as a whole, a sacrificial nation whose dolours have been unrivalled in our time. Karol Wojtyla's childhood and adolescence coincided with the brief, doomed moment of Polish independence: his early manhood with its savage martyrdom under the Nazis; his maturity with the long struggle to breathe under the suppressive tyranny of Soviet-imposed Communism. Nurtured in the very hothouse of suffering, acquainted with grief and forearmed against misfortune, this man born in the eye of the world's storm seemed peculiarly equipped by experience to be summoned to the chair of Peter at a moment of crisis in Roman Catholicism.

For a century and a half before 1918 Poland had had no existence as a nation. Karol Wojtyla was born on 18 May 1920, at Wadowice, in the foothills of the Carpathians, about thirty miles from Cracow. Three months later on the Feast of the Assumption, 15 August, the Poles secured the independence of their new state by winning the Battle of Warsaw, the so-called 'Miracle of the Vistula', against Leninist Russia. For a further nineteen precarious years the new state maintained itself, first as a bourgeois democracy, latterly as a military dictatorship, before being engulfed in the Second World War and its totalitarian aftermath.

Wadowice was then a town of 9,000 people. Wojtyla was baptized in the parish church on 20 June 1920. Against the entry which records it, successive parish priests have noted his progress in the church: priest, 1 November 1946; bishop, 28 November 1958; archbishop, 30 December 1963; cardinal, 26 June 1967; pope, 16 October 1978. By birth Wojtyla belonged to the lower middle class. His father, Karol Wojtyla, was a commissioned quartermaster in the army, an administrative official of no great social or military consequence. His mother, Emilia Kaczorowska, had been a school-teacher, and after marriage she took in sewing to contribute to the family income. The flat in which they lived was old but respectable – it had running water.[3]

The family's existence was hard-working, church-going, ambitious, but dogged by misfortune. Wojtyla's elder brother Edward, fifteen years his senior, was a gifted pupil who qualified as a doctor. Wojtyla himself was, according to the testimony we now have, an exemplary boy at school. One teacher, Father Zacher, states: 'He was the nearest thing to a genius I ever had the good fortune to teach.'[4] A surviving photograph, taken at primary school, shows a close-cropped little boy; he had, said Father Zacher, 'a sad, intelligent face'. There was much to be sad about. His younger sister died as an infant. In 1929, when he was nine, his mother succumbed to heart disease. Four years later his brother Edward, now working in a hospital, was swept away by a scarlet-fever epidemic. Wojtyla himself and his lonely, disappointed father, retired and living on an exiguous lieutenant's pension, were all that remained of the family.

Yet it does not seem that Wojtyla's childhood was dispirited. He was strong, healthy, industrious, clever, extroverted and gregarious – characteristics he has retained. He played football, went swimming and canoeing on the Skawa River. He walked, and later climbed and learned to ski, in the mountains. Skiing, indeed, became and remained a passion, and he learned and still speaks the dialect of the mountaineers, the Gorals. At the grammar school he attended from 1931 he showed outstanding aptitude for language, both the classics (he can still quote from memory passages of Homer and Virgil) and modern tongues, including and above all his own Polish. He also developed the capacity for abstract reasoning which is his great intellectual strength, delving into the obscurities of Kant's *Critique of Pure Reason* while still a schoolboy.

Hence he had no difficulty in qualifying for university, and in 1938, on the eve of war, father and son moved to Cracow so that Wojtyla could attend the great Jagiellonian University. This is the pearl and pride of Polish culture, dating from 1364 and, after Prague, the oldest university in east-central Europe. Among its *alumni* are Nikolaj Kopernik, or Copernicus, the early sixteenth-century astronomer and author of *De Revolutionibus Orbium Caelestium*, who made the first major Polish contribution to the corpus of Western knowledge; Johann Faustus, the original of one of the most persistent of European myths; and Lenin, the assassin of Europe's *ancien régime*, who, though never registered as a student, was a regular reader in the university library in the years 1912-14. Cracow is a city of haunting and fragile beauty, which the harrow of modern times, raking the rest of Poland so unmercifully, has somehow spared. There, on the far perimeter of the West, the late Gothic and the Baroque left a series of masterpieces, grouped around the vast Market Square and the *massif* of cathedral, palace and castle. The ancient university is part of this complex. It is without a trace of orientalism; it breathes the rationalism and humanity of the West.

The point is important, for the Poles have always been and are now more than ever anxious not to be corralled into a vague entity called 'Eastern Europe', and judged (or rather condemned) by its supposed standards. The Poles, and the Pope among them, are fond of pointing out that a stone in a Warsaw park marks the exact centre of the geographical entity called Europe. In one of the last articles he wrote before his election, Wojtyla stressed that Europe is a much larger and wider concept than the nations which compose the European Economic Community and belong to Nato.[5] There is an abiding fear among the Poles that history, which has been so cruel to them, will in some way be allowed to lock them out of the lighted circle of Western civilization and relegate them permanently to an orientalism they have always hated and resisted. The Jagiellonian is the gracious symbol of this resistance, and there Wojtyla absorbed its cultural ethic and programme.

For his main studies he chose Polish language and literature, mainly it seems because to do so allowed him the fullest scope for what was already a passion: the theatre. The histrionic tastes of the future pope have struck some as strange. Not so: the theatrical and the religious urge (and, indeed, the political urge) are closely related. All theatre has its origins in religious ceremonial; from the sacred dances of the Old Kingdom of Egypt, more than two and a half millennia before the birth of Christ, we can trace the first, distant adumbrations of a secular stage. Between dramaturgy and liturgy the dividing line is narrow. It remained so until the early modern age. For not only did the European drama evolve medieval mystery plays, but the theatrical content of the Catholic religion was powerfully and deliberately reinforced during the Counter-Reformation of the late sixteenth century. Roman orthodoxy stressed the histrionic not least to differentiate itself from the drabness and austerity of Calvinism.[6] Wherever it held the power, the church encouraged the Baroque; it patronized the theatrical art of Tintoretto, Veronese, Caravaggio, El Greco; it pressed the secular courts within its orbit to finance the burgeoning drama. The Jesuits, the court clerics *par excellence*, were foremost in legitimizing the theatre and encouraging academic performances in their proliferating colleges and universities. Poland, as an outpost of the Counter-Reformation, and Cracow as its cultural centre and capital, did not neglect the drama as an ideological weapon (even today Cracow has a dozen theatres). The stage was an arena where Polish Catholicism and nationalism learnt to differentiate themselves, in spectacular fashion, from Prussian Lutheranism and Russian Orthodoxy. The Counter-Reformation drama developed almost imperceptibly into the quasi-underground Polish national theatre of the nineteenth century, which briefly surfaced in the years between the wars, only to descend to the underground again during the Nazi occupation.

Karol Wojtyla was drawn to the theatre by his natural talents as well as by his religious and national upbringing. He was a fine and enthusiastic dancer of mazurkas, polonaises, krakowiaks and folk ballets, moving gracefully for such a well-built, powerful man. He has, to this day, an unmistakable presence: he seems to command the area around his body. Above all, he has a rich and expressive baritone voice, which in youth (we are told) had sweetness and pathos. The voice is paramount in Polish theatre, which learnt in the nineteenth century to operate clandestinely, with the minimum of props, lighting and machinery, performing if necessary in private houses. Wojtyla belonged to 'The Theatre of the Spoken Word', whose only aid was a piano. Writing in the weekly *Tygodnik Powszechny* under the pen-name Andrzej Jawien, he later praised the discipline of this dramatic form:

It prevents the young actor from indulging in a pernicious individualism, for it forces strict discipline on him. .... [It] requires a subordination of

7

the actor to the dictates of the great poetic word. This becomes particularly evident when the word expands in faultlessly spoken choral scenes. A group of people unanimously, as it were, subjected to the poetic word has a sort of ethical significance: solidarity and loyalty to the word.[7]

That is a very Polish expression; in Poland, play-acting is never far from moral and national values. In 1939, after the three-week destruction of the Polish armed forces, and the Fourth Partition of the country – this time between the rival atheisms of Hitler and Stalin – it was natural for the theatre to go underground again. Indeed it had no choice. Hitler was determined to destroy the Polish nation: 'I shall make Poland a forgotten name on old maps.' To him, the Poles were *Untermenschen*, sub-human. They were to be, as his Governor-General, Hans Frank, put it, 'slaves of the Reich'. For this purpose all expression of Polish culture was erased. Education was forbidden. Universities, even schools, ceased to function legally. Most of the teachers at the Jagiellonian were taken to Sachsenhausen concentration camp, from which they never emerged alive.[8] Against this background, Wojtyla and his closest literary friend, Juliusz Kydrynski, organized an underground version of their theatrical club which they called the Teatr Rapsody-czny (Rhapsody Theatre). Like the university itself, which also went underground, it led a difficult and precarious existence. But it was a matter of pride to Wojtyla and his colleagues that they contrived to stage twenty-two performances of Polish classics in private houses and apartments.

The shadows, however, soon encompassed him. In 1940 an able-bodied Polish male caught by Nazi police patrols without an *Arbeitskarte* (work card) was liable to instant deportation as a slave labourer. Hence, in the winter Wojtyla found himself a labouring job in a stone-quarry at Zakrzowek. The conditions were atrocious. The quarrymen worked in the open in inadequate clothing; to avoid frostbite they smeared grease or vaseline on their hands and faces. Wojtyla thought himself lucky when he was promoted shot-firer and allowed to work part of the time in a hut. Yet in some ways he found the experience rewarding. He became interested in stone as a material and as an image. Some years later, when he was already a priest, the curiously intimate relationship between man and stone, which formed the basis of our first culture, provided the theme of his longest and most striking poem, 'The Quarry'. The symbolism of stone, the notion that a church, as a building, and the church, as a society, are 'living stones', recur in his sermons. Another poem, 'Marble Floor', written about the pavement in St Peter's, meditates upon the New Testament text, *tu es Petrus*.[9] The idea of man acting upon a stone and in a sense animating it, while preserving the absolute distinction between human life and matter, became for him an important illustration of the existentialist philosophy he was shortly to embrace.

Moreover, working in the quarry, and in a chemical factory to which he moved in 1941, gave him a practical insight into the world of the industrial worker, which few priests possess, and certainly no pope before him. Wojtyla later investigated the worker-priest movement in France, and came to the conclusion that its dangers outweighed its undoubted merits since it undermined the sacramental nature of the priesthood – a view which, as pope, he has made authoritative. But he was grateful for his own industrial experience because it set him to exploring the concept of alienation brought about by the modern industrial process, a central element in Marxist philosophy and one to which Wojtyla himself has given an original and Christian vector. Alienation and powerlessness is the theme of several of his poems, such as 'The Car Factory Worker' and 'The Armaments Factory Worker'.[10]

As the war spread, and conditions in Poland grew progressively more horrifying, Wojtyla's own life took on a note almost of desperation. In 1941 his father died, leaving him without close relations. That winter he was knocked down by a tram and nearly crushed to death by a lorry, as he lay unconscious in the road. His skull was fractured and the stoop in his shoulders still reflects the gravity and pain of this accident. Slowly recuperating, Wojtyla made friends with a lay evangelist called Jan Tyranowski who, like his own grandfather, was a tailor. Tyranowski, who organized a 'rosary circle' in his flat, seems to have aroused contradictory feelings in those who knew him. He made, however, a profound impression on Wojtyla, who became chairman of the tailor's youth club and later described him, in a magazine article he entitled 'The Apostle'.[11] It was at this point, in 1942, that the combination of personal misfortunes and national tragedy, the reflections they provoked, and the talks with Tyranowski, persuaded Wojtyla that he had a vocation for the priesthood. The Jagiellonian was still functioning after a fashion, albeit illegally, and he was able to transfer to its theological school.

At this time Wojtyla was immersed in the poetry and mystical writings of St John of the Cross, the sixteenth-century Spanish Carmelite reformer. His first thought, after deciding his vocation was valid, was to become a Carmelite himself. The ecclesiastical authorities decided otherwise. They seem to have regarded him from the start as an outstanding candidate for the priesthood, with excellent potential: in Poland an able, right-thinking young man is always eyed by the church with a view to the hierarchy and steered away from the contemplative orders. So Wojtyla began training as a secular priest. In the circumstances, the Cracow seminary functioned surprisingly well. Wojtyla's existence was of course illegal, and he lived in a series of priest's 'hiding holes' in private houses. His name also figured on a Nazi blacklist on account of his activities on behalf of the Jewish community in Cracow and its neighbourhood. As recorded in the archives of the Anti-Defamation League of B'nai Brith, the Jewish organization, he belonged to an underground group which took Jewish families out of the ghettos, gave them new identity papers and, if necessary, found them hiding places.[12] This was very dangerous work indeed, but Wojtyla had witnessed the treatment of Jews at the quarry and in the chemical works, and he knew of the fate that awaited them in Auschwitz and elsewhere. Indeed, as the war progressed, the likelihood that Hitler intended to exterminate the entire Polish nation, as well as the Jews, increased. On 6 August 1944, following the Warsaw rising, the Nazis rounded up all males in Cracow between the ages of fifteen and fifty, and shot them without trial. Wojtyla narrowly evaded the death-net, and thereafter Monsignor Adam Sapieha, the Prince-Archbishop of Cracow, hid him and four other seminarians in his crumbling palace, which enjoyed a certain degree of immunity from Nazi house searches.

Prince Sapieha evidently thought highly of Wojtyla, whom he had the pleasure of ordaining on 1 November, All Saints' Day, 1946. The new priest, aged twenty-six, afterwards celebrated his

first masses in memory of his father, mother and brother, in the
crypt of St Leonard in Wawel Castle, among the tombs of the
Polish kings. The Prince seems to have been determined to give
Wojtyla the best possible preparation for high rank in the church.
He sent him to Rome to take a doctorate in divinity at the Pontifical
University, known as the Angelicum, run by the Dominicans. In
the vacations he made it possible for Wojtyla to travel widely in
Western Europe, both to broaden his outlook and to study pastoral
methods. At the Angelicum, in those days a temple of theological
orthodoxy, he worked under the Irish theologian Father Michael
(later Cardinal) Brown and the French Thomist Father Réginald
Garrigou-Lagrange. He delighted in Aquinas: 'His entire philosophy is so marvellously beautiful, so delightful and, at the same
time, so uncomplicated.'[13] Staying at the Belgian College, he
formed a friendship with a Flemish priest, Father Marcel Eulem-
broeck, secretary of a young workers' organization, the Jeunesse
Ouvrière Chrétienne, and it was under this auspice that he visited
France, Belgium and the Netherlands. These countries were then
(shortly before Pope Pius XII condemned theological adventurism
in his encyclical *Humani Generis*, 1950) rich in doctrinal and pastoral innovation. Though he had now abandoned any idea of
becoming a Carmelite, Wojtyla kept in touch with the order, which
published his first collection of verse, *Song of the Hidden God*, in
one of its publications (March 1946); and his interest in St John of
the Cross bore fruit in his doctoral thesis, which dealt with the
doctrinal concept of faith in St John's work. This particular study
has had a notable influence on Wojtyla's mature moral philosophy,
as I shall demonstrate later. At the time, the thesis enabled him
to obtain his doctorate, *magna cum laude*, in April 1948, the
degree being confirmed by the Jagiellonian in December the same
year.

On his return to Poland he served for three years as a parochial
clergyman, first in Niegowic, then in the parish of St Florian in
Cracow itself. It is a characteristic of Catholicism in post-war
Poland that there is an insatiable demand for new churches; and it
is a characteristic of the regime that it does everything in its
considerable power to prevent them from being built. At Niegowic,
Father Wojtyla successfully outwitted the authorities, mainly by

using volunteer labour, and put up the first of the churches he was to see consecrated by his efforts. He thus early established a reputation for administrative vigour. This was confirmed by the speed and thoroughness with which he set up parochial institutions and societies in a country just emerging from the bewildering horrors of attempted genocide. In these years Wojtyla formed the conviction that the family as the Christian unit, and the parish as the ecclesiastical unit, are the two indispensable elements in a Catholic polity, to which all other considerations must yield precedence. This remains the essence of his approach to church governance as pope. It is to him strange that any priest could be considered ready for senior office without thorough parochial experience.

However, the church in Poland has a complex strategy of survival. One of its objects since 1945 has been to establish a position of intellectual stature, even eminence, not so much within the Catholic Church as a whole - though this is certainly an important consideration - as in relation to the aggressive secular state which seeks to loosen its hold on Polish minds. Its prize institution is Lublin University, the only Catholic centre of higher education in the entire Communist world. It guards Lublin with jealous pride, and constantly furnishes it with its best talents, as students and teachers. In 1951 Wojtyla was granted sabbatical leave to resume his studies at the Jagiellonian, with a view to preparing himself for an eventual professorship at Lublin. He now turned to the philosophical studies which had been increasingly preoccupying him, and in particular to the attempt to reconcile existentialism, the leading philosophical mode on the Continent in the immediate post-war period, with Christianity.[14] He was particularly interested in the form of descriptive psychology known as phenomenology, developed by Edmund Husserl and his school. One of these thinkers became the subject of his philosophical thesis, entitled 'On the possibility of grounding Catholic ethics on the system of Max Scheler'.[15] This occupied him during the years 1952-8 and it was published in 1960 by Lublin University Press. In the meantime he had been lecturing in social ethics at the Cracow Theological Seminary (the Theology School of Cracow University had been closed down by the government in 1954). In 1956 he was appointed Professor of Ethics at Lublin, a chair which, in a technical sense, he still occupies. The impact of existentialism and phenomenology on Wojtyla's thinking about human behaviour has been considerable, and I will discuss it in later sections of this book. What should be noted at this stage is that, during the 1950s, Wojtyla established himself as one of Poland's leading ethical philosophers, with a reputation throughout the Catholic Church on the Continent, and indeed even beyond Catholic circles. His name became well known at international gatherings of phenomenologists. In Lublin he also established himself as an academic administrator, creating a new department of patristic studies.[16]

During these years, however, Wojtyla continued to do a great deal of pastoral work, chiefly in Cracow. He became a leading figure in the archdiocese. It was never the intention of the church authorities to lose him to academia. On 4 July 1958, when he was still only thirty-eight, he was appointed auxiliary bishop of Cracow, with the titular see of Ombi. As Poland's youngest bishop he took over much of the routine labour of this huge and growing archdiocese. When Monsignor Baziak, its elderly archbishop, died in 1962, Wojtyla was elected Vicar Capitular, or chief administrator, of the see, and on 30 December 1963 Pope Paul VI made him Archbishop of Cracow in name as well as in fact. This splendid appointment would have gratified his predecessor, Prince Sapieha, who had early recognized in Wojtyla a young man of outstanding gifts: for he was now, in his early forties, a major figure in the Polish church, indeed in Christendom as a whole. Inevitably, too, he was a principal actor in the continuing drama of church and state in Poland.

This has a very long history, of which the Poles are acutely conscious, for the church has been involved from the start in the emergence of a Polish national identity. The first baptized Polish kings, in the tenth century, sought the help of the church in establishing their independence of the German Emperor. In 972 Mieszko I sent Pope John XIII the hair of his son Boleslaw, born in 965, when it was ceremonially cut off on reaching the age of seven. Receiving the homage of a child's hair meant accepting moral parenthood for him, and Boleslaw, to whom we owe this story, all his life regarded himself as a vassal of St Peter. Polish kings paid homage to the papacy for the entire country, as a means of securing papal protection against the Emperor, and this was expressed in the collection and dispatch of Peter's Pence.[17]

It must be conceded that some of the links in the chain of evidence identifying Roman Catholicism with Polish nationalism are fragile. St Stanislas, the eleventh-century Bishop of Cracow who is the patron saint of Polish nationalism, is one of those mysterious early-medieval figures, like England's Edward the Confessor, whose biographical details were manipulated by later hagiographers to suit their own politico-ecclesiastical purposes. Boleslaw II, ruler of Poland, condemned the bishop to *truncatio membrorum*, and as a result Stanislas died on 11 April 1079. Latin Christendom was at that time plunged in the investiture contest between Pope Gregory VII and the Emperor Henry IV. As Boleslaw was a bitter enemy of the Emperor, we must presume that Bishop Stanislas was not a papalist, may indeed have been one of those bishops who supported the secular power against the new claims of the clerical order.[18] However, in the late twelfth century, stories about Stanislas, a brave bishop martyred for standing up to the secular power and rebuking a wicked king for his scandalous life, became conflated with the doings of St Thomas à Becket of Canterbury. By the early thirteenth century the Polish church had become a symbol of national unity. The chronicles of Master Vincent from about 1220 onwards gave the Poles a homogeneous account of its legends and traditions to explain its unity and its destiny. In 1249 Bishop Bogufal of Poznan set down in writing a dream in which the coming of Polish unity, with the help of the papacy, was predicted. The symbol of this revival was the canonization of St Stanislas, Bishop and Martyr, by Pope Innocent IV – a clericalist fire-eater – on 17 September 1253.[19] From that day to this, St Stanislas has occupied a central place in the Polish national epic, and he figures frequently in the invocations and prayers of Karol Wojtyla (who is, of course, aware of the complex historiography).

The papacy has not always, however, been a faithful friend to Polish nationalism: far from it. Vatican policy was to support the three iniquitous partitions, by Austria, Prussia and Russia, which dismembered Poland in the late eighteenth century, and it opposed the Kosciuszko revolt in 1794, in which three bishops met violent ends. In the early nineteenth century the popes put obedience to legally established authority before self-determination, and even supported Tsarist Orthodoxy in suppressing the Polish Catholics. By the 1860s, however, when the Poles rose once more, the Catholic Church was again identified with Polish nationalism. When the Polish state was founded in 1918, its interests were generally aligned with the church's. The concordat of 1921 limited taxation on church property (which included over a million acres of agricultural land), gave a number of legal privileges to the clergy and exemption from conscription, and made the teaching of religion compulsory in all schools.

However, inter-war Poland, where the church was not only free but privileged, was in essential respects less 'Catholic' than post-war Communist Poland. It is important to grasp this point, because it is a key to the present vitality of the Polish church and the influence it now exercises within world Catholicism. Inter-war Poland was a huge and heterogeneous state. Only two-thirds of her twenty-seven million population were actually Poles. There were over three million Jews, and huge minorities of Germans, Lithuanians, Russians and Ukrainians. In addition to the religious minorities formed by the Lutherans and the Russian Orthodox, the Ukrainian Uniates, though in communion with Rome, had a liturgy and tradition totally different from those of the Polish Latin Catholics, to whom they were incorrigibly hostile. Poland was internally a country deeply divided by race, culture and religion, and this was one cause of its downfall.

The Poland which emerged in the post-war period was smaller in area but a much more homogeneous country. Hitler had virtually destroyed Polish Jewry. To strengthen Russia's European frontier, Stalin had moved the whole of Poland west. The Poles were allowed to drive out the German inhabitants of their new 'western territories', as well as the old German minority of pre-war Poland. As a result, the Lutherans, too, were virtually eliminated. The Baltic shore, which had been Protestant since the sixteenth century, became Catholic; thus the Lutheran cathedral of Danzig (now Gdansk) passed into Catholic hands and the mass was again celebrated there for the first time in nearly four centuries. At the same time, in the East, Stalin annexed vast stretches of pre-war Polish territory, and with it nearly all the Orthodox and Ukrainian-Uniate populations, most of the Polish Catholics from these areas being driven to the West. Thus a succession of brutal and arbitrary events solved, or rather eliminated, Poland's minority problems, and turned it into the most homogeneous Catholic state on earth. Of course the immediately apparent contrast with pre-war Poland was that the church, far from being a legally privileged entity under a concordat, was now the object of systematic hostility, indeed persecution, by the state. To this day, no new concordat has been signed, nor any general constitutional agreement giving the church a legally secure position. In a totalitarian state, where a body without legal status is, *ipso facto*, treated as an enemy of society, this is a grievous handicap. Indeed it is plain that, in 1945, the architects of the new Communist regime intended to destroy Catholicism completely and believed it was possible to do so. During the war 30 per cent of the clergy had been murdered. The church had lost nearly all its property. It was now deprived of its schools, and of the opportunity to conduct any religious instruction within the framework of the public system of education. Many of its churches had been destroyed or damaged. It was almost impossible to get permits to rebuild or repair them, let alone to build new churches made necessary by the vast upheavals in population. Laws specifically framed to entrap clerical opponents were applied with rigour. When Wojtyla began work on his philosophical thesis, Polish prisons held over 900 priests and eight bishops, including Archbishop Baziak himself (he was then the papal representative in Poland). Wojtyla's first course of lectures on ethics, to the seminarians at Cracow, was conducted underground, as in wartime under the Nazis.

Progressively, however, the sheer weight of Polish Catholicism began to tell against a regime which, from the start, was narrowly based and unsuccessful. Each time the government aroused the open anger of the population by its economic failures, it was forced to turn to the Catholic hierarchy for assistance in urging restraint on opposition forces. Its attempt to create a rival power-centre to the hierarchy, in the shape of the pseudo-Catholic Pax movement, under Boleslaw Piasecki, was a failure.[20] The Catholic bishops were gradually released from gaol as the 1950s progressed. They proved willing to assist the regime, *in extremis*, but naturally extracted a price. The first unofficial agreement between church and government came during the 1956 crisis; thereafter, the church gradually strengthened its institutional position, working through informal deals, through Catholic deputies in the Sejm, the Polish parliament, and opposition groupings, which invariably took on a Catholic colouration.[21]

As a result, the church not only kept its own university but was able to expand its seminaries and so its numbers of full-time workers. By the 1960s, the Catholic clergy was back to its pre-war strength of 18,000, with far higher educational standards. With 6,558 parishes, a figure of one priest for every 2,300 faithful was maintained. The percentage of vocations became much higher than in the pre-war period, and by 1970 there were 4,070 students in Polish seminaries, as against 2,078 in 1937. The number of religious, chiefly nuns, grew from about 22,000 in 1939 to over 36,500 in 1960. By the end of the 1960s there were 50 per cent more monastic foundations, priories and convents than before the war. The growth of religious was most marked in the new orders, including the Pallotines, who engage in pastoral duties among special deprived groups of the population, and the Salesians, who evangelize among the industrial workers.[22] These developments not only reversed the pattern of Catholicism in every country behind the Iron Curtain; they run counter to the secularizing trend in every country in Western Europe. They are the product of many special factors, but they testify, not least, to the vigour and growing self-confidence of the Polish bishops, among whom Wojtyla soon became outstanding.

Numbers of clergy are not the only sign of the resilience of Polish Catholicism. An analysis of polls, surveys and studies undertaken by state organs such as the Polish Radio's Research Centre of Public Opinion, and Catholic institutes such as the Academy of Catholic Theology in Warsaw, reported in a variety of publications, lay and religious, shows that, while secularizing forces are at work in Poland as everywhere else, the mass base of Polish Catholicism is overwhelmingly strong. Virtually all children are baptized Catholics. From 92 to 95 per cent receive holy communion after suitable instruction, given at more than 18,000 catechetical centres.

In the countryside, virtually all marriages are Catholic, and more than 80 per cent of the peasants claim that the church is 'an intrinsic part' of their lives.

It is true that the rural population, 72.6 per cent of the whole in 1931, is now below 50 per cent, and peasants moving into the towns are sometimes inclined to drop their religious observances. Surveys show a correlation between employment on state farms, whose workers tend to be rootless, and declining religious belief. This is one reason, of course, why the church has opposed, so far successfully, any collectivization of the peasantry, which owns and works 90 per cent of the land. But if urbanization produces some attrition of belief among ex-peasants, the process also works the other way, for the great majority of peasants moving into the towns retain their faith and so strengthen urban Catholicism. Thus between two-thirds and three-quarters of town-dwellers are married in church, and weekly Sunday mass attendance is over 50 per cent. Over 90 per cent of Poles are buried according to Catholic rites. It would be hard to match these figures anywhere in the world.[23]

The coming of the Communist regime may, paradoxically, have strengthened Catholicism among the Polish intelligentsia, not only for the obvious reason that it gives religion the invaluable attraction, among intellectuals, of the opposition role, but also because about half of those officially classified as belonging to the intelligentsia are of lower-class (chiefly peasant) origins, where faith is stronger. Poland is perhaps the only country on earth where religious fervour among intellectuals is higher than it was half a century ago.

This specifically Polish background to Wojtyla's approach to the problems of contemporary Catholicism is of crucial importance. Unlike Catholic leaders in the advanced Western-style countries, where Catholicism has been in general decline, or those in the poorer countries, where the church is almost overwhelmed by overpopulation and poverty, Wojtyla comes from a highly successful and immensely self-confident Catholic community, whose strength has been increasing, whose hold over people's minds has never been more secure, and which feels history is on its side. Moreover, this success has been achieved, and this confidence created, not by offering concessions to prevailing fashions but, on the contrary, by the steadfast reassertion of traditional Catholic teaching, on all occasions and in the most uncompromising manner. The Catholic Church is the most respected institution in Poland precisely because, on essentials, it is seen to be unbending, unchanging and sure of itself. Wojtyla is a religious conservative not least because he has seen conservatism work.

Success, however, has not come easily. The church, and the hierarchy in particular, has had to fight every inch of the way. Though the regime is intrinsically weak and often demoralized, it disposes of an infinity of legal and physical powers and will stoop to any device, however contemptible, to damage the church. It cuts the microphone wires and switches off electricity at big church gatherings, or arranges big sports events to cut down attendances. It not only refuses licences to Catholic publications and, when it finally grants them, imposes direct censorship, but makes it difficult for them to obtain adequate supplies of paper. It confiscates foreign Catholic publications. Wojtyla, an avid, indeed compulsive, reader, had his luggage searched and volumes confiscated every time he returned to Poland from visits abroad. Many of the hundreds of articles he published in the 1960s and early 1970s were censored. Sometimes he was unable to obtain printing facilities or paper for the books, pamphlets and magazines he encouraged or sponsored. He hates censorship, and that is one reason why he repudiates the old Holy Office adage, 'Error has no rights'.

State control over material supplies and permits has been the chief weapon in the regime's attempts to prevent church-building. The twenty-five-year struggle to build a church in the new industrial town of Nova Huta near Cracow has become an epic in the history of post-war Polish Catholicism. Transferring people to new centres where no churches exist, and then preventing them from being built, is one way in which the regime tries to stamp out religious observance. In Nova Huta officialdom used every weapon in its armoury; the church responded accordingly; there were arrests, demonstrations, riots. It was Wojtyla who led the building campaign to its triumphant conclusion, and when the church was finally built he told the congregation of 50,000 who attended its consecration: 'This city of Nova Huta was built as a city without God. But the will of God and the workers here has prevailed. Let us all take the lesson to heart. This is not just a building – these are living stones.' The foundation-stone had been taken from St Peter's itself, and since its opening the church accommodates fifteen packed congregations every Sunday.[24]

As Archbishop of Cracow, Wojtyla became, inevitably, the chief lieutenant to the embattled Polish primate, Cardinal Stefan Wyszynski, Archbishop of Warsaw. There is some evidence that the regime initially saw Wojtyla as a liberal alternative to Wyszynski, who was essentially a man of the pre-war church. Both men were active in the Second Vatican Council, 1962-5, which the cardinal and the fifteen Polish bishops were permitted to attend. But whereas Wyszynski was clearly unhappy about the Council's decision to embark on drastic liturgical reforms, which involved the virtual abandonment of Latin for routine services - the Latinity of the mass has always been, for Poland, a symbol of its links with the West - Wojtyla, a man of the post-war world, had taken all this in his stride. He was, from the start, an enthusiastic conciliarist, and on this superficial basis the regime concluded he would be an easier man to deal with. It quickly realized its mistake, and was soon making it clear it hoped Wojtyla would not succeed Wyszynski as primate.

A number of characteristics made him formidable in Communist eyes. He was much more outgoing and approachable than the primate. He was a great mixer, who loved to move among the crowds, shaking hands, remembering names, recognizing faces. He enjoyed sing-songs, dance-festivals, in both of which he would join with gusto - 'a man for dancing and the rosary', as an admirer put it. His wartime experiences gave him a definite *rapport* with audiences of workers, a real threat in Communist eyes, for they then believed - this was before the day of an independent trade union movement - that their strength lay on the factory floor.

Wojtyla showed notable energy and enthusiasm in putting through the administrative reforms laid down by the Council to promote lay participation at every level of church activity and even government. In 1971-2, for instance, he triumphantly organized an archdiocesan synod, following meticulous preparations, including detailed consultations with junior clergy and the laity. Though Wojtyla, both as bishop and pope, has given unwavering support to the traditional hierarchical structure of church government, power lying with the episcopate and ultimately with the papacy, and though he has always insisted on the decisive role played by the priesthood in all church activities – he draws a fundamental distinction between priest and layman – he has shown a vigorous belief in the Council's notion of the church acting as a community, with layfolk playing their full part. As bishop he was particularly energetic in getting priests to organize regular parish meetings and the laity to attend and speak at them. He regarded lay participation not only as an important engine of spirituality, which it undoubtedly is, but as adding to the unity and weight of the church in its dealings with the authorities. While conserving the dominant role of the clergy in church government, he was shrewdly anxious to demonstrate that Catholicism spoke not for the special interests of a clerical caste but for nearly thirty-four million ordinary Poles.

The government soon learnt to fear the skill with which he used the changes introduced by the Council to reinforce the traditional populism of the Polish church. They were dismayed, also, by the rapid growth of his own, personal popularity, the expertise he quickly developed in handling crowds and the enthusiastic response he evoked from them. In Poland there is none of the bifurcation, so often found among Catholics in the West, between 'intellectual' and 'popular' Catholicism. Wojtyla, though an intellectual by any standards, shared not just in form but in his heart all the devotional practices of the people: the rosary, intense affection for the Blessed Virgin, always seen as 'the Queen of Poland', the cult of the saints, a passion for pilgrimages. As Archbishop of Cracow he promoted and shared the religion of the people. While he might, in his study, share all the theological subtleties of a Karl Rahner or the ethical perceptions of an Yves Congar, in church or on his knees, in procession or on pilgrimage, he spoke the spiritual vernacular of the humble peasant.

Yet at the same time Wojtyla was well aware that the Polish church must maintain and reinforce its reputation as an intellectual institution. It must appeal to the intelligentsia and the mass of the educated young who, while increasingly alienated from Communism as theory and practice, would not turn wholeheartedly to the church unless it could offer them a sinewy alternative philosophy. As archbishop, he kept up a substantial portion of his academic work. He remained a familiar figure on the Lublin campus and at the Jagiellonian. He continued to mix with students, seminarians and young lecturers, playing tennis and squash with them, and going on canoeing and, above all, skiing holidays with young people from university circles. His output of academic papers, philosophical as well as theological, remained formidable, and he kept up his reading of new books and learned journals. Wojtyla has never been a man to waste time: he had a reading-light fitted to his car so that he could continue to study while visiting his archdiocese. He also continued to write dramatic sketches and poems (as well as articles in the Catholic press) and to keep a sharp eye on the cultural scene.

Hence, when in 1968 young Polish intellectuals shared the effervescence of that famous year, and demonstrated against censorship of the Adam Mickiewicz play *Ancestors*, dealing with Russian imperialism, Wojtyla took an important part in the dispute. The church as a body, following the leadership of Cardinal Wyszynski, adopted no position. The cardinal tended to reflect the views of the Polish workers, who evinced no sympathy for the students (in 1970 when the workers rioted over food prices, the intellectuals responded with similar indifference). Wojtyla took the part of the students, partly as a matter of general strategy, but chiefly because the issue, of academic freedom, was a vital part of his whole view of human rights. Indeed, he went further and intervened in a dispute between the cardinal and Catholic intellectuals, himself producing a carefully reasoned paper setting out the rights and the duties of Catholic writers. This was published in the magazine of the Catholic intelligentsia, *Tygodnik Powszechny*, and had the effect of defusing an angry little affair which might have inflicted lasting harm on the church. He also wrote privately to Pope Paul VI, to whom the cardinal-primate had complained, explaining that on all essentials Polish Catholic intellectuals were loyal to the church.[25]

Wojtyla was able to take this action without endangering in any way the close working relationship he had established with Wyszynski. The two men were very different and the old primate inclined to be prickly. But the profound respect (and considerable tact) with which Wojtyla invariably treated his senior averted any chance of real friction, which the government would have been swift to exploit. Indeed they tried to do so in 1967, during General de Gaulle's state visit. The authorities blocked a meeting between General and Primate, offering Wojtyla as a *pis-aller*. But Wojtyla refused to have anything to do with this mean little ploy: if the primate were not permitted to meet the distinguished visitor, neither would he – a point of view de Gaulle understood perfectly.[26] Subsequent Communist efforts to engineer a breach between the two prelates proved equally futile.

Wojtyla has always taken a keen professional interest in Communist tactics. He became one of the few senior Catholic clergy who developed a thorough theoretical grasp of Marxism-Leninism. He judged it essential not only to understand the nature of its intellectual appeal, such as it was, but to use it as a guide to the behaviour of the Polish (and Soviet) authorities. In nearly two decades of dealing with them at a high level, he developed an extraordinarily sensitive nose for what might be termed their negotiating propensities. He adopted two general principles. The first was always to drive a hard bargain, especially on practical matters like public meetings, publications, the building and repair of churches, the establishment of catechetical centres and the general enforcement of the church's legal rights. The Communists treated voluntary concessions as a sign of weakness, so Wojtyla learned not to make them without a *quid pro quo*. At the same time, he was careful never to drive them into a corner from which their only exit was by force, which in the last resort they would never scruple to use. The truth, as he discovered, was that he, the representative of the Latin Western tradition, was dealing with a system of orientalized gangsterism. Hence his second principle was always to stand on ceremony. He would insist on dignified gestures and formal marks of respect which in other circumstances he might willingly have forgone. It always paid to make a fuss. Thus he protested furiously when representatives of the church were excluded from the celebrations marking the six-hundredth anniversary of the foundation of the Jagiellonian, saying publicly: 'Proud, small and arrogant men came and ordered that not a single mention of the church and its work must be made at these festivities.'

In negotiating with the Communists, Wojtyla based his case essentially on a thoroughgoing doctrine of human rights, which he first formulated to himself under Nazi occupation, which was greatly strengthened and enriched by his philosophical studies, which was articulated – thanks in part to his own efforts – in many of the documents of the Vatican Council, and which, finally, acquired some practical leverage from the Helsinki Accords, signed by the Communist bloc. The notion of freedom and human dignity had Christian roots, he argued: 'At the heart of the organization of the people of God is a profound awareness of the value of the human person.... We must strive to preserve this awareness of our human dignity, even to the point of shedding our blood, as Christ shed his blood for us.'[27] Religious freedom was the very essence of human freedom, since it embraced the whole man, his soul and mind as well as his body. To deny it was not merely a moral and civic outrage, but in a deeper sense impossible: 'One can understand that a man may search and not find. One can understand that he may deny. But it is incomprehensible that a man should be told: "You may not believe".'[28]

In the religious sphere, the doctrine of human rights, as he developed it in negotiations, in speech and in print, found practical expression in the right to worship – and therefore to build churches – in the right to process peacefully on feast-days and for pilgrimages, in short to carry on all the traditional expressions of Polish Catholicism. There was also the right to educate children in their faith. He fought bitterly against the compulsory atheism classes in the state school. Nearly all the teachers were Catholics: thus they would be forced to expound a doctrine they believed to be false and hateful: 'Such an act of suicide inflicted on the human conscience and on human personality cannot be demanded.'[29] Equally, he protested loud, long and repeatedly against the regime's monopoly use of mass communications for propaganda and distortion: 'We want to see a true picture of ourselves in newspapers, on the radio and on TV ... what we read and what we hear through the media is not a true picture – it is as if Poland were an atheistic country.'[30]

Indeed, a crucial point in the case Wojtyla developed against the restrictions imposed on Catholicism is that they denied the centrality of the church in Poland's history and national character. When the regime got itself into messes, as in 1956, 1968 and 1970, the importance of the church was unofficially recognized, as ministers made desperate private appeals to the hierarchy to use their influence in counselling moderation. That was all very well: but why wasn't the church given regular access to the media? 'We are often approached by the authorities', he noted in a sermon on Christmas Day 1977, 'and asked to help to combat the spread of immorality. But in that case the church must first be given the necessary means ... including access to the radio and TV.' The case he put to the Communist leaders was essentially this: the fact that you need, appeal for and obtain our assistance in keeping Poland on an even keel - so avoiding a showdown with Soviet imperialism and the fate of Czechoslovakia - implies recognition of our place in society. What we have a right to ask for in return are the practical expressions of that place, including an assured legal position to enable us to carry out our role without endless bickering and difficulty. Time and again he returned to this argument.

Thus the state powers found Wojtyla a formidable antagonist, who appeared to them, as it were, in full canonicals, with a thousand years of tradition and history behind him, acutely conscious and indeed jealous of the respect owed to his church, and adamantly zealous in upholding its rights and dignity. But to ordinary Catholics of the Cracow archdiocese he was quite a different person. He moved into the old palace with some reluctance and lived there in frugal fashion. He took a great deal of exercise as well as working hard, so his appetite was healthy. But his interest in food was minimal. He drank very little. He did not smoke. He possessed no TV or radio, though he played his guitar occasionally, and was always ready to sing. His books were his joy. His clothes were a disgrace. When, in June 1967, he went to Rome to receive the cardinalate Paul VI had awarded him on 29 May, he was virtually penniless. To buy his cardinal's outfit, his secretary, Father Pieronek, had to borrow 200 dollars from the Polish College, where they stayed. Expenditure on the robes was grudged. But, for Wojtyla, being made a prince of the church, and a papal elector, was more than formal acknowledgement of the historic dignity of his see. It marked the recognition of his growing prominence and influence in the central councils of the Roman Catholic Church.

2

The Summons

IN THE 1960s AND 1970s, first as bishop, then as archbishop and cardinal, Wojtyla became a well-known figure in the international church. He was often in Western Europe, and especially in Rome itself. He made repeated visits to North America, visiting the Polish emigrant communities in the United States and Canada. He visited the Middle East and Africa, South and East Asia, and Australia. One of the concessions the Polish church wrung from the authorities in its many bitter bargaining sessions was greater freedom to travel for its leading clergy. Wojtyla took full advantage of this, as did other Polish bishops. They were anxious to play their full part in international Catholicism, recognizing the danger that the Vatican in its pursuit of *détente* with the Communist world might be tempted to strike bargains from which Catholics behind the Iron Curtain, and especially in Poland, would suffer.

Under Wojtyla's influence, it became the policy of the episcopate to ensure a Polish 'presence' at every important international gathering of Catholics, and there to stress the identification of the church with freedom – freedom for others and freedom for herself. In 1976, at the Eucharistic Congress in Philadelphia, for instance, the Poles provided a strong delegation and Wojtyla took an active part. His main speech was typical of many he made abroad in the effort to get Poland's message across. Everybody, he argued, has a right to freedom, self-determination and choice of career, and to act in accordance with his convictions. There was a hunger for freedom in a world where old forms of colonialism were merely being replaced by new ones. There were, he said, many forms of 'underprivileged' people: and one consisted of those underprivileged in terms of religious freedom, indeed actively persecuted because of their religious convictions.

The Summons

Wojtyla became identified with the cause of religious freedom at the Second Vatican Council (1962–5), which marked his own entry on to the international stage and the first emergence of the Polish episcopate as a force in world Catholicism. Among the more than 2,000 prelates who attended the Council, few can have been more enthusiastic about its work and more in harmony with its inner spirit than Wojtyla. As Cardinal Benelli, Assistant-Secretary of State and later Archbishop of Florence, put it: 'If there was one man who believed in the Second Vatican Council and had a firm will to carry it out, it was Cardinal Wojtyla.'[1]

Although Wojtyla made eight formal Council speeches altogether, his most substantial contribution, the one that other participants remembered, was in the debate on religious freedom which led to the promulgation of the Declaration on Religious Freedom, *Dignitatis Humanae*, on 7 December 1965. It was and is his contention that the church must concede to others (where it has the power) the liberty of action and thought and speech and writing it demands for itself. In taking this line, which triumphed at the Council against the arguments of the conservative Cardinal Ottaviani, Prefect of the Congregation of the Faith, he felt he was acting in an honourable Polish tradition. For, at the Council of Constance (1414–18), the then rector of his old university of Cracow, Pawel Wlodkowic, had spoken out strongly against the policy of the Teutonic Knights of making forcible conversions to Catholicism among the pagan Lithuanians, with whom the Poles felt some affinity. Wojtyla often quoted the example of Rector Wlodkowic,[2] arguing that, whatever happened in the past, the church must now be seen to have clean hands in the matter, in doctrine and in usage; for, if she conceded that 'even error has rights', could she not argue on behalf of herself that, *a fortiori*, truth has rights too? The point was taken, and conceded by the Council Fathers, and it is perhaps too often forgotten that Wojtyla played a notable part in persuading the church to change its practice on this central libertarian issue.[3]

On the related subject of the church's access to truth, Wojtyla also took what was regarded as a liberal line. In the debate on the Pastoral Constitution of the Church in the Modern World, he argued that the church spoke with authority but should not present itself as authoritarian: 'Let us avoid all suggestion that the church has a monopoly of truth,' he said. His speech on religious liberty had led to an invitation to join the steering group (or Mixed Commission) on this *schema*, and he persuaded his colleagues to include a chapter on 'Marriage and the Family', expressing the doctrine of the 'community of life', in the final document, *Gaudium et Spes*. This constitution, also published on 7 December 1965, quickly established itself as the most popular of all the Council documents.[4]

In the aftermath of the Council, Wojtyla took a leading part in implementing its recommendations and machinery, in Rome as well as at home. He attended four out of the five general synods of bishops, the main constitutional instrument set up by the Council to ensure the continuous application of its teaching. The synods are consultative and advisory rather than legislative; and they are in no sense sovereign. Their existence leaves papal authority intact. But Wojtyla dismissed the notion that pope and bishops were rivals for power. At the 1969 synod he argued that bishops in synod or in their national episcopal conferences (or regional conferences such as the decennial Latin American meetings) complement and re-inforce, rather than challenge, the rights of the Holy See. In his view the Dogmatic Constitution on the Church, promulgated in November 1964, put the point admirably: 'Together with its head, the Roman Pontiff, and never without this head, the episcopal order is the subject of supreme and full power over the universal church.'[5]

His activities at the 1969 synod evidently impressed his episcopal colleagues. At the 1971 synod he was elected a member of the Secretariat of the Synodal Council, its steering group, coming ninth on the list with ninety votes. He was again elected to the Secretariat at the October 1974 synod, coming fourth with 115 votes (out of a possible 184); and he acted as *rapporteur* to the full synod for the study group on 'The Gospel in the Modern World'. At the 1977 synod, on Catechesis, a topic on which the Polish bishops are thought to be particularly proficient and enterprising, he not only led the Polish delegation but was elected Chairman of the Secretariat, and was in many respects its dominant figure.

During these years Cardinal Wojtyla became as conversant with the workings of the central government of the church, and as adept at manipulating elements in its power-structure, as any prelate can be who is not himself actually a member of the bureaucracy. While not exactly an insider, he was in form at least a member of the establishment, acquiring membership of various Congregations which are, in effect, the ministries of the Vatican, for the Eastern Churches, for the Liturgy, for the Clergy, for Catholic Education and Divine Service.[6]

This work in the central organs of the church, and his necessary involvement in Vatican *Ostpolitik* diplomacy, brought him into increasingly close contact with Paul VI. Here there was a background of distrust and some animosity between the Polish episcopate and the Vatican. Pius XII, pope during the years 1939-58, that is, throughout the war and the post-war settlement, had always been accused of possessing a pro-German bias. The Polish church had taken a strongly nationalistic line over the 'Western Territories' taken from Germany and awarded to Poland as part of the settlement. On 24 May 1948, the then Polish primate, Cardinal Hlond, had written a pastoral letter on the subject, presenting the territories as Poland's rightful heritage: 'The hour has come', he wrote, 'to balance the centuries-old accounts.' In September 1965, his successor, Cardinal Wyszynski, celebrating the twentieth anniversary of the creation of a Polish church organization in the territories, had preached a sermon in Wroclaw (once German Breslau) proclaiming: 'The stones of Wroclaw now speak Polish.'[7]

Unfortunately, the failure of the Allies to agree on any kind of formal peace treaty with Germany made the Vatican reluctant to recognize the finality of Poland's occupation of the territories, and therefore to give a permanent status to Polish diocesan frontiers in these areas. In Poland this was attributed to Pius XII's Germanophilia, and later Paul VI, who had served under him for many years, was accused of sharing his prejudices. In the event the problem was resolved, or very much eased, by direct dealings between the Polish and German episcopates. Here, Wojtyla, who had visited Germany often, who had excellent contacts in the German church and (unlike most Polish bishops) a thorough understanding of German culture and modes of thought, played a decisive and constructive role. He was one of the instigators, and the principal author, of the letter of

18 November 1965, signed by all the Polish bishops and addressed to the German episcopate, which offered forgiveness and asked for reconciliation. The letter asserted the right of the bishops to speak on behalf of the nation in a formulation which bears the Wojtyla stamp: 'In Poland the symbiosis of Christendom, Church and State existed from the very beginning and was strictly speaking never dissolved. . . . Polish means at the same time Catholic.'[8]

The letter was not popular among ordinary Poles, and it was denounced root and branch by the Polish government, eagerly seizing on an opportunity, for once, to drive a wedge between the church and Polish national sentiment. But as Wojtyla explained repeatedly from his pulpit in Cracow Cathedral, Christianity stood for forgiveness, or it was nothing: forgiving enemies is what Christianity is all about. Moreover, it quickly became apparent that the gesture was not only courageous but well judged. It evoked an enthusiastic response not only from the German bishops, but from rank-and-file German Catholics and Lutherans. It was an important staging post on the route which has led most Germans to accept the loss of their Baltic and Silesian territories to Poland, and German finance to invest so heavily in the Polish economy. Needless to say, the Polish regime never gave the church the credit for taking the lead in this unpopular but necessary process of reconciliation. But in the Vatican at least it was greeted with relief and gratitude, and Wojtyla's part in it was appreciated both there and in Germany. He became a much-respected figure in German church circles and a frequent visitor and speaker; indeed, he led a Polish delegation to Germany in September 1978, just before his election to the papacy.

Wojtyla was also deeply involved in the Vatican's general *Ostpolitik*, and especially in protecting Poland from the damaging consequences of its over-enthusiastic pursuit. Pius XII had waged an unrelenting cold war against the Soviet bloc governments on behalf of the beleaguered Catholics of Eastern Europe, what he liked to term 'the Church of Silence'. John XXIII modified this policy, opening windows to the east, partly to secure the freedom of such prelates as Cardinal Slipyi, Patriarch of the Russian Uniates, who had spent eighteen years in Soviet camps and gaols: partly also to enable bishops from Eastern Europe to attend the Council.

Paul VI continued and broadened this policy, sometimes with more zealotry than wisdom. It was the contention of the Polish episcopate that the Vatican's Secretariat of State, in its lack of experience in dealing with Communist regimes, was simply not tough enough: it got far too little in return for what it conceded. In the late 1960s Cardinal Wyszynski complained bitterly that the Polish church, the chief victim if the Vatican struck a poor bargain with Moscow, was kept in the dark about much of the negotiations and its warnings and protests went unheeded: if he represented the 'church of silence', he said, the Vatican was 'the church of the deaf'.

What the dispute, which came to a head in the years 1969-71, was really about was the Vatican's reluctance to recognize the true weight of the Polish church, now the largest and most homogeneous Catholic community in the whole of Europe, the extent to which its vital interests were involved in any talks with the Communists, and the degree therefore to which it must be a party to any agreements reached. It was Wojtyla who, by virtue of his growing status and reputation in Rome, was best placed to put the Polish case privately. He did so with great skill and persistence, and by 1972 he had got the Pope to accept it.[9]

Thereafter the policies of the Vatican and the Polish episcopate were much more closely co-ordinated, and the Poles were given, in effect, a veto on Vatican initiatives in the East. Wojtyla's object throughout was to secure for the Polish church, in default of a full concordat, a clearly defined legal status, which would allow it to sue for constitutional rights in the courts. His tactics were to exploit the Polish government's recurrent difficulties to obtain concessions, and prevent the Vatican from blundering in and offering to help without extorting anything significant in return. His object was not to overturn the Communist government. 'The church does not combat the regime in Poland,' he insisted. 'We ask one thing only: that in our homeland Christ has his place, and that the church is respected in its mission and vocation.' He set out his objective more fully in 1974: 'For us, next to God, our first love is Poland. After God one must above all remain faithful to one's homeland, to the Polish national culture. All we demand is the right to live in accordance with the spirit, history, culture and language of our own Polish land: that same culture which has been used by our ancestors for centuries.'

Wojtyla was making a characteristic point: just as the state must recognize the dignity of each individual, so it must concede to the church the dignity it has earned by its contribution to Polish culture and nationhood. 'Dignity', the public recognition of essential worth, is one of his favourite concepts. He kept pushing for the 'dignity' of the church throughout the seventies. A new phase opened in the summer of 1976, when world inflation finally hit Poland. The troubles that followed led to the so-called 'summit' between Wyszynski and the Polish dictator Gierek on 29 October 1977. Gierek begged for the cardinal's help, which was reluctantly granted. A month later, on 1 December 1977, Gierek had an audience with Paul VI in Rome. Complicated negotiations followed. In June 1978, the head of the Vatican's Polish desk, Archbishop Luigi Poggi, reported after a visit to Warsaw that the Polish government would not yet concede the church full statutory recognition. The Polish episcopate had a long 'shopping list' of grievances they wanted satisfied, and on 17 September 1978 they made a joint demand for the removal of censorship on church publications. These requests, too, remained largely unmet. On the other hand, the general power of the government *vis-à-vis* the church declined steadily throughout the seventies, and Catholic demands were increasingly conceded in practice if not in form. Wojtyla's policy of exerting continuous pressure, while never going too far, now that he had succeeded in aligning Vatican diplomacy behind it, brought results which were more gratifying than he was prepared to admit, at any rate in public.

He also developed a certain personal relationship with Paul VI, which their growing concordance on *Ostpolitik* helped to nourish. In 1960 he had published *Love and Responsibility*, a pastoral and ethical treatise on human sexuality, dealing with marriage, parenthood and such issues as abortion and birth-control. The masterly style in which Wojtyla produced what might be termed a unified theory of sex and procreation, seen through Christian eyes, made the book a notable success and it was translated into Italian, French and Spanish. Paul VI read it while awaiting the report of the technical commission of theologians and doctors which John XXIII had appointed to study the birth-control issue. The intellectual rigour with which Wojtyla's book demolished the case for artificial contraception stiffened Pope Paul in his resolve to reject the majority findings of the commission, which recommended that artificial means were sometimes permissible to supplement the approved Catholic 'rhythm' or 'natural' method of birth-control. When he came to write his own encyclical *Humanae Vitae* (25 July 1968) on the subject, much of Wojtyla's thinking reappeared in the argument and gave the document an original and positive content which a simple reiteration of traditional Catholic teaching would have lacked. Most Catholics, having learnt that the Pope's verdict had gone against artificial contraception, did not trouble to read any further, and in the immense and noisy controversy which followed, some of the central arguments in the encyclical went almost unexamined. The rage and incomprehension which greeted *Humanae Vitae* helped to form a defensive bond between the Pope and the young cardinal.[10]

It was not surprising, then, that in 1976 Wojtyla was honoured by being invited to give the traditional series of Lenten sermons, twenty-two in all, to the Pope and the pontifical household. There are two versions of how this came about. One has it that Paul VI wanted a Pole to give the series, and the Polish bishops accordingly nominated Wojtyla; another is that he was the Pope's personal choice. At all events, the sermons were delivered, to great acclaim. Wojtyla already had the reputation of being a powerful and profound preacher, the only criticism being that, when addressing a well-educated audience, he tended to go on too long and lapse occasionally into obscure philosophical jargon. But the 1976 Lenten series was written in advance and carefully timed. As published under the title *Sign of Contradiction*,[11] it offers a fresh and sparkling set of insights into some of the central issues of religion – our perception of God, the object of creation, free will, sin and evil, and the significance of the redemption. Wojtyla showed himself an original biblical commentator, especially on the Book of Genesis, and spiced his reinterpretations with references to the Marxist theory of alienation, French structuralism and even the works of Hans Küng. The performance might have seemed merely brilliant and adroit, had it not also given the impression of heartfelt *gravitas*.

It certainly raised Wojtyla's reputation among the curialists, who welcomed this revelation of a powerful and original mind not afraid to defend orthodoxy, and with novel arguments, clearly at home among modern intellectual concepts without displaying the fatal *stigmata* of trendiness.

When Paul vi died, a little over two years after this notable Lenten series, Wojtyla was established as one of the most formidable diocesans in the entire church and a familiar and much-respected figure on the Roman scene. But it should not be thought that, when the 111 cardinals began to gather in Rome, in August 1978, to elect Paul vi's successor, Wojtyla was regarded by any of the experts as a likely or even a possible choice. The conclave was clearly an important one. The last seven years of Paul's long pontificate had been remarkably inactive, compared with the bustle of the 1960s. The church had been changing indeed, perhaps more swiftly than ever, during these years; but the changes had been self-generating and anarchic rather than directed by the papacy itself. In particular, during his last two or three years Paul had given the impression of being a resigned and sometimes a helpless spectator of a post-conciliar church which had slipped out of his control.[12] There was clearly a need to choose a pope who would reassert the authority of the Holy See, and if necessary give the church a new direction. But there was no general agreement what that direction should be, or who could provide it.

The period August–October 1978, which ended with the election of Wojtyla as Pope John Paul ii, should be seen as a whole, and as a historic convulsion in the way the Roman Catholic Church conducts its affairs. It can be seen as a whole; but it is difficult, even at this distance of time, to see it clearly. Paul vi may have governed the church loosely in his last years, but on one point he had exerted his authority in all its plenitude. In 1975 he had written and published an Apostolic Constitution, that is a papal legal directive, entitled *Romano Pontifici Eligendo*, describing in great detail how the papal conclave following his death was to be conducted.[13]

The primary aim of this fiercely worded set of rules was to preserve intact the personal autocracy of the new pope, and in particular to prevent any group of cardinals, or the college as a whole, from imposing any conditions on the new pope before electing him. Thus Section 82 forbade the cardinals to seek to impose on any candidate 'any form of pact, agreement, promise or other commitment of whatever kind'. If such a promise were extracted, even on the most solemn oath, it would be utterly null and void, and those responsible were to suffer automatic excommunication, *latae sententiae*, that is without trial or formal judgement. Furthermore, under Section 83, the cardinals were likewise forbidden 'to underake commitments of common accord to which they agree to be bound should one of them be elevated to the pontificate', and any such pacts would also be null and entail excommunication of those who made them. Paul VI seems to have reasoned that it was his last duty to the church, after a pontificate which he admitted to himself, and sometimes privately to others, had been in many ways unsatisfactory, at least to hand over the absolute powers of the papacy intact to his successor, so that he might start with a *tabula rasa* and repair the damage unfettered by any collegiate restraints. He evidently believed that this object was more likely to be achieved if the conclave were conducted in the greatest possible secrecy. Hence the second object of the Apostolic Constitution was to reinforce the security surrounding the election and prevent the cardinals, or anyone else, from ever disclosing what went on during it, under pain of ferocious spiritual punishment in this world and the next. The cardinals were forced to adhere to these provisions by taking a blood-curdling series of oaths, before and at the commencement of the conclave itself. The Constitution was up to date in the sense that it took account of such modern practices as electronic 'bugging'; in every other respect, however, it breathed the spirit of the Middle Ages.

Paul VI's posthumous instruction did make one concession. 'We do not, however,' he provided, 'have the intention of forbidding the exchange of views concerning the election during the period when the see is vacant.' What he had in mind, presumably, was discussion among the cardinals during the conclave itself, but they took him literally at his word. Throughout the pre-conclave period they held daily general congregations of the college, in the Sala Bologna of the Apostolic Palace, under the chairmanship of Cardinal Jean Villot, the tall, self-effacing Frenchman who combined the offices of Secretary of State with papal *Camerlengo*, or Chamberlain, in charge of arrangements during the vacancy.

Villot's decision to hold these meetings proved important and prudent for two reasons. Of the 111 cardinals, only three had been appointed by Pius XII and eight by John XXIII. No fewer than 100, therefore, had never before taken part in a conclave. The old collegiate intimacy no longer existed. Only twenty-seven were Italians. Of the rest, twenty-nine came from Europe outside Italy, eleven from North America, nineteen from Latin America, thirteen from Asia and Oceania, and twelve from Africa. Some had never even met before. They were a very diverse group of men, with a high average age (sixty-six) but a variety of experiences: most were diocesans, but there were a round dozen with a background in the regular orders, including three Jesuits, three Franciscan and two Dominican friars, a Benedictine monk, a Salesian, a Redemptorist and an Oblate of Mary. The series of pre-conclave meetings allowed the cardinals to get to know one another better, and exchange thoughts on the future of the church, in a relaxed and leisurely manner, before they were engulfed by the daunting regulations, the tensions and the discomforts of the conclave itself. But equally important, these gatherings offered the members of the college a degree of protection, not to say insulation, from the propagandist hubbub and pressures in and around St Peter's Square.

Of the four post-war conclaves, all of which I have observed, the one in August 1978 was the most conspicuous for the activities of pressure groups. Despite the August heat, not only thousands of journalists of press and TV, but large numbers of Catholic activists of all persuasions, descended on Rome. There were numbers of daily press briefings and an impressive output of propaganda material. The 'traditionalist' supporters of Monsignor Lefebvre, the former Archbishop of Dakar – who had been a prickly thorn in Paul VI's side – were particularly vociferous. But their intervention, by its nature, was ineffective since it revolved round their objection to Paul VI's decision to prevent cardinals over eighty from voting in the conclave (though they were allowed to attend it). Fr Ducand-Bourget, the parish priest of Saint Nicolas-du-Chardonnet in Paris, which had been 'occupied', as it was termed, since the previous year by Lefebvre's supporters, described this exclusion as 'moral euthanasia' and claimed it invalidated the conclave. Precisely the opposite objection was voiced, at the other end of the political spectrum, by a left-wing pressure group under the former Benedictine prior, Jean-Claude Besret. He complained of the conclave's being limited to cardinals and demanded the inclusion of 'representatives' of the entire church. 'In the walled enclosure of the conclave', as he put it, 'the psycho-drama of Christian alienation is being played out.'[14]

Such voices were easy to ignore. More persuasive, or so it seemed, were the efforts of the liberal-modernist wing orchestrated by the German *Concilium* group, with which the Professor of Theology at Tübingen, Father Hans Küng, was associated. Küng was active on his own account, giving newspaper and TV interviews, in which he stipulated, among other things, that the new pope must reverse Paul VI's ruling on birth-control. Speaking on behalf of the world, he warned against the 'damaging error of settling for a mediocre pope'.[15] He and his friends also drew up a more formal list of criteria for the new pontiff, signed by ten theologians of very varying degrees of eminence. They included such well-known names as Yves Congar and M.-D. Chenu of Paris, but also the Peruvian Gustavo Gutiérrez, already associated with the ultra-left system known as 'liberation theology', the heterodox Flemish christologist Father Edward Schillebeeckx, and the American publicist Father Andrew Greeley. Their manifesto insisted that the cardinals should first settle a programme of action, including the abandonment of the papal prerogative and the substitution of the synod of bishops, assisted by national conferences and diocesan councils, as the decision-making authority in the church. Only when this programme had been agreed should the cardinals proceed to elect a pope to carry it out.[16]

This kind of propaganda, needless to say, was accompanied by a good deal of personal lobbying in Rome itself, as well as by immense daily publicity in the press and on television, in which the liberal side had the overwhelming advantage. Had each of the cardinals, awaiting the conclave, been isolated in exposure to this din, it might well have influenced their thinking. As it was, meeting regularly among themselves for confidential, serious and informed discussion, they confronted the reality of the choice before them, as opposed to the illusions of special pleading, which they tended increasingly to ignore as the conclave itself approached. In the event all the propaganda efforts proved futile.

In the 1963 conclave, Cardinal Montini of Milan had entered it a favourite and emerged a pope.[17] There was no apparent favourite in August 1978, but the voting was confined to three (possibly four) ballots and the proceedings ended, to the astonishment of all those outside the Sacred College, on the evening of the first day. Cardinal Benelli of Florence, a former curialist, was regarded as the most likely choice if the cardinals decided they wanted someone associated with the central machinery of the church, like Pius XII or Paul VI. But Benelli was only fifty-seven; and in any case the feeling was that the church's problems were pastoral rather than diplomatic or administrative, and that the cardinals must turn not to a curialist but to a diocesan. Assuming that the choice must or should be an Italian, the field narrowed to four: the cardinal-archbishops of Genoa, Naples, Palermo and Venice. Of these, Salvatore Pappalardo of Palermo was regarded as too young (only fifty-nine), Corrado Ursi of Naples as too insignificant, and Giuseppe Siri of Genoa, though a formidable and vastly experienced figure (he had been a bishop since 1944), as too much the candidate of the committed right wing. According to one source, Siri received twenty-five votes, which represented virtually a full turn-out for the right, on the first ballot.[18] Thereafter, opinion moved irresistibly in favour of Albino Luciani, the Patriarch of Venice, whose age (sixty-five) was considered about right and whose views corresponded with the centre-right majority of the cardinals. In a subsequent interview, the Belgian cardinal Léon-Joseph Suenens said that the first ballot was inconclusive, the second eliminatory, the third pointed the way and the fourth produced 'an extraordinary, unexpected majority, a royal two-thirds' – that is, about ninety out of 111. The only cardinal to admit he voted against Luciani was the Argentine conservative Juan Carlos Aramburu.[19] But his was doubtless a 'favourite son' vote for the Argentine-Italian curialist, Cardinal Pignedoli, who was certainly a contender.

In varying degrees the cardinals believe that their deliberations and voting are guided by the Holy Spirit. The election of Luciani was so speedy and decisive, and it caused the college such evident satisfaction, that we must assume that his character, record and views fitted with rare exactness what the princes of the church considered the right profile of a pope in August 1978.

Luciani came from the north of Italy, the great provider of twentieth-century popes - Pius x, Pius xi, John xxiii, Paul vi. Like the saintly Pius x he came from a poor family in the Veneto. His tutors at the Belluno seminary had included Alfredo Ottaviani, the witty traditionalist who ran the Holy Office for so many years. The liberal Pope John had made him a bishop; the more conservative Pope Paul had sent him to Venice and given him a cardinalate in 1973. This implied a man of the centre; in fact, his views, which had been expressed at Italian episcopal conferences (of which he had been Vice-President 1972-5), at the 1974 synod on evangelization, and at the Pescara Eucharistic Congress in September 1977, tended towards the right. He had a habit of stressing the *magisterium*, reflecting his training at the Gregorian University in Rome. He had publicly insisted that the general synod was a consultative body only - so much for Father Küng and his allies.

However, what seems to have been decisive in the election of Luciani was the known evidence of his intellectual formation and tastes. Contrary to the popular supposition, the Catholic Church is not averse to reform. On the contrary, its ruling élite tends on the whole to be predisposed in favour of reform and reformers, provided these operate within the assumptions of Latin Christianity. It hates reforms which reflect secular criteria and standards, but it welcomes reforms from within. One of the great insider heroes of the modern Catholic Church is St Charles Borromeo, the Counter-Reformation bishop who in the late sixteenth century first produced a systematic *curriculum* for the training of priests - invented, in fact, the seminary, which had not existed in the Middle Ages. John xxiii's well-known devotion to Borromeo, whose biography he wrote, was one reason his colleagues were ready to elect him pope. Luciani was also a member of the Borromeo cult; indeed his episcopal motto, *Humilitas*, was copied from the saint's.

More decisive in Luciani's case, however, was his interest in the nineteenth-century Italian reformer Antonio Rosmini-Serbati (1797-1855), who had been Vice-Rector of Luciani's Belluno seminary. Rosmini's work is little known outside the Catholic clergy, but within it, and especially in Italy, it is much admired. In 1848 he had published a famous book, *The Five Wounds of the Church*, calling for reforms of the type which now evoke nods of approval even from conservative cardinals – an end to the ostentatious display of church wealth, greater contact between priests and people, better training of the clergy, an end to secular influence in the appointment of bishops, and the need to promote episcopal unity.[20] At the time they had seemed highly controversial. Rosmini fell foul of the Jesuits; was accused of Jansenism and had his works placed on the Index; was cleared; then, after his death, attacked again, some forty of his propositions being condemned by Leo XIII in 1887–8. But Rosmini and his work survived. The order he founded, the Fathers of Charity, or Rosminians, flourished, and though they were unable to obtain his canonization, his teaching came back into fashion, especially his stress on catechetics. Catechetics became a Catholic vogue-word in the 1950s and 1960s. As a method of instilling Catholic ideas and values it was raised, by the Second Vatican Council, almost to the level of an art. Indeed, from being simply the teaching of the catechism by rote, it was now treated as a serious branch of theology, an example of a humble clerical trade being semantically upgraded. Luciani, himself a most diffident and self-effacing man, who never once ventured to speak at the Council, thus found himself the unexpected beneficiary of ecclesiastical fashion. Of such is the kingdom of heaven.

Unfortunately, no one thought to inquire about his medical record, or indeed whether he had any. He later volunteered the information himself, telling a regular Wednesday general audience in St Peter's that he had been in hospital eight times and had had four operations. At the time of his election, however, all was euphoria. The cardinals rejoiced that the conclave had been so brief, conclusive and painless. Had not the Holy Spirit spoken in no uncertain fashion? The crowd was relieved that the papacy had remained in Italian hands and delighted by Luciani's simple manners. Many Catholics throughout the world were surprised but not displeased to read in the newspapers about his warm-hearted if naïve contributions to parish and diocesan magazines – 'open letters' to a curious mixture of real and imaginary characters, ranging from

Christopher Marlowe and G. K. Chesterton to Mr Pickwick and Mickey Mouse. Others were a little disturbed. So this was 'catechetical theology'!

Luciani's choice of John Paul for his papal name was a well-meaning if clumsy and inelegant device, adopted without much consideration, to show that his pontificate would seek to combine the innovative values of John XXIII and the stabilizing authority of Paul VI, thus getting the best of all possible worlds. On Sunday 27 August, the day after his election, he warned the crowd in St Peter's Square: 'I do not have the wisdom of heart of Pope John. I do not have the preparation and culture of Pope Paul.' John Paul I was clearly among those who believe that the best, or at any rate least controversial, way for the church to 'modernize' itself is to abandon the ancient ceremonies and liturgical elaborations with which, over long centuries, it has emphasized the historic dignity of its mission to the world and its sacral character. Thus he declined to be 'crowned' or 'enthroned' and a comparatively simple ceremony, held on 3 September 1978, saw him merely invested with the pallium, the short shoulder-band of authority denoting his primacy, dating from Roman times. Why this secular and pagan symbol should be retained, while others of Christian origin were abandoned - Pope Paul VI had already discarded and sold the three-tiered papal tiara - was never explained to the public. Ending the coronation, of course, meant relinquishing not merely a rite but a sacrament, and seemed to imply lack of confidence in the process whereby the church had, over one and a half millennia, invoked a special blessing and sacramental grace for Christian rulers charged with exercising authority, lay or ecclesiastical.[21]

John Paul I's minimalist attitude to the more majestic aspects of the liturgy, however, by no means implies that he had the itch for change. Such evidence as we possess suggest the opposite. His first speech to the cardinals setting out his intentions was a routine and lack-lustre affair, in which he pledged himself to continue the work of the Council, to proceed with the revision of canon law, to pursue the cause of ecumenism and to forward the work of evangelization. What pope could say less? It later turned out, as Cardinal Siri revealed in a newspaper interview, that the speech was the work of Cardinal Benelli and the curia, and was an example of bureaucratic contingency planning.[22] That John Paul I would have undertaken certain initiatives of his own seems probable, but it seems equally probable that he would have left the government of the church largely in the hands of the curia, avoiding alike the spectacular interventions of John XXIII or the close personal supervision which marked the early years of Paul VI. In short, his pontificate promised to be eminently 'safe' from a curialist viewpoint. Indeed, even on liturgical matters, his decision to scrap the coronation seems to have been more a gesture of humility than a foretaste of reform. His sole personal expression of opinion during his pontificate occurred on his first and only visit to St John Lateran, the ancient and splendid cathedral of Rome, on 23 September, when he criticized the ill-considered and unauthorized liturgical changes which had occurred in recent years.

John Paul I's pontificate lasted only thirty-three days. He seems to have been stunned by his elevation, bewildered by the variety and complexity of the tasks facing him, shocked by the number of decisions required of him, each day, from rising to repose, and perhaps above all disheartened by being wrenched from familiar faces and surroundings and placed in the splendid and impersonal isolation of the Apostolic Palace. No doubt in time he would have achieved some sort of control over his court and surroundings - after all, he had been a more than adequate Patriarch of Venice, always regarded as a difficult and unmalleable see. As it was, his manifest disorientation seemed to confirm the complacent curialist view that, while pastoral experience might be desirable - was, indeed, very desirable - experience of central government was essential. As the pressures mounted, he was occasionally seen about the palace and Vatican gardens, a wan and etiolated figure. Was he praying for guidance or relief from his burdens? His life was Spartan: rising at five, retiring at nine; he ate, as the Romans say, 'like a canary'. On 5 September he had a shocking experience when the Orthodox Metropolitan Nikodim of Leningrad, paying him a courtesy call, collapsed and died in the papal study. A little over three weeks later, at 5.30 a.m. on Friday 29 September, the Pope himself was found dead in his chamber, after he had failed to respond to his morning call. The lights were still on. He had evidently been reading Thomas à Kempis's

Imitation of Christ. Medical examination suggested he had died at about eleven the previous night. The knowledge that the Pope had been dead for many hours before his condition was discovered added a chilling pathos to his distressing end.

As the Catholic Church elects as its head men of an age at which, in most other walks of life, they are accustomed to retire, it is inured to short pontificates. No fewer than fourteen earlier popes had died within a month of election. The eighth-century Stephen II had reigned only three days. All the same, the abrupt and totally unexpected extinction of John Paul I, fatuously baptized by the press 'the smiling pope', was a numbing blow in a church where superstition is never far below the surface. If the Holy Spirit had guided his election, why had the sustaining hand of Providence been so abruptly withdrawn? Had he failed or offended in some way? Had his election been a misinterpretation of the divine will?

The cardinals, who had left Rome rejoicing, returned in sombre mood. The October conclave had none of the gaiety and warmth of its August predecessor. There were fewer visitors in Rome. The propaganda efforts of the rival factions lacked conviction this time. Though the pre-conclave consistories were resumed, the preparatory period was cut to a minimum. The emphasis was on businesslike decision and dispatch.

The problem which faced the cardinals when they were walled up in the conclave was in all essentials the same as in August; but it was seen through a different prism of experience. Then, a man in his mid-fifties had seemed too young. Now, comparative youth, and still more robust health, seemed an advantage. The requirement of a man with ample pastoral experience still seemed important; but strength, endurance, a broad range of capacities now emerged as essential qualifications. In August it was taken for granted that if a suitable Italian pastoralist were available, he should be chosen. But Luciani had been the only one, and he was now dead. In October, therefore, the unthinkable automatically placed itself on the agenda: a non-Italian pope.

Once the issue was raised, it was immediately seen that the election of a foreigner was virtually a non-problem. It was true that the last had been Hadrian VI, a Dutchman, elected in 1522; a 'habit' of more than four and a half centuries had thus been formed. But in a church accustomed to thinking in millennia, the full perspective of history gave a different picture. Of the 262 popes, it is true that 132 might broadly be described as Italians. But the papacy was a much older institution than the national state; it antedated the most obscure origins of all the great European languages; it was already venerable when distinctive national cultures began to emerge. For many of the earlier popes the problem of nationality did not exist; it is not clear where they came from or what they considered themselves. Often we have little more than their place of birth; sometimes not even that. Among the popes whose culture we can identify, there have been seventeen Frenchmen, fifteen Greeks, seven from Syria and Palestine, five Germans, four Spaniards, three from Sicily, two each from North Africa, Sardinia and Dalmatia, and one each from Hungary, Portugal, the Netherlands and England.[23] A large number of the Italians did not see themselves as Italians but as Florentines or Romans or Neapolitans or Genoese or Venetians. Italy as a concept had not existed until the reign of Pio Nono – indeed, had come into being in the teeth of his resistance and over his indignant protests. The papacy had not recognized 'Italy', created at the expense of its territorial patrimony, until 1929. What, then, was Italy to the papacy or the papacy to Italy?

The answer was custom, language, distance; nothing fundamental. During the twentieth century, a number of non-Italian curialists had been *papabili*: for instance, the Anglo-Spanish Cardinal Merry del Val, Pius x's brilliant Secretary of State, or the French Cardinal Tisserant, *camerlengo* in the last years of Pius XII. It is true that the pope is bishop of an Italian see and has a special relationship with the bishops of the other Italian dioceses, but a good pastor with a working knowledge of Italian should find no difficulty in coping with such duties. A more substantial objection in the post-war period had been the papacy's delicate involvement in Italian domestic politics, especially the close links forged between Pius XII and the Christian Democrats, who had formed the core of all Italy's governments since 1945. Yet even Paul VI, a warm supporter of the Christian Democrats, had recognized the objections to this *liaison* and had gradually freed himself from it. By 1978 it was no longer the foundation of Vatican domestic policy.

Once the cardinals had admitted to themselves that a non-Italian pope raised no real difficulties, the range of choice widened considerably. There was, however, a further factor in their minds, which had not been present to the same degree in August. The brevity and abrupt termination of the Luciani pontificate had disturbed and shocked the church, already rendered uneasy by the lack of direction during the last years of Pope Paul. Those who had called for a strong and energetic man in August now found themselves the majority.

Of course, if strength of will were now considered more important than pastoral qualities, an Italian curialist might still be the choice. Here, Cardinal Benelli might seem the obvious contender. It was later said that he, having organized the election of Luciani, entered the October conclave on his own account, as it were. He undoubtedly had considerable support; according to one version he came close to election on the fourth ballot.[24] His weakness was that the Italians - even the Italian curialists - were by no means united behind him. Those who had been foremost in urging the need for a 'strong' pope - Cardinals Siri, Ursi of Naples, Felici, the former General-Secretary of the Council - who were, in fact, accused of creating a 'strategy of tension' to elect one, did not agree that Benelli fitted this description.[25]

In the meantime, support for Cardinal Wojtyla had been growing. He had received some votes even at the August conclave.[26] As a synodal activist and energetic globetrotter he was well known to most of the college, admired and, not least, liked. Despite his comparative youth (fifty-eight), he was a very experienced diocesan bishop. No one who had any knowledge of his record could dispute his strength of character, his toughness as a negotiator or his loyalty to Catholicism. His evident robust health was a distinct advantage. In one important respect, however, he had exactly the same appeal as Luciani: he was known to be a reformer within the Catholic *ethos*. His interest in St John of the Cross and St Teresa of Avila, the two Carmelite reformers of the sixteenth century, was a pointer in this direction. Equally important was the effort he had made over many years, both in his own archdiocese and in Rome, to apply the reforms ordered by the Council in the spirit in which they had been adopted, that is, as renewal, not *carte blanche* for doctrinal and liturgical adventurism. His orthodoxy on all essentials was established beyond possibility of doubt. To the cardinals, many of them elderly men who had become increasingly alarmed by the drift to anarchy within the church, Wojtyla must have seemed – as the balloting proceeded and they contemplated the possibility of his election – a young and virile champion of the church's true interests, not afraid to welcome and use change, but wedded to that changelessness of the spirit which is the very heart and essence of Catholic traditionalism, and can be summed up in four words: the acceptance of authority. Here was a paladin from the church's far-flung and embattled frontiers, steeled in action, fervent in duty, born to obey but willing to command.

It must not be supposed, however, that Wojtyla appealed strongly only to apprehensive conservatives. His candidacy was promoted just as energetically by European liberals like Cardinal König of Vienna. It is a small footnote to history that the first Pole to be made pope almost certainly received the vote of every German-speaking cardinal. But the election was overwhelming anyway – 103 votes out of 109 (I exclude Wojtyla's own) on the last ballot. There are four different accounts of how he received the news that he had been decisively elected, but all agree that he was visibly shaken, indeed uncharacteristically flustered for a man accustomed to taking decisions promptly and with confidence. He insisted on receiving the personal endorsement and approbation of his superior, Cardinal Wyszynski. It is an unfortunate custom of the conclave that the pope must choose his pontifical name in the perturbation of spirit which immediately follows his election, when humble astonishment is often uppermost of judgement. Hence the many Clements, Innocents and Piuses. The new pope said, nearly a year later, that when John Paul I had told the cardinals who elected him that he would take those names, 'to me personally it seemed to be charismatic'.[27] That was his *ex post facto* justification for perpetuating the awkward combination commemorating two popes, one of them likely to be soon forgotten.

Wojtyla was elected on the evening of 16 October 1978, and appeared on the balcony of St Peter's at about 7.20 in the evening. The crowd had received the announcement of his name thirty-five minutes earlier in some bewilderment. Commenting later, Cardinal

Benelli said: 'There was not the convergence of votes on an Italian needed to be elected pope. But this did not matter: in the church there are no foreigners.'[28] To the Romans, however, there are foreigners. The pope is their bishop. I well remember hearing on the wireless the exultant shout which went up from the crowd when one of their own, a Roman born and bred, Eugenio Pacelli, was elected in 1939. But the Roman crowd is volatile. When the new pope addressed them in slightly accented but otherwise flawless Italian, they melted. His words were well chosen and are worth repeating: 'The cardinals have summoned a new bishop of Rome. They have called him from a far-away country: far-away yet close, because of our communion in the traditions of the church. ... I was afraid to accept that responsibility. Yet I do so in a spirit of obedience to the Lord and total faithfulness to Mary our most holy Mother.'

With this simple and heartfelt statement – the reference to the Virgin was absolutely characteristic and well received by the Romans – Wojtyla became the youngest pope since the election of Pius IX in 1846, the first non-Italian since 1522, the first pope from the Slavic east and the first pope with direct experience of the greatest challenge Christianity has ever faced, totalitarian atheism. The titles he assumed on 16 October 1978 were sonorous: 'Bishop of Rome, High Priest of the Universal Church, Patriarch of the West, Primate of Italy, Archbishop and Metropolitan of the Roman Province and Sovereign of the Vatican City State'.[29] But the reality of the task awaiting him was grim.

3

The Mission

THE PAPACY has the longest continuous history of any religious or spiritual institution on earth, and it remains by far the most influential. John XXIII, not a vainglorious man, saw it as the pivot of three concentric circles: the broad inner circle of Catholicism itself, the wider circle of Christianity as a whole, and the general orbit of human monotheism. The papacy, as he conceived it, had a divine responsibility to all three, indeed to mankind as a whole, and a wise pope could win a hearing even in the outer circles. It was John's achievement that, in his short pontificate, he won that hearing. It was Paul VI's secret sorrow that he knew he had largely lost it, even within the inner circle of Latin Christianity.

There can be no doubt that when John Paul II assumed the papacy he had John's thoughts very much in mind. How could he not? All Polish leaders have been driven by the harsh facts of their geographical and historical predicament to look beyond their borders for relief: their salvation lies not in their national faith, valorous though it be, but in international hope. John Paul was and is an internationalist by interest, by inclination and by faith. His perspective is global; his parish is the species. Six months after his election, on Sunday 11 March 1979, he told the noon-time crowd in St Peter's Square that his first encyclical, *Redemptor Hominis*, which he was about to publish, reflected what he called 'the central task of my new ecclesiastical service', which was 'to interpret the connection between the redemption and the dignity of man'.[1] This interpretation of his pontificate, the implications of which we shall examine shortly, clearly refers to his wider role as the high priest of the planet. John Paul was saying that his work was designed to offer benefit to every single human being.

However, the pope also has a more direct and specific responsibility to some 750 million Roman Catholics, the largest religious community on earth. This duty has inevitably thrust itself on his attention from the first second of taking office. How best to serve the church? How, indeed, to save it from destruction?

The Roman Catholic Church has throughout its history tended to throw a superhuman burden on the person of the pontiff, believing he has superhuman assistance in carrying it. The health of the church has revolved around the activity of the papal office and the policies and judgement of the men who discharge it. Christian Rome had been synonymous with spiritual autocracy and centralized direction even before its bishops inherited the residual authority of the Western Roman emperor. Their efforts to exert this authority were inhibited only by distance and their own exiguous means.

From the mid-eleventh century, and especially during the pontificate of Gregory VII (1073-85), the popes built up the international system of canon law, with their own court (or curia) in Rome as the ultimate court of appeal, which was the basis of the papal triumphalism of the later Middle Ages. The church triumphant was the communion of the saints in heaven; triumphalism was the notion that some of the potency of the heavenly court was discharged in Rome. There, the pope exercised vicariously the authority of Christ and dispensed justice to monarchs as well as their subjects, his decisions ultimately determining every aspect of human behaviour. This form of Latin-Christian totalitarianism came closest to realization under the Italian jurist Innocent III (1198-1216), though it reached its ultimate expression in the Bull *Unam Sanctam* (1302) of Boniface VIII (1293-1303).[2] Long before the Reformation, however, papal pretensions were being challenged both from within the church - by the reformers and the conciliar movement in the early fifteenth century - and from without by secular nationalism.[3]

The Reformation destroyed papal authority in northern Europe but provoked in turn an internal reformation within the rump of Latin Christianity during the Council of Trent (1545-53). Tridentine Catholicism, as it is sometimes called, is the foundation of the modern Roman Catholic Church, based upon a reformed but still authoritarian papacy, a well-trained priesthood and the strength of new élite orders such as the Jesuits (founded in 1534).[4] During the Counter-Reformation, which extended from 1550 to the end of the Thirty Years' War and the Peace of Westphalia (1648), the papacy and its secular allies, chiefly the Habsburgs, stemmed the Protestant Reformation. They consolidated Roman Catholicism in Italy, Spain and Portugal and their overseas dependencies, France and southern Germany and the Austrian Empire, as well as outlying bastions like Ireland and Poland. But northern Europe could not be brought back to Roman allegiance by force or persuasion and the Catholic monarchs tired of the effort to do so. When the papacy refused to accept Westphalia and the doctrine it embraced, *cuius regio eius religio* (the religion of a state is that of its prince), its influence in Europe and the world abruptly declined and remained slight for 150 years.[5]

It was Pope Benedict XIV (1740-58) who first demonstrated the possibility of a modern-minded and adaptable papacy. But not until the French Revolution and the Napoleonic Wars had demonstrated the need for an institution of international legitimacy and traditional authority more durable than fragile secular dynasties, did the papacy take on a new vigour. It also acquired a new populism, appealing directly to the parish congregations, by-passing secular courts and national hierarchies alike.[6] The coming of railways and the growth of the modern pilgrimage, especially to Rome itself, and the rise of Catholic newspapers, made Pius IX (1846-78) better known and loved among ordinary Catholics than any of his predecessors. He celebrated this resurgent and democratic triumphalism by convening the First Vatican Council (1869-70) which formulated the traditional belief in papal infallibility as dogma.[7]

From 1870 to the death of Pope Pius XII in 1958, the papacy and so the church remained committed to neo-triumphalism, that is, to the notion that all authority in the church in dogmatic and moral teaching, no less than in administrative rule, lay in the papacy. This meant that the degree to which the church adapted to the modern world was determined from above, by the pope himself. The views of the popes varied, but within fairly narrow limits. In an appendix to his encyclical *Quanta Cura* (1864), Pius IX

condemned eighty erroneous propositions, embracing rationalism, socialism and communism, liberalism and various forms of
modern thought, including the assertion that the 'Roman Pontiff
can and ought to reconcile and adjust himself to progress, liberalism
and modern civilization'. However, his successor Leo XIII (1878–
1903), while never repudiating the Syllabus of Errors, proceeded to
adjust himself to progress in a series of encyclicals dealing with
social problems, including the famous *Rerum Novarum* (1891),
which became the basis for modern Catholic teaching on capitalism,
industry, trade unions and wages.[8] But Leo was rigid on many
aspects of dogma, condemning Rosmini (1887), Anglican Orders
(1896) and 'Americanism' (1899). The doctrinal screws were
tightened still further under Pius X (1903–14); he condemned
the 'Modernist' movement in the encyclical *Pascendi* (1907) and
imposed an anti-Modernist oath on the clergy.[9]

With Benedict XV (1914–22) there was a return to some degree
of liberalism, and this pattern was, broadly speaking, maintained
under his successors Pius XI (1922–39) and Pius XII (1939–58).[10]
Pius XI signed the Lateran Treaty, which regularized relations with
the Italian state, and reaffirmed Leo XIII's social teaching. Pius XII
modernized the church on many points of detail during his long
pontificate. But under both men there was no devolution of authority, little encouragement of internal discussion and a recurrent
tendency to pounce on efforts at doctrinal innovation, exemplified
by the Pius XII encyclical *Humani Generis* (1950), which led to the
silencing and scattering of progressive theologians. The same year
Pius published his encyclical *Munificentissimus Deus*, which defined
the Assumption of the Blessed Virgin as dogma (the first and so far
the only use of the formal powers invested in the papacy by the
infallibility decree). This was widely regarded as a gesture of
defiance towards the other Christian churches and towards liberals
within Roman Catholicism. During the final years of Pius XII the
church in its external aspects seemed healthy; it had never been
more numerous or, apparently, more self-confident or stable. But
the brighter spirits within found its atmosphere of uncreative
conservatism oppressive, and its immobility dangerous. There was
a widespread feeling that the church had run out of dynamism,
both intellectual and spiritual, and that it might become the victim

either of an unpredictable explosion from within, or more likely of gradual and ultimately uncontrollable apathy spreading from below. So, once again, the papacy determined on an act of leadership, of reform from above: John XXIII (1958–63) 'opened the windows' of the Vatican as he put it, summoned the Council and began the latest epoch in Roman Catholic history.

There were clearly both opportunities and risks in this procedure. The risks in calling a council with no specific agenda in mind – nothing more than a vague desire to 'update', as John put it – were pointed out to the Pope by the curia, who feared it would serve as an open invitation to radicals of every kind to press their claims. The opportunities, however, received much more attention. The Council was undoubtedly 'popular', in the sense that most of the informed élite who take a strong personal interest in the affairs of the church, from bishops to ecclesiastical journalists, welcomed the event. During the first session, Pope John intervened decisively to prevent the curialists from stifling free and wide-ranging discussion.[11] After his death, Paul VI continued the Council, though pressed by the curia to wind it up quickly. He did withdraw from its deliberations two inflammatory subjects, clerical marriage and contraception, but he allowed the gathering to take its natural course of four full sessions, and to produce a very substantial body of work covering almost every aspect of the church's beliefs and activities.

The Council cannot be described as inspirational. It disappointed the progressives, in that it did not reverse the verdict of the First Vatican Council, introduce a 'conciliar era', downgrade the pope from autocrat to constitutional sovereign, and perpetuate itself in some form as a legislative body. The general synods which followed it remained consultative and advisory only, and their summons and dismissal a matter for the pope's decision. In other words the church remained, in this respect, a fragment of the *ancien régime*, without a formal constitution binding on its head, who retained his powers intact.

On the other hand, the pope's freedom to use these powers, or rather to use them without open opposition and defiance, was evidently much diminished. This became evident when Paul VI in 1968 reaffirmed the church's ban on artificial contraception by publishing his encyclical *Humanae Vitae*. The Council might not have limited papal authority in theory; but it undermined it in practice. Hence, though the results of the Council seemed meagre to radical spirits, they were quite enough to alarm the traditionalists. They lamented many grievous losses: Latin as the primary language of the liturgy; the Tridentine liturgy itself, now changed almost beyond recognition; many ancient services and devotional practices; and many famous saints from the early centuries, now dismissed as spiritual fictions, canonized non-persons. If Paul VI was more conservative than Pope John in protecting the inner power structure of the church, he was far more ruthless in changing or scrapping its external fabric. He not only cast away his own tiara but took from the cardinals their splendid red hats, festooned with tassels. He turned the altar into little more than a communion table. Some modernizers went much further. In many churches the neo-baroque altars which had been such a prominent expression of nineteenth- and twentieth-century ultramontanism were gouged out and put on the bonfire. Laymen and laywomen were encouraged to take prominent roles in the new vernacular masses. Many of the old triumphalist hymns were banned, being replaced by ones less likely to impede the cause of ecumenism, or by 'folk hymns' accompanied by guitar music. There was, in short, a systematic dismantling of the devotional aesthetic of the Counter-Reformation, a deliberate dispersal of the mysterious opacity and the evocation of the supernatural with which Catholicism had designedly surrounded herself. At the same time, the absolute distinction between priest and layman, which the church had maintained throughout the Dark and Middle Ages, and indeed reinforced in the Tridentine reforms, was now obscured. While plain daylight replaced the numinous, the demotic began to infringe upon the hieratic. The combined result of all these changes was to banish the reverential awe with which Catholics had always regarded the machinery of their church and the men who worked it.

From the perspective of today, the Council can be seen as merely one manifestation of the world-wide challenge to authority in every field which was the outstanding characteristic of the 1960s. It was a decade of illusion, in which eager spirits were led by long-continued prosperity to believe and propagate many Utopian notions: that poverty could be abolished, cruelty and violence legislated out of existence, every freedom infinitely extended and voraciously enjoyed, and some kind of democratic and egalitarian paradise established on earth. The vast and unconsidered expansion of higher education was both a product and accelerator of these illusory forces, pouring on to the scene countless armies of young graduates, who shared these fantastic hopes and set about elbowing aside the obscurantist and authoritarian elders who alone, it was argued, prevented their realization.

As a result of the Council and the forces it unleashed, the Catholic Church too became a victim of this youthful and radical frenzy. The liturgical reforms authorized by the Council were treated as a mere platform on which to erect a superstructure of experimental worship. Layfolk, men and women, invaded the altar, preached, sometimes dispensed communion. Priests abandoned their clerical garb, often even their vestments. Even bishops were seen to flaunt secular clothes and habits. Seeking to involve themselves more in the lives of their congregations, the clergy embarked on varieties of social work, became consequentially involved in politics and so progressed to militant political activism, not excluding violence. The notion of prayer, devotion, intercession and grace, of a church revolving round the sacraments, and of a clergy whose principal duty was to administer them, was pushed into the background.

Moral theology was revised, often on a do-it-yourself basis. The teaching of *Humanae Vitae* was very widely disregarded, and many priests and even bishops ceased to press the point. That was not surprising. More remarkable was the increasing willingness to obscure the church's presentation of the moral law over the whole range of issues covered by the Sixth and Ninth Commandments, a presentation which had hitherto been crystalline and unvarying. Catholic clerics were now found willing to exculpate adultery and fornication, acquit the divorced, extenuate homosexuality and other sexual perversions and apologize for the milder forms of pornography. To some extent this growing licence was paralleled by a relaxation of discipline by the church's own canonical organs. The annulment of defective marriages, widely regarded as the church's own form of divorce, became much easier and less expensive. More remarkable still, a new leniency was displayed, on an ever-increasing scale, in releasing members of the clergy, regular and secular, male and female, from their vows of lifetime service, without the least ecclesiastical penalty. So a trickle of ex-priests and monks, and of ex-nuns too, quickly became a torrent. And those thus released on the world, with the full blessing of the church authorities, remained in full communion – often as hyperactive lay persons – and promptly agitated for yet more fundamental changes in the way Catholicism conducted itself.

Inevitably the passion for change invaded the sphere of dogmatic theology. The victims of Pius XII's purge in the early sixties had long since been rehabilitated; had, indeed, taken a prominent, even predominant, role among the *periti* or experts of the Council. Now, they became the honoured doctors of the new, liberated church. Their pupils and disciples, raised to high positions in Catholic seminaries, universities and schools, began to enlarge the frontiers of orthodoxy to encompass ever-widening territories hitherto regarded as dubiously speculative or plainly heterodox. The church's *magisterium*, or teaching authority, came under special challenge, as was to be expected. More disturbing, though following a pattern long since established in the Protestant churches of the West, fundamental axioms of Christianity, such as the incarnation, were brought under suspicion. The fear grew that there was no tenet of the faith of ordinary Catholics which was now immune to reinterpretation and representation, often in unrecognizable guise, or indeed outright abandonment.

The decade of illusion was succeeded by the decade of disillusionment. During the mid-1970s, the collapse of the great post-war economic boom demolished the easy Utopianism which had been so prevalent in the secular sphere. Extravagant hopes were now abandoned, ambitious policies reversed. Religion was not immune from this returning sobriety. As the seventies progressed, the risks which were pointed out to Pope John when he summoned his Council were now seen to have been only too real. The bill for 'renewal' was being paid: damaged authority, lost certitudes, lower discipline, above all a thinning out in the ranks of the faithful. During the decade 1965–75, the Roman Catholic Church, hitherto impervious to the ravages of secularism which had afflicted all the

Protestant churches, began to experience declining congregations for the first time. There was also a fall in vocations to the secular priesthood, to the orders of monks and friars, and among women's orders. As departures from the clergy continued to increase, there was a growing shortage of priests, and indeed of religious staff of all kinds, which in some areas assumed the proportions of a catastrophe.

This disturbing trend can be illustrated by two striking examples. Throughout the reign of Pius XII, the Jesuits, the largest, best-trained and most highly disciplined body in the church, had continued to expand. In 1939 there had been 26,000 of them; there were 30,000 in 1950, 34,000 in 1958. When the Council opened in 1962, there were no fewer than 36,000 Jesuits on station throughout the world, a doubling in size since 1920. By the end of the 1960s, this impressive expansion had been reversed. In the 1970s, the Society declined by a third, and the number of students and novices from 16,000 to a mere 3,000. When Pope John Paul II took office, there were fewer Jesuits than at any time since the 1920s.[12]

Again, at the accession of John Paul II, he found his own diocese of Rome in a state which, in embattled Poland, would have been regarded as deplorable. To serve its three million Catholic inhabitants there were only 1,153 priests, half of them from religious orders and many of them foreign. Very few indeed of these priests were born in Rome, the diocese itself producing only a handful of ordinands each year (seven in 1978). Rome, *mirabile dictu*, even lacked churches: some seventy of its parishes had no proper sacramental building. Not surprisingly, some 25 per cent of Romans were now contracting civil marriages, a figure which would once have seemed incredible.[13]

These two examples highlight a world picture which was in many areas much less disconcerting, but where contraction and crisis could be discerned almost everywhere. Traditionalists blamed the dwindling numbers on the Council and its changes. Progressives argued that the decline was part of an irresistible trend towards secularization, and would have been still more pronounced if the changes had not been made. They blamed the church's policy on such issues as contraception, and the continued ban on married or women clergy, for the reduced congregations and the shortage of priests. To which the traditionalists retorted that the Protestant churches had surrendered on these and most other issues, and were in a still worse state.

Both factions heaped the responsibility on the shoulders of Paul VI, especially during his last years, when the magnitude of the crisis became apparent and his efforts to deal with it increasingly feeble. It is characteristic of John Paul II that, since taking over and grasping the scale of the problem himself, he has always referred to Paul's efforts with conspicuous loyalty and generosity. On 8 August 1979, on the first anniversary of Paul's death, he spoke of his continuing 'to toil indefatigably for the transformation of man, society and political systems'.[14] A month later he referred to Paul as 'the Peter of our times' and said he admired the way in which he stood up, rock-like, to the shocks in the aftermath of the Council.[15] He clearly feels that the criticism of Paul VI has been largely unjustified and grossly misinformed; that the critics have no conception of what it means to rule the Roman Catholic Church.

The Roman Catholic Church is, in truth, an enormous organization. When John Paul II took office there were 739,126,000 Catholics out of a total world population of 4,094,110,000 – about 18 per cent of mankind. Diocesan returns (the true figures are somewhat higher) put the number of the clergy at 1,556,754, with 403,801 priests, 4,456 deacons, 68,426 lay religious, 946,398 nuns and lay-sisters, and 133,673 catechists in the missions. There were 331,960 parishes, composing some 2,372 ecclesiastical territories: 1,640 dioceses, 402 metropolitan sees, 54 archbishoprics and 12 patriarchal sees. The church runs an astonishing variety of different institutions, ranging from newspapers and radio stations to hospitals; but above all it is a major educational force in the world, running 79,207 primary schools, over 28,000 secondary schools, and universities which, at the end of 1977, contained 986,000 students.[16]

The administrative pyramid which controls this vast conglomerate has a very narrow apex. From time to time the pope must take a direct interest in the affairs of each diocese. Certain issues always go to the pope and he may, at any moment, be forced to cudgel his wits over the affairs of a troubled priest or nun ten thousand miles away. As both head of government and head of state, he is involved in the explosion of inter-government activity which has been such an expensive and time-consuming feature of our age. When the Vatican's diplomats attended a private summit meeting at Frascati in September 1973 they numbered thirty-six nuncios, thirty-six pro-nuncios, sixteen apostolic delegates and one *chargé d'affaires*. State visits to the Vatican increase steadily: ten under Pius XI, twenty-six under Pius XII, thirty-four under John XXIII, ninety under Paul VI.[17] The effect of the Council has been greatly to increase the number and activities of devolved and consultative organs within the church and so, paradoxically, the work of its central government, and not least its size, which trebled under Paul VI. All these developments have increased the work of the pope, who remains of course an autocrat, directing policy personally, and not a constitutional sovereign.

However, autocrat though he may be, the man in charge of a world body of this size is at the mercy of demographic forces which he cannot control or even influence. That, I think, is one reason why John Paul II is so anxious to exculpate Paul VI from responsibility for the church's troubles, which are as much the result of nature as of policy. For virtually all its existence the Catholic Church has been predominantly a European institution, reflecting the cultural assumptions, in the widest sense, which Europeans – and especially southern Europeans – take for granted. On the eve of the Council, the Catholics of what might be termed the heartlands (Europe plus North America) were still the majority, 267 million or 51.5 per cent of the whole. Catholics from the poorer countries, the so-called 'Third World', numbered 251 million or 48.5 per cent. By the time John Paul II was elected, this ratio had been decisively reversed. Of the sixteen countries with Catholic populations of more than ten million, eight were 'Third World' – the order being Brazil (with over 100 million Catholics), Mexico, Italy, the Argentine, Colombia, Peru, Venezuela, France, Spain, Poland, West Germany, Czechoslovakia, the United States, Canada, Zaire and the Philippines.[18] By the year 2000 relative birth-rates will ensure that 70 per cent of all Catholics will live in the poor countries, with Latin America and Africa providing more than half.

The biggest single problem facing the church is how to look

after these vast congregations. Latin America, for instance, is already grievously short of priests: less than 1.5 for every 10,000 Catholics in Central America, against a world average of 5.5 and a North American figure of 11.6.[19] The demographic shift, moreover, contains a social change of equal importance. Until very recently, the Catholic Church was a church of peasants, both in Europe and in Latin America, with all that implies in terms of devotional and cultural attitudes. It is rapidly becoming a church of city-dwellers, even of big-city dwellers. The problems of the Rome diocese, already described, reflect this process in miniature. Between 1870, the end of the First Vatican Council, and 1965, the end of the Second, the city of Rome's population rose from 200,000 to nearly three million. By the end of the year 2000 about half the world's population will live in big cities, 252 million in cities with over five million each. Many of these monster cities will be Catholic, including the two biggest, Mexico City with thirty-one million people, and São Paulo with nearly twenty-six million. How will the church accommodate itself to these vast megalopolitan congregations? Or will it, in practice, lose them? And how will the Vatican, once the geographical and cultural centre of Catholicism, modify its role as, increasingly, it sees itself pushed to the periphery?

John Paul II had seen such demographic changes at work in Poland, albeit on a more modest scale, and had acquired twenty years' experience of coping with them. He had first become aware of the need for urban evangelism, for instance, in 1947 when he visited France and read Father Henri Godin's remarkable book, *La France, pays de mission*, which set in motion the *prêtres-ouvriers*.[20] He had formed his own views, during his years as a bishop and a world traveller, of the extent to which papal policy could master these trends and turn them to account, and the extent to which they were stronger than any human agency. But then, in his belief, the Roman Catholic Church, and the papacy, are not, or not wholly, human agencies. Therein lies a dilemma. To what extent should the church allow itself to be prudently guided by a sociology of religion, with all the relevant statistics and graphs? And to what extent should it put its trust in its supernatural mission, to which sociological considerations are irrelevant? The dilemma was adumbrated in St Augustine's great work, *The City of God*, written just after the fall of Rome, in which all earthly constructs are presented as ephemeral and unimportant beside the shining transcendency of the celestial metropolis. This book remained the most influential of all throughout the Middle Ages, but the church flourished mightily in earthly Rome, which it embellished and enriched, and could never bring itself to follow St Augustine's advice.

At John Paul II's accession, two broad courses lay open to him. The first was to continue the policy of adjusting Catholic attitudes to changes in the world, to reflect sociological patterns in the church's pastoral and moral theology, and intellectual trends in its dogmatic theology. This would involve what might be termed 'responsive evangelism', in which the church answered appeals and met needs as articulated by those who claimed to speak for the Catholic rank-and-file, even against its own better judgement. Another, and more pejorative, description of this strategy was 'consumer evangelism', as practised by some Protestant churches in the United States. So far as Catholicism was concerned, it had not worked very effectively, perhaps because it was attempted under Paul VI with insufficient enthusiasm and confidence, by men who did not really believe in it. But it could be given a few more years to prove itself, and more vigorous support from above.

The alternative course was to assume that the policy of the sixties and seventies was fundamentally misconceived. The great majority of Roman Catholics did not want constant change and adjustment. They had been harried into accepting it by a self-appointed militant élite. What most Catholics wanted was for the church to reaffirm its traditional teaching, offer them not doubts but certitudes, not debates and arguments but dogmatism, not responses but leadership, not politics but apologetics, not the prosaic but the supernatural, not democracy and social justice but grace abundant, not Utopia on earth - let alone Subtopia on earth - but life eternal.

By instinct and training, by intellectual conviction and personal experience, John Paul II was aware that the second policy came closer to that prudence which is the first of the cardinal virtues those holding high office in the church are expected to possess. But in adopting it he was aware it was unlikely to succeed unless he could give to the church's traditional view of the world an inspirational strength and intellectual transcendence which was new and vigorous. Was this beyond his powers? It was not. The faculties he had been given, and the life he had been allotted, had prepared him for this task. He set about it without prolonged hesitation and with enviable confidence.

Part Two

THE FIVE EVILS
OF THE AGE

4

The Crucifixion
of Man

ONCE JOHN PAUL II assumed the papacy, it quickly became
apparent that, at the very centre of his reinterpretation of the
Christian message, is a new kind of Christian humanism, a philosophy of man which might almost be termed a form of Christian
Prometheanism. Man is the greatest of God's creations, and the
most precious to Him. John Paul often repeats the great text from
St John's Gospel which is the key to the Christian dynamic: 'God
so loved the world, that he gave his only begotten Son, that
whosoever believeth in him should not perish, but have everlasting
life.'[1] Man is peerless in creation; but also fallible and vulnerable.
It is God's design that man should be cherished and protected, not
least from himself; the primary function of his church, therefore,
acting vicariously for God on earth, is to defend man. It does this
by teaching man about his nature, clarifying his rights and duties,
and showing him how to defend the former and how to discharge
the latter. In this process the church reveals the ubiquity and
transcendence of God in all man's acts and aspirations.

The defence of man: those four words describe the mission
which John Paul sees for himself as the principal Christian spokes-
man on earth. He sees man as threatened by a variety of malign
forces which, for the purpose of this book, I have grouped together
under five heads. Far and away the most potent of these evils – in
his opinion, the one most likely to bring about a veritable crucifixion of mankind on earth – is totalitarian atheism. It threatens to
accomplish both the intellectual and the physical enslavement of
man. It is a dagger pointing at man's heart, poison for his brain,
suffocation for his spirit. Of all the evils encompassing man, this is
the one of which John Paul has the most personal experience,

which is never far from his thoughts and fears, and which – if a spiritual Armageddon is approaching – will be, in his view, the chief enemy.

At his installation, John Paul remarked in his address, which he gave in a number of languages (including, be it noted, Ukrainian and Lithuanian), 'With what veneration the Apostle of Christ must utter this word: "Man"!' I call John Paul's view of man Promethean because he appears to see man as a creature of almost limitless gifts and unimaginable destiny. Now here is the poignancy of the threat which totalitarian atheism poses: for it, too, takes a Promethean view of man but, by depriving man of his true origins and destiny, threatens to turn him into a collective Frankenstein's monster.[2]

John Paul is well instructed in the theory of Marxism-Leninism. He brought with him to the October conclave, and was observed reading it there, the latest issue of a quarterly review of Marxist theory.[3] Unlike most Catholic priests, he has taken the trouble to master the Marxist theory of religion. (Indeed he often uses expressions familiar to Marxist-type thinkers, such as 'contradictions', 'distortions', 'negative forces', and so forth.)[4]

Marxist religious theory has as its basis Hegelian notions of progress. The world is infinite in time and space, with nature the absolute, and in this world the principle of emergent evolution is at work, marked by 'dialectical leaps' or breaks, producing new qualities. In this process, the only point at which nature, the absolute, achieves consciousness is in the emergent consciousness of man. This consciousness is a product of matter, a superstructure on the physical process, and social consciousness, too, depends on matter, that is, the economic life of society. Consciousness can penetrate everything and in the end know everything. Therefore the task of man, as the bearer of consciousness, is progress; he does consciously what nature does unconsciously, accelerates evolution by scrutinizing nature and society with his reason. So each individual has a task which transcends his personal desires, and only when he is capable of identifying these desires with the aims of society as a whole (the absolute) can he be really happy.[5]

It is this notion of man as alone responsible for progress, being the only conscious being in nature, transforming himself and his world in an unending effort of heroism, which led Marx – like many other late-eighteenth- and nineteenth-century thinkers who turned against religion – to see Prometheus as the model of social man. Prometheus, the Titan who stole fire from the gods and gave it to man – and was horribly punished for it – was described by Marx in the foreword to his doctoral dissertation as 'the most eminent saint and martyr in the philosophical calendar'.[6] Indeed, Marx saw himself as Prometheus, chained to a printing-press and attacked by the Prussian eagle. The myth of Prometheus was the beginning of human understanding and progress. 'All mythology', he wrote, 'overcomes and dominates and shapes the forces of nature in the imagination and by the imagination; it therefore vanishes with the advent of real mastery over them.' The duty of modern man is to move beyond myth and 'reproduce its truth at a higher stage'.[7] The myth of Prometheus, rather than the myth of Christ, adumbrates the true programme of action for man, and his proper relationship with 'God': 'The confession of Prometheus, in simple words "I hate the pack of Gods", is its own confession, its own aphorism against all heavenly and earthly gods who do not acknowledge human self-consciousness as the highest divinity.'[8]

Marx's presentation of Prometheus is in fact based upon a misreading of Aeschylus's *Prometheus Bound*, an error perpetuated by Marxist scholars to this day.[9] The comparison with Christ is further misleading, since Marx is confusing myth with history. However that may be, Prometheus serves him as a launching-point for an attack on religion itself, as a pseudo-science. It is a false and obsolete science, refuted by true, empirical science; a false metaphysic, too, since it is dualistic, admitting an 'other' world, beyond and above nature. It denies the possibility of an earthly paradise and distrusts human reason by revolving around mysteries which are inaccessible to man's understanding. Its moral values are false since it presents salvation as individualistic, personal rather than social. As salvation is presented as beyond, rather than on, earth, it inhibits man from performing his appropriate social duties here. Some of its precepts may be benevolent but they are egotistically directed towards securing personal happiness. By presenting God as the absolute, religion is anti-humanistic, denies man his Promethean vocation, and degrades him into the mere tool or plaything of a superior being.[10]

Marx's theory of historical materialism then goes on to argue that the notion of religion is not autonomous but a reflection of the economic life of society, part of the 'superstructure' of art, morality, philosophy and religion, reflecting a set of social relations corresponding to a particular mode of production. Modes of production are dominated by class struggle, and each antagonistic class has its own type of social consciousness. Religion is a characteristic feature of a society where exploitation is the norm: for the exploited it is an opiate, for the exploiter it offers a passport to paradise. Hence, in a society where there is no exploitation, religion will have no function and will disappear.

Now if Roman Catholicism were dealing simply with pure Marxist regimes, the problem would simply be a matter of argument, not of physical conflict. Marx despised religion and regarded its importance as minimal compared with other anti-social forces. Once the modes of production were changed, worship would gradually cease and even the word and concept 'God' would pass from human minds, so society could easily afford to tolerate vestigial religious practices. Unfortunately, Lenin took religion much more seriously than Marx. It was a gigantic conspiracy. Religious motives were behind virtually every philosophical opinion. Philosophers were the learned lackeys of the theologians. There was, he wrote, nothing more abominable than religion. Marx saw religion as pathetic. For Stalin, a typical anti-clerical, it was corrupt. But Lenin hated and was obsessed by religion; he had an intense personal dislike of any religious manifestation. In his view, the purer and more disinterested religious faith and observance are, the more dangerous they become. Since those who are saintly and selfless have more influence than the immoral and egotistical, clerics who make common cause with the proletariat against the capitalists are much more dangerous than those who defend exploitation.[11]

It was Lenin, therefore, who gave to the Soviet system and its manifestation in the Russian satellites its characteristic of intense, systematic and violent hostility to religion. Religion will not just disappear, or rather will not disappear quickly enough for the health of society, may indeed even be perpetuated by outside assistance from the capitalist world which rightly recognizes its value to the bourgeois cause. Hence it must be actively stamped out, by propaganda and repression. It was Lenin's obsession which led to the creation in the Soviet Union of a whole series of academic institutions devoted to anti-religious propaganda, with the Institute of Scientific Atheism at the Academy of Social Sciences as the intellectual driving force. Most Communist universities have readerships or chairs in Scientific Atheism; all Soviet institutes of higher education have regular courses in this subject; and an enormous number of general and specialized textbooks on atheism are kept in print.[12] This effort has never been relaxed; indeed, it was given a fresh impetus by Nikita Khrushchev's decree of 7 June 1954 which ordered the intensified study of the subject, leading to multiple conferences and the publication of the magazine *Science and Religion*.

Religion might survive this intellectual assault. But of course propaganda is only one prong of the Leninist attack. The other takes the form of direct legal and physical restraints. As Lenin put it, 'Under no circumstances can we consider religion to be a private matter with regard to our own party.'[13] Hence the exercise of religion is in practice, and to a great extent in law too, treated as hostile to the party monopoly (or 'leading role' as it is called) of power and influence.

Communist tactics, however, vary a good deal. In Albania, religion has been officially abolished. The Communist seizure and consolidation of power there, in the late 1940s, was marked by terrible violence against clerics, whether Orthodox, Catholic or Moslem. Muftis and Grand Muftis were systematically executed or murdered, including even leaders of the Moslem Bektashi sect who supported the Communists during the war. Two Catholic archbishops and many priests were executed for 'leading terrorist bands'. Orthodox bishops were deposed or sent to prison. This process seems to have culminated in 1967, when the Albanian official monthly *Nëndori* wrote that the remaining 2,169 churches, mosques, monasteries and all other religious establishments whatsoever had now been closed; Albania had thus become 'the first atheist state in the world'.[14] The Albanian Communist dictator, Enver Hoxha, told the Sixth Party Congress in November 1971 that the final closing of all places of worship was 'a decisive victory'.[15]

Next to Albania, the Soviet Union itself has come closest to placing religious manifestations completely under state control or eliminating them. As the 1970 Tashkent Moslem Conference showed, Moslem dignitaries tend to act as propagandists for the regime, insisting that Soviet laws are essentially based on the Prophet's.[16] The Russian Orthodox authorities have long been quasi-bureaucrats of the Soviet regime. This was why, in the late 1940s, when the Soviet regime had to deal with the religious consequences of the post-war frontiers, they decided on the forcible reunification of the Uniate churches of Eastern Europe with the Orthodox Church. This involved placing four million Uniates in the Ukraine, 460,000 in Carpathia, 1.57 million in Rumania and 320,000 in Slovakia – all of whom had been in communion with Rome since the early seventeenth century – under the 'spiritual direction' of the Orthodox authorities. Their only valid religious activities are carried out underground, therefore, and are illegal. The Roman Catholic Church organization in Russia was effectively destroyed in the 1930s purges, and was never allowed to re-establish itself after 1945. No religious instruction is permitted, and there is not a single Catholic monastery or convent, school or welfare institution in the entire USSR, though it includes Lithuania, with two million Catholics, and Latvia with half a million.[17] There are no Catholic publications (though an edition of the Bible was printed in 1968) and churches were still being demolished in the 1970s.

During the late 1940s and throughout most of the fifties, there was direct religious persecution of Catholics all over Eastern Europe. In 1955 an estimated 5,000 priests and 10,000 nuns were in prison or forced labour camps.[18] An easing-up began on 8 December 1956 when a desperate Polish government came to a *modus vivendi* with the Polish church. Over the last quarter-century, the more obvious forms of persecution have been progressively abandoned in Poland, and to a lesser extent in East Germany. In Czechoslovakia, persecution has varied with the degree of servility to Moscow: thus, in 1968, as a result of the 'Prague Spring', eighty-seven churches were under construction in East Slovakia alone; by 1970, all church construction had been halted completely.[19] The Catholic Church in Czechoslovakia is still effectively a church under state persecution.

Even where direct persecution has been suspended, Soviet-type bureaucracies and legal systems circumscribe religious activities. These regimes usually have a Department of Religious Affairs, or similar, charged with the supervision of a general law on religious associations. Thus the 1949 Czech decree setting up the department charges it with 'issuance of general rules, and direction and supervision in all matters of church and religion', regulating 'personnel matters and emoluments of clergymen, teachers and employees of the theological schools', the instruction of youth, censorship of church publications, and all appointments, elections and transfers of clergymen.[20] The religious association laws (sometimes accompanied with forms of 'financial support') have their origins in Stalinism and are designed to limit the influence of the churches in society, to control their legal activities and to compel leading churchmen to declare their loyalty to the regime. In other words, a church is better off without this type of law (and especially without state money). Such laws make the churches submit all their statutes for approval, register any body, however tiny, get approval for all meetings other than regular church services, themselves determined in conjunction with the state authorities, and submit pastoral letters and other announcements to censorship. Any church contacts abroad must be made through the Foreign Ministry, and clerics are forced to take loyalty and administrative oaths, which makes it easier to fine or imprison them.

The Polish church has been the most successful in the fight against the restrictions and controls of this regulatory network. It raises its own funds and has even managed to get back some of its property. Thus it has been able to reject financial support while still maintaining a wide range of activities. It controls its own religious teaching centres, up to seminary level - and even, as I have already noted, its own university - and, since it has helped to prevent the collectivization of the peasants, it still has a solid rural base. Yet most of what it has obtained is a matter of political bargaining, not undoubted legal right, and could be capriciously removed if circumstances changed. Such toleration as it enjoys depends solely on the regime's needs for its assistance in crises, and not on any recognition of its rights. Were the Soviet Union to assert its military power, everything the church has regained would be lost overnight. Thus, to John Paul II, who knows the balance of forces in Poland down to the smallest nuance in a paragraph in *Trybuna Ludu*, the party paper, the church there is still under official sentence of death, even if execution has been suspended. He has a burning sense of the injustice done to man's right of spiritual freedom by the Communist regime in Poland and, *a fortiori*, elsewhere behind the Iron Curtain.

Moreover, coming from Poland, and having survived the Second World War there, he has a sense of the violence totalitarian atheism does to the rights of man, and the scale of the horrors to which it can lead, which transcends the mere experience of life under a Communist regime. He has known not just one but both the egregious godless tyrannies of the twentieth century. Hence his remarks to the Polish bishops at Auschwitz: 'Can anyone on this earth be surprised that a pope who came from the archdiocese which contains this camp started his first encyclical with the words *Redemptor Hominis*, and that he devoted it in full to the cause of man, the dignity of man, the threats facing man, the rights of man?'[21]

This encyclical, a long and complicated document, was issued in March 1979 and was John Paul's first measured statement of his philosophy of Christian humanism.[22] It opens with a resounding assertion which, at one and the same time, affirms the Pope's belief in the central relevance of Christianity today, the centrality of the incarnation in Christianity, and Christianity's origins not in myth but in fact: 'The redeemer of Man, Jesus Christ, is the centre of the universe and of history.' The encyclical is based essentially on St John's Gospel, which not only unequivocally asserts the divinity of Christ but also stresses the links between the redemption and human freedom. The key text which dominates the encyclical, and to which John Paul refers most frequently is: 'And ye shall know the truth, and the truth shall make you free.'[23] To John Paul, Christianity is about freedom. That freedom is internal as well as external. Indeed, that internal freedom which we secure by the understanding of our natures and the purpose of life, and by the subjugation of our baser instincts, is more complete and durable than any external freedom of action. But the inner freedoms cannot be wholly separated from the external freedoms, and in particular that freedom to hear the word, and to practise it, which makes inner freedom possible, and which we call freedom of religion. John Paul sees it as his primary mission to explain how important freedom, in its widest sense and in its multiplicity of senses, is to the church, and to identify the church with human freedom, and with the dignity and rights of the individual. A great part of the encyclical, therefore, is concerned with the exposition and explanation of the Vatican Council's Declaration on Religious Freedom promulgated on 7 December 1965.[24]

In framing *Redemptor Hominis*, it was clearly John Paul's aim to publicize it behind the Iron Curtain. Hence his insistence on an early visit to Poland, which he was able to arrange, despite great difficulties, in June 1979. The October before, his election had been greeted by official Poland with a mixture of pride and consternation. After a meeting of the Polish politburo the then party boss, Edward Gierek, said the election 'has caused great satisfaction in Poland'. But the press was instructed that no photograph of the Pope was to be wider than one column, or headline wider than two columns. The weekly Catholic paper *Tygodnik Powszechny*, in which John Paul II had a special interest, had to struggle hard to get an extra paper allocation to raise its print from 40,000 to 55,000 copies, and the censors cut one article in it and suppressed a photograph. The Polish government was represented at the Pope's installation, but travel visas were refused to three leading Catholic intellectuals, one of them a close personal friend of the new Pope.[25]

John Paul's original proposal was to visit Cracow in May 1979, for the nine-hundredth anniversary of the martyrdom of St Stanislas, an excellent occasion, as he saw it, for publicizing his encyclical. The Polish government saw this flaunting of a figure identified with the resistance of the church to an overweening state as deliberately provocative, and refused to agree. Indeed, when the Pope sent a message to his former archdiocese in December 1978, all references to St Stanislas were cut from it, and restored only after *Tygodnik Powszechny* threatened a public scandal by refusing to publish the cut version (it was eventually read out in full in all churches of the archdiocese).

An eight-day visit was eventually agreed, beginning on 2 June 1979. There were further compromises over the itinerary. John

Paul's wish to say a triumphant mass in his church at Nova Huta, built after so much resistance by the party, was too much for its pride, and he was persuaded to say mass instead at Czestochowa, Poland's most famous shrine. The regime did its best to limit the impact of the visit without provoking the anger of the population. It agreed to his celebrating eight open-air masses, and making thirty-two speeches or sermons. It accredited about 900 foreign journalists. To the popular astonishment, it even provided a giant cross for the papal appearance in Victory Square, Warsaw, though it was taken down immediately afterwards. It authorized the transmission on nationwide TV of the Pope's arrival, his reception at the government's Belvedere Palace, the open-air mass in Victory Square, and a mass he celebrated at Auschwitz. But all other coverage was only local, one reason being that Polish national TV can be seen in Czechoslovakia, Soviet Lithuania, East Germany, the Ukraine and Byelorussia, in all of which there are substantial Catholic (or Uniate) populations. The camerawork consisted mainly of papal close-ups and avoided long shots of the enormous crowds. The regime did its ineffective best to keep numbers down. Apart from indispensable announcements, official media sources were silent about the visit, and the itinerary was not published except in the Catholic press. An official document entitled 'Principles of accreditation for Polish journalists and of press coverage of the papal visit to Poland', later made public by Radio Free Europe, revealed the fears of the regime and its clumsy use of state journalists to orchestrate the coverage to its own tunes. At lower levels, officials, long used to obstructing Catholic festivities, refused coaches to special trains and closed roads leading to places where the Pope was to appear. All the same, twelve million Poles contrived to see him in the flesh.[26] At Czestochowa itself 3,500,000 were present.[27]

The Pope refrained from any provocative words or gestures. He repeatedly drew attention to his encyclical, but he made no attack on the regime for denying human rights – that was simply implicit – and he dealt with the issue directly more in the context of Auschwitz and the Nazis than in terms of the Communist denial of religious and political freedom. His object was to secure for the Catholic faith the public recognition and acceptance of its centrality in Polish history and contemporary life which the regime had hitherto denied.

In this aim he plainly succeeded. Before the immense crowds, all his actor's skills, his magnificent voice in particular, were used to great effect. His balcony appearances in the evening, impromptu but prolonged, demonstrated his ability to conduct what can only be described as an emotional dialogue with the people, in which exchanges, ejaculations, hymns, short sermons and folk-songs are blended into a highly charged performance. No other public figure today possesses this peculiar skill to the same degree: there is in fact something reassuringly old-fashioned about it, an echo of the pre-war, pre-TV age, when great men made personal, visual and aural contact with those they led. But there is none of the demagogue about John Paul. There are many flashes of humour and of humanity, but the general tone is of high seriousness. He conveys *gravitas*. He may possess the skills of an actor, but he never sounds like one. He sounds like a pope, and a great pope, discussing the most important issues human beings face in the course of their lives, and paying his audience the compliment of treating these issues at the level and length they merit. Some of his Polish sermons lasted an hour or more.

The background to nearly all his remarks was the notion of the inseparability of a people and its religious belief: religion was a fact of life, not a waning myth. The need for the divine is the most human thing about man, the heart of his humanity – and Christ, with his two natures in one person, expressed this need and its realization. No theory of man can be complete without God. No history of man can be complete without God. At Victory Square in Warsaw, on 2 June, he said: 'Christ cannot be kept out of the history of man in any part of the globe. The exclusion of Christ from the history of man is an act against man.' There could not be silence on such issues. On 3 June, at Gniezno, seat of Poland's oldest bishopric, he said he had come to cry out with a loud voice, to speak 'before Europe and the world, of the often forgotten nations and peoples', the lost peoples of Eastern Europe. He told the assembled Polish bishops on 5 June: 'Any authentic dialogue must respect the convictions of believers, ensure all the rights of citizens and the normal conditions for the work of a church, in the fullest sense as a social community to which the vast majority of Poles belong.' At Auschwitz he spoke of human rights and the centrality of religion in illuminating and securing those rights. At Czestochowa he spoke for an hour on the transcendence of Christianity in Polish history. At the same shrine, in an address on the priesthood, he gave an impassioned defence of the notion of a clergy dedicated to service by its celibacy and separateness – a point to which we shall return – and spoke of Poland's role, with its massed battalions of eager priests, to serve as missionary to the world, of which his own pontificate was to be seen as the harbinger.[28]

The net effect of the papal visit was to consolidate the church's central position in Polish national consciousness and to emphasize its role as arbiter. The regime was in gracious mood when the Pope departed, congratulating itself that the visit had proceeded without disturbing the sullen tranquillity of life in Communist Poland. At the airport, the regime's president, Henrik Jablonski, kissed John Paul's hands. In fact their complacency rested on an illusion. The visit had a double effect. It clearly contributed to the self-confidence and unanimity with which, next year, the Solidarity Movement of the workers swept away the government's trade unions. Secondly, it inspired that movement, with the help and guidance of the church, to behave with a restraint and self-control which allowed it to keep and consolidate its gains and extend them to the farming sector.

It is John Paul's view that the Poles have often thrown away opportunities to secure their independence by a foolish ardour. It is one of his axioms that a man must accept responsibility for the consequences of his acts, and therefore weigh them well in advance. Responsibility, indeed, is the other side of the coin to rights. Throughout the gestation of the Solidarity Movement, it was a paramount asset to its leadership to feel that there was, in Rome, a concerned, watchful and potent figure, strengthening their resolution to win but counselling moderation in victory. John Paul refrained from exulting when the agreement reached between Solidarity and the regime in November 1980 created, in effect, free trade unionism in an Iron Curtain state for the first time. But he made his feelings plain enough. At his general audience on 12 November 1980, he expressed 'joy' at what he called 'this wise and mature agreement' and added the wish that 'this maturity which in the last few months has characterized our fellow countrymen's way of acting' would 'continue to be typical of us'. Thus with quiet satisfaction did he gather the harvest of his visit.[29]

We must not, however, presume from this that John Paul has any illusions about the possibility of a permanent accommodation between Christianity and any society based on Marxism-Leninism. He is familiar with the Leninist text which makes it clear that any arrangement between a Communist state and the church is merely a tactic better to accomplish the destruction of religion.[30] Marx himself demanded 'the decisive and positive abolition of religion'. He wrote: 'The criticism of religion ends with the doctrine that man is the highest being for man, that is, with the categorical imperative to overthrow all circumstances in which man is humiliated, enslaved, abandoned and despised.'[31] Those who advocate a Christian-Marxist reconciliation tend to omit the first half of this sentence.[32] John Paul, on the basis of his Polish experience, doubts the existence of a 'grey area' which totalitarian atheists and practising Christians can peacefully cohabit. 'In Poland', he said at Toronto in September 1969, 'people have a clear choice between atheism and Catholicism.' To him, the choice is bleak and obvious: 'One cannot be a Christian and a materialist. One cannot be a believer and an atheist.'[33]

Even leaving aside the dedicated and violent hostility of Marxism-Leninism to religion, there are many aspects of its theory and practice which John Paul finds utterly abhorrent. His Christian humanism rejects its repudiation of the universalist principle of human rights, its deliberate creation of privileged élites and viewpoints. Thus in a sermon in December 1977 he thundered: 'No one can say: *You* have these rights because you are a member of such and such a nation, race, class or party, but *you* are denied these rights because you do not belong to this nation, race, class or party.... Every man by virtue of being man has a right to social advancement in the framework of his community.' Or again, in a sermon in September 1978, just before he became pope: 'It is intolerable that public institutions which belong to the whole nation should be used for the benefit of only one philosophy, or a single political view.... It is intolerable that people should be divided into privileged and unprivileged categories according to their political beliefs.'[34]

It is John Paul's view that Marxism-Leninism is a false humanism. Through its misunderstanding of man's nature it somehow contrives to get the worst of all worlds, combining the caste system of the *ancien régime* with some of the worst features of capitalism, and the beneficent aspects of neither. He sees 'socialism' as practised in the Soviet-type states as horribly, visibly impersonal: 'In the name of socialization people are herded into ever vaster industrial establishments and housed in multi-storey blocks where they are hermetically separated from each other. It is not only the walls that separate them, it is the whole atmosphere of distrust, indifference and alienation. In such an atmosphere, the human heart withers.'[35]

Nor, in John Paul's view, is such impersonality an accidental blemish of Communism: it is the direct and inevitable consequence of a disastrous false theory, which denies man his free will and insists that culture and society spring deterministically from the modes of production. Such an analysis is the opposite of humanism: it degrades man. He told the staff of Unesco in Paris on 2 June 1980: 'A culture without human subjectivity and without human causality is inconceivable. In the cultural field, man is always the first fact. Man is the prime and fundamental fact of culture.' He added that man and his culture cannot be explained exclusively either by a materialist or a spiritual analysis, but by both together. Religion and culture, he said, are inseparable, because both are centred on man.[36] Communism, therefore, is not a new culture: it is an anti-culture.

One of the aspects of Marxism which John Paul has studied most carefully, because of its relevance to his interest in phenomenology and existentialism, as well as his beliefs as a Christian humanist, is the Marxist theory of alienation, central to its critique of capitalism. In his view, alienation, which makes a man feel a stranger in the world he inhabits, is at least as much a characteristic of Communist as of capitalist societies, and springs from secularism rather than a particular form of economic organization. In a 1976 address to the Harvard Divinity School on 'Participation or Alienation' he called Marxism 'the anti-catechism of the secular world'. In so far as it is a totalitarian atheism, rather than a liberal-pluralist society of the type characteristic of capitalism, it increases secularity – indeed compels it – and so deepens the alienation of man. Moreover, its programme of action divides rather than unites men; it preaches hatred rather than reconciliation and love. In his great Lenten series of 1976, he described what he called 'anti-love', leading to the abuse of man, as the 'real alienation'. This anti-love could be brought about 'by production, by consumption, by the state in various totalitarian and crypto-totalitarian countries, under various regimes which start with lofty humane declarations and end by violating elementary human rights. It is this anti-love which divides communities into classes, which incites nations and nationalities to fratricidal clashes, and splits the globe into oppositional "worlds".'[37]

Indeed it is John Paul's view that Marxism-Leninism is not a humanism at all, but a form of paganism. In prehistory and in pagan antiquity, he argued in the 1976 series, men saw divinity in the wonders of the natural world. But, as the Book of Wisdom put it, if men were so impressed by natural phenomena as to call them gods, how much more powerful is he who made them.[38] St Bonaventure argued that even primitive men derived an intuitive knowledge of God from the contemplation of nature. But mere empirical knowledge is not enough: God is realized through love. When the Book of Wisdom says that men who do not know God are fools, it is making, according to Aquinas's commentary, a distinction between empirical knowledge and wisdom. As St Paul puts it, 'Knowledge puffeth up, but charity edifieth.'[39] Knowledge as a human construct is a ramshackle building, but knowledge through love is on sound foundations. Marxism is a reversion to paganism in that it sees natural phenomena, such as modes of production, as the ordering forces of the world. To make the forces of nature divine, to regard matter as absolute, is pagan. Even man is not an absolute, but a being who is relative and contingent; only God is the absolute, the complete being. Modern creatures, denied knowledge of God by totalitarian systems, still intuitively move towards Him, as did the pagans in ancient times.

John Paul was much struck by an episode in 1945, which he relates in this sermon, when a young Russian conscript, part of the occupying forces, made his way to the seminary in Cracow to seek instruction. He told them he had never been taught about God, but 'I always knew that God exists'.[40] Thus God was found even in the new paganism. Even ignorant men search for God because they know by instinct that they are not complete without Him. John Paul often pursues a line of argument well expressed by the French theologian Henri de Lubac, that the failure of atheistic humanism lies in its destruction of man's transcendental character and so his ultimate significance as a human being. It is not, therefore, a humanism at all.[41]

John Paul's Christian humanism does not contain a theory of the state. But he puts forward some clear general ideas about social behaviour. In the last chapter of *Redemptor Hominis* he indicates a middle way between collectivism and pure individualism, what he terms 'acting together' in community. In this section 'solidarity' is a key word, and it is no accident that 'Solidarity' was chosen as the name of the Polish free trade union movement, which was plainly influenced by this encyclical. John Paul argues that society must permit men to 'act together', even in opposition; and such opposition has the right not merely to exist, but to exist effectively. 'The structure of a human community', *Redemptor Hominis* says, 'is correct only if it admits not just the presence of a justified opposition but also that practical effectiveness of opposition required by the common good and the right of participation.'

Opposition has rights because above and beyond the claims of the state are the claims of the moral order. In *Redemptor Hominis* he contrasts 'surrender to the prevailing climate of opinion' or mere conformity or 'opportunism' (the dirtiest word in the Polish language today) with 'surrender to the perceived good', which is the essence of morality. Indeed, opposition may embody solidarity, neighbourliness, love, which are the 'perceived good', while the state denies them, the deepest form of alienation – a view, expressed in Chapter 15 of *Redemptor Hominis*, which rests on the more complex arguments put forward in Chapter 7 of *The Acting Person*, John Paul's one major essay in philosophy. He cites St Stanislas as an example of opposition to the state embodying the 'perceived good'. The saint was 'the defender of the freedom that is the inalienable right of every man, so that the violation of that freedom by the state is a violation of both the moral and the social order'.[42]

The Marxist notion that men are compelled towards a just social and moral order by a collective class consciousness is to John Paul totally unacceptable because it is based on moral relativism and denies the paramountcy of the individual conscience, which lies at the very core of man's being. 'The dignity of the human person', he said in his 1976 Lenten series, 'has its foundation in the conscience, in that inner obedience to the objective principle [of morality] which enables human "praxis" to distinguish between good and evil.' This conscience is the basis of man's kingliness, dominion, the key to his moral grandeur and so the monitor of true social and moral order.[43]

The thrust of John Paul's Christian humanism is to expose the inadequacy of any doctrine of man which excludes the divine, and especially of totalitarian atheism which denies it by force. For it is of the essence of his humanism that man is not sufficient unto himself. *Redemptor Hominis* stressed the greatness, dignity, importance and rights of man. By the autumn of 1980 John Paul felt it necessary to elaborate the exposition of his humanism by stressing the role of God and the impingement of the divine on human values. The result was his magnificent encyclical *Dives in Misericordia*, published on 13 November 1980.[44]

John Paul believes that knowledge of God and of man is complementary: the path to God leads through man, the path to man through God, Christ being the bridge. 'Man', he writes, 'cannot be manifested in the full dignity of his nature without reference to God, not only at the level of a concept but also in an integrally existential way' (by 'existential' he means the power of the notion of God to illuminate human existence, and its derivation from human experience). Hence, he goes on, 'the more the church's mission is centred upon man, the more it is, so to speak, anthropocentric, the more it must be confirmed and actualized theocentrically, that is to say, be directed in Jesus Christ to the Father'. The error of secular philosophy tends to be to 'separate theocentrism and anthropocentrism, even to set them up in opposition to each other'. But the church, following the pattern of Christ, 'seeks to link them up in human history, in a fundamental, organic way'.[45]

John Paul illustrates this thesis by what is, in effect, a philosophical essay on justice and mercy. The mission of Christ was to embody and dispense mercy: Christ is mercy incarnate. What exactly is mercy? It is a form of love, love in a social context. When love manifests itself in the human condition, the reflection of man's limitations and frailty, both physical and moral, it is called mercy. Mercy, then, is social love. The incarnation of Christ is mercy made visible: 'He himself, in a certain sense, is mercy.' Many human systems, especially totalitarian ones, 'seem opposed to a God of mercy, and in fact ... exclude from life and remove from the human heart the very idea of mercy'. There is, indeed, no place for mercy in determinist systems such as Marxism. Mercy, like free will, is an anti-determinist idea. There is nothing about mercy in Marxism-Leninism. It is, literally, merciless. So-called 'history', as the dynamic of Marxism, has no mercy because it is an impersonal idea and mercy implies a person. The notion of 'socialism with a human face', though superficially attractive, is self-contradictory in terms of Marxism. Mercy is thus greater than justice and it can be so because it is non-deterministic and embodies free will.[46]

John Paul uses the parable of the prodigal son to show that the church is not so much centred round social justice (which is impersonal) as around mercy (which is personal). Mercy, he explains, involves two different Old Testament terms, *hesed*, implying faithfulness to oneself (mercy is implicit in God's character), and *rahmim*, denoting the kind of love expressed by a mother to her child. Both contain a personal element. When the father in the parable receives the prodigal back, justice is expressed by his brother, but mercy (in both senses of the term) by his father. Whereas justice is cold and impersonal, mercy is joyful and personal. The most that a secular system can offer, at its best, is justice. God, through his church, offers mercy.[47]

The parable, John Paul continues, illustrates another aspect of mercy: conversion. This again embodies a non-deterministic, indeed an anti-deterministic concept, involving free will. In a striking passage he writes: 'Conversion is the most concrete expression of the working of love and of the presence of mercy in the human world ... mercy is manifested in its true and proper aspect when it restores to value, promotes and draws good from all the forms of evil existing in the world and in man.' Marxism-Leninism makes no provision for conversion in the workings of history. Evil is dependent on impersonal systems of production and cannot therefore be eliminated until they are abolished: in Marxist eyes conversion is a type of 'reformism' and so anathema. But in the teaching of the church, the cross prefigures the elimination of evil and the ultimate perfection of justice. Even in this world, under the shadow and inspiration of the cross, and with the example of the Saviour, mercy incarnate, before it, the church offers to the world a work of mercy. Unlike Marxist eschatology, based on impersonal forces, it offers not a withering away of the state but the coming described in Revelation,[48] 'a new heaven and a new earth', when God 'will wipe away every tear from their eyes, there will be no more death, or mourning, no crying, nor pain, for the former things will have passed away'. This coming time is adumbrated by Christ in the Sermon on the Mount, the process 'in which love, containing justice, sets in motion mercy, which in its turn reveals the perfection of justice'.[49]

How does the church express this process in the world as we find it? First, it bears witness against injustice. Second, it teaches that justice is inadequate – indeed, its pursuit can (and in the case of totalitarian atheism invariably does) descend to horrifying things: 'The experience of the past and of our own time demonstrates that justice alone is not enough, that it can even lead to the negation and destruction of itself, if *that deeper power which is love* is not allowed to shape human life in all its dimensions.'[50] It is not simply the inadequacy of justice as perceived by Shakespeare: 'Use every man after his desert, and who should 'scape whipping?'[51] The secular mind sees mercy as a unilateral act, and therefore prefers justice. Hence the preference for impersonal and reciprocal social welfare systems which 'free social relationships from mercy and base them solely on justice'. This is to ignore that 'true mercy' is 'the most profound source of justice'. Mercy, in fact, is 'the most perfect incarnation of "equality" between people … The equality brought by justice is limited to the realm of objective and extrinsic goods, while love and mercy enable people to meet one another on the plane of humanity, with a dignity proper to man's estate.' Mercy has a metaphysical dimension which justice lacks. When we do justice between persons, it needs to be humanized by that love which, as St Paul puts it, 'is patient and kind'.[52] Mercy, in fact, is a form of divine justice, and it is as the advocate and practitioner of mercy that the church transcends purely secular ideology. An earthly regime, even the most enlightened, can only dispense a form of justice. The church, being a divine as well as a human society, signposts the higher path to mercy.

In these two remarkable encyclicals, every word of which he wrote himself, John Paul has exposed and condemned the crucifixion of man by totalitarian systems which, even in their theoretical pursuit of noble aims, suffer from calamitous misunderstandings of man's nature, and therefore in practice degrade and destroy him. He demonstrates the superiority of a mercy which is divine to a justice which is human.

But if John Paul is distrustful of secular Utopias, he does not accept the world as he finds it. He talks about the rights of man on both sides of the Iron Curtain. Almost exactly a year after he addressed three and a half million Poles in Czestochowa, on 31 May 1980, he concelebrated mass in the basilica of Saint-Denis near Paris, the burial place of the old French kings, and quoted those formidable and sonorous lines from the *Magnificat*: 'He hath shewed strength with his arm, he hath scattered the proud in the imagination of their hearts. He hath put down the mighty from their seats, and exalted them of low degree. He hath filled the hungry with good things, and the rich he hath sent empty away.'[53] John Paul sees very clearly that the secular world must be changed, often radically, and that the church has a divine mandate to urge and even assist such changes. The question is: how can rights be secured without violence? How can social justice be brought about in the spirit of mercy and love? We come now to the second great issue of his pontificate.

5

The Temptation
of Violence

IF POPE JOHN PAUL has been careful to prevent the church from becoming directly involved in Polish politics, his reasons spring not just from a careful balancing of the issues in Eastern Europe, but from a comprehensive world view of the church's proper role. The church must be consistent. It cannot engage in politics in one region and forbid it in another. John Paul has always been anxious to emphasize that the church operates at a higher level than the purely political plane. For the church, as he sees it, 'commitment' and 'justice' are not enough: it sets its sights higher, on love and mercy. This is the message both of *Redemptor Hominis* and *Dives in Misericordia*: without love there can be no 'perfection of human rights', and without mercy no 'perfection of justice'. Jesus Christ was not a revolutionary, at any rate in a political sense. Rejecting this interpretation in his 1976 Lenten series, he added: 'Any objective examination of the Gospel shows Jesus to have been above all a teacher of truth and a servant of love; and it is these characteristics of his which explain the real meaning of all that he did and all that he set out to do.'[1] Politics are liable to lead the church into a denial of Christ on both scores: by the temptation of polemics, the negation of truth, and by the temptation of violence, the negation of love. Indeed, next to totalitarian atheism, John Paul recognizes in the politics of violence the greatest evil of the age.

Almost from the start of his pontificate he has had to face this evil in acute form in Latin America. In 1968 Paul VI had attended the conference of Latin American bishops at Medellín in Colombia. Ten years later, John Paul I had been engaged to go to its successor, at Puebla in Mexico, when his death led to its postponement. It was finally held in January 1979, with John Paul II presiding at its opening – by far the most important of his early engagements. As we have seen, Latin America is now the most potent and numerically dynamic region in world Catholicism, and will become steadily more crucial to the faith as the years go by. Of all the regions of the world it has been the most thoroughly penetrated by Catholicism. For more than three centuries, Spain and Portugal, under concordats with the Vatican, granted the church an absolute monopoly of religion in their Latin American colonies and associated the church directly and closely with government. All the advantages and the evils of this system are now coming to maturity.[2]

A recent secular analysis of the history of the Catholic Church in Latin America presents the problem as follows.[3] The church's desire to preserve its monopoly has always determined its political posture. As it was ineffective as a spiritual instrument, and so unable to create a basis of autonomous religious strength when faced with the challenge of change, it has tended to realign itself with whatever groups have been in power, striving energetically to secure both the legal basis of privilege and the support of political élites.

According to this analysis, the church has passed through four stages. In the first, derived from its earlier experience in Spain and Portugal, the church identified itself with political society as a whole – the 'Christendom' ideal. The church underwrote the powers-that-be and helped them to exercise social control, receiving legal advantages in return. This pattern was universal until the first half of the nineteenth century and has continued to flourish in places: under Getulio Vargas in the Brazil of the 1930s, under Juan Perón in Argentina in the 1940s, under Alvarado Velasco in Peru after 1968, and in the Chile of Augusto Pinochet since 1973. But the drive behind this form now comes largely from secular rather than from ecclesiastical forces, since the church is increasingly suspicious of conservative regimes even at their most ingratiating.

In the second phase, most marked in the latter part of the nineteenth century, there arose a 'political church', locked in bitter conflict with anti-clerical regimes which advocated liberalism, secularism, democracy and the end of Catholic monopoly, especially in education. This phase lasted broadly from Pius IX's Syllabus of

Errors in 1864 to the death of Pius x in 1914. During it the church was identified with pre-capitalist obscurantism, and with peasants and landowners, while the Protestant churches of North America were held up, even by liberal agnostics, as apostolates of capitalist progress and bourgeois enlightenment. This was unfair, since the church, and especially the Jesuits, had been an economic innovator in Latin America, introducing both the first capitalist enterprises and the first collective farms of the modern era.[4] Despite its record, however, the church was forced by liberals into alliance with the most secular elements. This second phase culminated in the ferocious church-state battles in Mexico between the wars, when the assault on clericalism became total and the church had to fight for its very existence – to the point indeed where it entered a third phase, finding an identity of interests with the lowest echelons of society, also persecuted and exploited, and so seeing itself as a 'servant church'.

This phase was in line with one stream of Catholic thought, expressed in papal 'social' encyclicals, from *Rerum Novarum* of 1891 and *Quadragesimo Anno* of 1931 to John XXIII's *Mater et Magistra* in 1961 and Paul VI's *Populorum Progressio* in 1967. Generally speaking, it is not true that the Catholic Church in Latin America has been backward in supporting social and economic reform. The charge is belied by study of the documents, such as pastoral letters. Thus, the Chilean collective episcopal letters of 1910, 1931, 1937, 1949, 1962 and 1971 reflect a continuity of radical social ideas, and a similar pattern developed in the 1950s and 1960s in Brazil, Venezuela and Peru, as shown in episcopal papers. In the 1950s, the Chilean church developed advanced notions of land reform and in 1961 sold 13,000 acres of its own properties to occupiers. The church promoted rural unions in Chile, Mexico and Brazil long before 1939, and in 1954 it provided the drive behind the foundation of the Latin American confederation of Christian Trade Unions.[5] In the 1960s, Latin American Christian Democracy, of which the Chilean president Eduardo Frei was the archetype, basing itself on Jacques Maritain and the modern Thomists, rejected both Marxist collectivism and liberal capitalism.[6]

Unfortunately, the dominant secular forces preferred the earlier, compulsory version of Christendom in their 'national security states' as they are called, which the church was no longer prepared to underwrite. When Perón broke with the church in 1954 he adumbrated a *renversement des alliances* which has since occurred, for instance, under Stroessner in Paraguay, Romero in El Salvador, Pinochet in Chile and Videla in Argentina, to list only four cases. The realignment of forces is full of paradoxes. Conservative clergy and layfolk, still numerous, now find themselves fighting shoulder to shoulder not only with military dictators but with what is left of liberal capitalism, and looking for salvation to North America, home of the once detested Protestant heretics.

Meanwhile a large section of the church has been pushed, or has moved itself, much further to the left, opening a fourth phase, the emergence of a so-called 'pastoral church', seeking for popularity among the masses by identifying itself with the secular goals of radical politics. Catholic radicals make common cause with movements and regimes whose avowed aim is to stamp out Christianity altogether – and which actively persecute it the moment they get the opportunity – while at the same time they sanctify the violent overthrow of governments, such as the national security regimes, which are publicly pledged to uphold Christian values and guarantee Catholic worship. In the nineteenth century it was the liberal anti-clericals who drew the distinction between Christian idealism, which they endorsed, and the church, which they pronounced corrupt. Now it is the paladins of *seguridad nacional* who say there is nothing wrong with Christianity as such, were it not for the pestilential clergy who claim to speak for it. In this process, church and clergy have been split down the middle.

How did Latin American Catholicism get into this crisis? As we have seen, its roots are deep in history. The beginnings of the present phase go back to the 1950s, to the decision of Catholic universities, in Europe and the Americas, to establish courses in social science, which immediately fell into the hands of priests who were committed to political activism, such as Roger Vekemans in Chile and Camilio Torres in Colombia. They were quickly joined by radical clerics from abroad, especially from the University of Louvain and American Catholic campuses.[7] These progressive élites within the church adopted the secular moral idealism of the left, and their sources of inspiration were essentially not only non-

Catholic but non-Christian: Marxism, Castroism, liberalism and democratic socialism. In 1962, Brazilian Catholic activists founded the revolutionary Ação Popular. In Colombia the activities of men like René García and Manuel Alzate Restrepo were difficult to distinguish from Marxism itself. In Havana the Apostolic Nuncio, Cesare Zacchi, was persuaded to say that Castro was, from the ethical viewpoint, a Christian. When Salvador Allende was elected President of Chile, the primate, Cardinal Silva Henríquez, assured him that the church supported the basic programme of his Unidad Popular. The turning-point, at which the ultra-radicals captured a section of the episcopate and first acquired a major voice in policy, was precisely the conference of Latin American bishops held in Medellín in that fatal year 1968, the high tide of 1960s illusions.

Latin American Catholic radicalism expresses itself in a variety of ways but, above all, in the institutional structure of the *comunidades de base* (basic Christian communities) and the philosophical system of 'liberation theology'. The communities are in origin a legitimate device, being plausibly presented as an answer to the shortage of priests in impoverished rural areas. They are said to have five main aims.[8] The first three, gathering the people for mass, promoting mutual help and providing education, especially preparation for first communion, confirmation and marriage, reflect the mainstream catechetical movement and are essentially the same as the work of catechetical centres set up in Poland and elsewhere. But the fourth aim, promoting trade union activity, is wholly secular and political, and the fifth, founding new centres – which gives the movement its dynamism – together with its regional structure of meetings and so forth, gives the communities some of the characteristics of soviets, on which they seem in part to be modelled. Moreover, some of the devotions and services of the communities are tendentious if not actually uncanonical. Private prayer, the rosary, the use of statues is discouraged; all services have to be communal; the 'Our Father' is recited with joined hands and the kiss of peace is a universal embrace. The 'Service of the Word' is celebrated without a priest, omitting the eucharistic prayer and communion (unless the host has been 'reserved'). The moral theology of these centres has been taken over by quasi-political concepts expressed in sociological-Marxist jargon. Thus, a pastoral letter from one of the bishops associated with these communities reads: 'For sin read sinful structure, for holiness read brotherly society, for grace read human dignity and human rights, for redemption read freedom.'

This approach is not likely, in itself, to prove attractive to the genuine poor of Latin America. They have their own popular cultic faith, a syncretism of Catholic piety and Indian religious practices, which evolved in the countryside and has now been carried into the towns. It is characterized by a multiplicity of unofficial saints and miracles, as well as official ones, of which the most famous is the Virgin of Guadalupe, dating from 1531. The 'theology of liberation' is an attempt to harness this popular religiosity (*religiosidad popular* or 'the church of the disinherited' as it is sometimes called), give it political aims and turn it into a revolutionary force by means of the cell-structure of the 'basic communities'.

Like most new theological ideas, liberation theology has German origins. In 1967 Professor John-Baptist Metz, a pupil of Father Karl Rahner, coined the term 'political theology'. The fundamental problem of theology, he wrote, is not 'how dogma stands in relation to history, but what is the relation between theory and practice, between understanding the faith and social practice'. In other words, the job of theologians was to work out theological justifications for certain definite courses of political and economic action.[9] A number of German theologians, such as Jürgen Moltmann and Wolfhart Pannenberg, worked along these lines. Between 1968–71 they produced, for the benefit of the Third World, what was termed 'theologies of development'. This did not catch on: it was dull, it did not embody an element of hate or violence, it did not draw any moral distinction between the New and the Old World.

Only when the concept passed to Latin America did it catch fire, in the form of liberation theology. The 'theolibs' adapted Marx's criticism of Feuerbach: 'The theologians have only interpreted the world in various ways; the point is to change it.' Thus, one theolib, the Chilean Juan Luis Segundo, accused Metz and his school merely of 'revolutionizing the way we formulate problems' whereas what needs to be changed are 'the concrete circumstances in which people work and live'. It was the Peruvian theologian, Gustavo Gutiérrez, who first thought of marrying Metz's ideas with Marxism and *religiosidad popular*. He saw in these cults a 'potential for liberation', the 'popular expressions of the faith' which 'reveal the sufferings of a subjugated people'. There was in it 'a resistance and a protest against the domination exercised against the popular classes, as well as a vigorous manifestation of hope in the God of the Bible'.[10]

To Gutiérrez, the 'central question in theology' is 'What relation is there between salvation and the historical process of liberation of man?' There are, he argues, only three possible answers to the question. First, that there is no intrinsic connection between religion and politics, but this is dualism. Second, that salvation is only another name for human liberation, but this is mere reductionism. The third answer is the formula adopted at Medellín in 1968, the 'clear perception that in man everything is mediated politically', which is 'not to be confused with the unfounded and totalitarian assumption that everything is politics'. Medellín also went on to recognize and encourage *religiosidad popular*, according to Gutiérrez's analysis. 'In our evaluation of popular religion', the bishops declared, 'we may not take as our frame of reference the Westernized cultural interpretation of the middle and upper classes; instead, we must judge its meaning in the context of the subcultures of the rural and marginal urban groups.'[11]

It will be evident that there are profound intellectual confusions in this approach, confusions of the type Marxists are skilled in exploiting. The theolibs called Medellín 'the new Pentecost'. They planned to make Puebla another 'Council of Jerusalem', in which their views would become an official policy of action. The conservatives and the moderates within the Latin American churches fought back. The result has been a long and bloody battle, with casualties on both sides. At the end of 1977 the conference secretariat produced a 'consultative document' for the Puebla meeting, which was promptly attacked by Gutiérrez and his allies as a rejection of the Medellín principles. Foreign support was orchestrated: a letter came from Yves Congar and seventy other 'progressive theologians' in France, and similar letters from Canada, the United States, Belgium and Spain. The last was signed by two bishops, fifty-five theologians and 700 other ecclesiastical personages, and asserted: 'In Spain with the triumph of Franco the church fell into the same trap of establishing a "New Christianity": a society ruled by church principles with an institutional church joined to the power of the state, which has caused such lamentable consequences.'[12] This campaign was designed to influence comments on the document made by individual bishops' conferences, which were collated from May 1978 onwards and incorporated in a final working document of 200 pages drawn up by the progressive Cardinal Aloisio Lorscheider, Archbishop of Fortaleza in Brazil, the President of the conference. Among its fourteen appendices was one on liberation theology.

The theolibs nevertheless continued to claim up to and during the conference that they were being excluded from its deliberations. They protested that the twenty conference theology experts included only one theolib, Lucio Gera from Argentina, and pointedly omitted Gutiérrez himself. They said it was a scandal that delegates to the conference did not include Sergio Méndez Arceo, the mutinous Bishop of Cuernavaca in Mexico who is a prominent advocate of 'dialogue with Marxism', and Miguel Obando Brava, Archbishop of Managua, who played a notable role in assisting the left-wing Sandanistas to take over Nicaragua by force. To make their affiliations clear, they also protested at the presence in Puebla of certain invited guests, such as representatives of the International Institute of the Sacred Heart, Wisconsin (judged 'pietist' and therefore right-wing), and Help for the Suffering Church, which organizes relief in Eastern Europe (and is therefore judged anti-Soviet). In fact, excluded or not, everyone who wished was present in Puebla. The theolibs set up a rival 'centre of information and debate'. In any case, many of them were on the staffs of individual progressive bishops, one of whom brought with him, as a theological 'expert', a simple peasant, to provide 'spiritual insights'. The progressive delegates destroyed the confidential character of the conference's closed sessions by regularly providing accounts of them to be published in the Mexican radical paper *Unomasuno*, and they even stole a dictaphone tape of private letters sent by the conference's General-Secretary, Archbishop

López Trujillo, judged hostile to their ideas, and published that too.[13]

Into this fevered atmosphere, John Paul II introduced a note of magisterial calm and pontifical authority. There can be no doubt that he would have preferred a much longer time to prepare himself, to be briefed on the arguments and personalities involved, and to give careful thought to his principal speeches. As it was, there was sometimes an air of improvisation about his remarks. The papal programme was very crowded and the strain was increased by the fact that musicians arrived to serenade the Pope promptly at 5.30 each morning. But he did not falter. Everything he said was shrewdly judged and absolutely consistent with his central strategy: he will have no cause to regret any of his remarks. It has been argued that the theolibs and other progressives can take encouragement from what John Paul said on his visit. But that is a fairly tortuous, not to say desperate, interpretation of the texts.

In fact the essential burden of the Pope's remarks was to stress that the church's work of evangelism must utilize its traditional hierarchical structures, and revolve around the long-established certitudes of the faith. He arrived in the Dominican Republic on 25 January 1979 and from there proceeded to Mexico. At the basilica of Our Lady of Guadalupe, addressing 6,000 Mexican priests and religious, he commanded them to be loyal to their bishops. It was not to be permitted, he said, 'that priests and religious should exercise a teaching authority independent of the bishops, the only authentic guardians of the faith, or of the episcopal conferences'. As for the work of the priests themselves, he told them: 'You should be spiritual leaders, priests and religious, not social or political leaders, or servants of a temporal power.... Secular matters are more properly the field of action of the laity.'[14]

On 28 January, opening the Puebla conference, John Paul made his principal statement of policy.[15] The conference, he said, must take as its point of departure the conclusions reached at Medellín, 'but without ignoring the incorrect interpretations at times placed on them'. They must be guided by the working document, but also by Paul VI's apostolic exhortation *Evangelii Nuntiandi*, 'into which he put his whole pastoral soul as his life drew to a close'.[16] The conference was 'not a parliament of politicians' but 'a fraternal meeting of pastors'. It was concerned with truth, 'the truth which shall make you free', the only solid basis for 'praxis', and the only basis of truth was 'purity of doctrine'. That was the concern of the bishops, 'the careful and zealous transmission of truth'. He denounced 'false re-readings' of the Gospel which 'cause confusion and diverge from the central criteria of the faith', and in which 'Christ's divinity is passed over in silence' or shown as 'politically committed, as one who fought against Roman oppression and the authorities, and as one engaged in the class struggle'. Jesus himself regarded such attitudes as 'a temptation' and he 'unequivocally rejected recourse to violence'.

The real perspective of Jesus's mission was much deeper: 'It consists in complete salvation through a transforming, peace-making, pardoning and reconciling love.' Other interpretations of Jesus's work were clever but 'fragile and inconsistent', and against them it was necessary to affirm the true faith, 'the vocation to harmony and unity which must expel the dangers of war in this continent of hope'. It was this faith which enabled the church to make its positive contribution to improving the world, 'to transform hearts and to make systems and structures more human'. Then followed a key sentence: 'Any form of silence, disregard, mutilation or inadequate emphasis of the whole of the mystery of Jesus Christ' which diverged from the church's teaching was a false form of evangelism.

The church, then, must teach the faith, the whole faith, and nothing but the faith. The bishops must ensure this was done. They must 'proclaim unceasingly' and with 'special vigour at this moment' the central truth of the church's mission: 'The church was established by the Lord as a fellowship of life, love and truth.' The guide was *Lumen Gentium*, the dogmatic constitution officially laid down by the Council.[17] He commanded that all the bishops 'assent to this document'. Evangelization was not an individualistic, *ad hoc* affair but a concerted effort based on 'ready and sincere reverence for the sacred *magisterium*', the teaching authority of the church, which alone was 'objective' and reliable. He denounced the attempt to separate the church and the kingdom of God. God's kingdom could not be secularized. It was reached by 'faith and membership in the church' not by 'changing of structure and social and political involvement' and 'certain types of activity for justice'. He deplored the creation of mistrust towards the 'institutional' or 'official' church, presented as alienating, as opposed to a so-called real church 'springing from the people' and 'taking concrete form in the poor'. This was to expose the church to all-too-familiar forms of 'ideological conditioning'. Christ's truth could not be reduced to a mere 'system of philosophy' or 'purely political activity'. That would be to 'forget it – or to betray it'.

John Paul II then returned to his idea of Christian humanism. Atheistic humanism was 'an inexorable paradox', not a true humanism at all. It was based on 'an inadequate view of man' which deprived him of 'an essential dimension of his being, his search for the infinite'. Thanks to the Gospel, the church has the truth about man: 'The primordial affirmation of this anthropology is that man is God's image and cannot be reduced to a mere portion of nature or a nameless element in the human city.' Each man is 'an individual being, unique and unrepeatable'. So the church rejects 'all forms of humanism imprisoned within a strictly economic, biological or psychological view of man'. The church must proclaim the whole truth about man, and must not be prevented from doing so either 'by external compulsion' or through 'contamination by other forms of humanism' or 'by lack of confidence in her original message'. The best service a Christian pastor can render to any human being is to proclaim Christ's truth about man 'clearly and unambiguously'.

In this task, he went on, the church must be united. The bishops must preserve their collegiate unity. Priests must stand united under their bishops. The bishops must have 'the responsible and active but also docile and trusting' support of the religious orders. Everybody concerned in evangelization must support the church's *magisterium* and no other. Of course bishops must defend the human dignity of their flock, but the church had no need of 'ideological systems in order to love, defend and work together in the liberation of man'. The church has always had a duty to defend human rights and must steer clear of all the competing political systems 'in order to opt only for man'. A mere change of political system will not end the gap between rich and poor: 'There is no economic law capable of changing these mechanisms by itself.' The church must invoke the aid of ethics, justice, above all the primary commandment of love: 'The first place must be given to what is moral, to what is spiritual, to what springs from the full truth about man.' What was this full truth, the truth about the 'liberation' of man? In its 'internal and profound meaning, as Jesus proclaimed and realized' it, liberation was freedom not only 'from everything which oppresses man' but above all 'from sin and the Evil One in the joy of knowing God and being known by him'. He rejected the notion of liberation 'reduced to crude and narrow economic, political, social or cultural dimensions', a liberation 'based on ideologies which make it incompatible with the evangelical view of man'. Christian liberation was on a grander scale altogether. The church already had 'a rich and complex heritage' of social doctrine. It was the duty of bishops to make the faithful aware of it. As a rule, 'secular duties and activities properly belong to lay persons'. Let the clergy then stay clear of such things, except in special cases for which 'reasonable grounds' must be provided.

John Paul II added two footnotes to this majestic exposition of the church's view of 'political commitment'. The first came in Mexico City on 29 January, when he spoke of the 'basic communities'. He conceded that they 'can be a valid educational instrument and form of religious life within a new environment of Christian impulse'. But they must be conducted strictly within the criteria laid down in Paul VI's *Evangelii Nuntiandi*. They must be united with the church, not separate from it. Above all, 'they must not place themselves in opposition to the church as a whole, to its regular pastors and to existing ecclesiastical bodies and structures'.[18]

The following day, in a speech to landless Indians at Culiacán in Mexico, he tackled directly the question of land reform. Already on his first arrival in Latin America in Santo Domingo, he had spoken of a just world where 'there will be no peasants without land'.[19] John Paul regards the whole notion of a landless peasant as a kind of insult to nature. He regards the collectivization of the peasantry – from which Poland has been mercifully spared so far – as perhaps the biggest single crime of the Soviet Union, next to the denial of God (the two, in his mind, are connected). Scarcely any better are the conditions under capitalist ownership in parts of

Mexico, of which he was passionately reminded in Culiacán by an Indian catechist, speaking in the local dialect. He responded with a measured statement on land reform. 'The agricultural worker', he said, 'has the right to be respected. He must be defended against deprivation, using legal manoeuvres which are often tantamount to theft, of the little that he has.' There were 'barriers of exploitation' often 'constructed by intolerable selfishness' between man and man. They must be removed: 'Action must be prompt, and get to the root of the problem. The changes to be carried out must be bold and radical.' The church, he said, 'does indeed defend a legitimate right to private property. But she also teaches no less clearly that there is always a social mortgage on all private property, so that possessions must serve the general purpose God gave them. Hence, if the common good requires it, there should be no hesitation even at expropriation, provided it is carried out in just and legal form.'[20]

The Pope's many references to politics, economic conditions and clerical activism in his first Latin American visit had a remarkable internal consistency. There were two points he was determined to hammer home. First, the church has always been interested in social and economic conditions, has clear views about, and is continually updating them – as, for instance, in the question of land reform. Hence he repeatedly emphasized the continuity of Catholic social teaching with detailed references to *Mater et Magistra*, *Populorum Progressio*, documents issued by the Council, especially *Gaudium et Spes*, and the corpus of social teaching contained in the Gospel itself. John Paul becomes impatient at the suggestion that the church is a late and reluctant warrior on the field of social reform; it has always been there. Secondly, he does not think the church should shy away from radical solutions at times; but when it embraces them it must do so in unity, using its established processes of consultation and chains of command. That is the only way in which terrible errors of judgement can be avoided. In John Paul's church there is no room for spiritual egotists, moralizing prima donnas and quasi-political *exaltés*. No man has a private line to the deity. When the church moves it moves with the full force of its collegiate wisdom, which is the real basis of its collective strength. The church's voice is the voice of the Holy Spirit, which must be listened to in silence, not forced to make itself heard above a cacophony of strident and self-deceiving voices.

There was one further point John Paul wished to make clear: in no circumstances could the church support, still less engage in, violent courses. Addressing 100,000 industrial workers in a sports stadium in the Mexican state of Jalisco – famous for its loyalty to the faith in the persecutions of the inter-war years – he rejected absolutely and without qualification the recourse to violence as a solution to economic and political problems.

It was, however, during his visit to Ireland, at the end of September 1979, that he took the opportunity to condemn political violence in the most emphatic, categorical and comprehensive terms. It was, he said, the exact antithesis of the 'ministry of love' he had proclaimed for the church on his accession. He recognized that Ireland is a holy land, with a peculiar gift for sanctity, a pious zeal which is almost unparalleled, a passionate loyalty to the faith and, with all these, a fatal propensity to violence. Hence he made the castigation of violence the theme of his visit.

At Drogheda on 29 September, addressing 200,000 people, many from Northern Ireland, he denied that the root of the evil in Ulster was a religious one.[21] How could it be? For Christianity forbids us to seek solutions to such divisions 'by the ways of hatred, by the murdering of defenceless people, by the methods of terrorism'. Christianity is 'decisively opposed to fomenting hatred and to promoting and provoking violence for the sake of "struggle". The command, "Thou Shalt Not Kill", must be binding on the conscience of humanity. Otherwise we fall into the tragedy and destiny of Cain.' Of course, peace must be founded on justice. As he had said in Mexico and in Poland, 'Every human being has inalienable rights that must be respected. Each human community – ethnic, historical, cultural, religious – has rights that must be respected. Peace is threatened every time one of these rights is violated.' The moral law, John Paul said, was supreme. It was 'the guardian of human rights, the protector of the dignity of man'. It cannot 'be set aside by any person or group, or by the state itself, for any cause, not even for public security or in the interests of law and order. The law of God stands in judgement over all reasons of state'. All that was true. But if peace cannot endure without moral justice, it cannot be established by violence either: 'Peace can never flourish in a climate of terror, intimidation and death.'

There followed a passionate *réquisitoire* against violence: 'Violence is evil. Violence is not to be accepted as a solution to problems. Violence is unworthy of man. Violence is a lie. It goes against the truth of our faith. It denies the truth of our humanity. Violence destroys what it claims to defend – the dignity, the life, the freedom of human beings.' How could violence be used in the cause of human rights, when the most basic of human rights is the right to live? 'Violence', he asserted, 'is a crime against humanity. It destroys the very fabric of society.' He prayed that 'the moral sense and Christian conviction of Irish men and women may never become obscured and blunted by the lie of violence, that nobody may ever call murder by any other name than murder, that the spiral of violence may never be given the distinction of unavoidable logic or necessary retaliation'. Those who lived by the sword would perish by it. So he appealed to the men of violence to desist: 'Return to Christ, who died so that men might live in forgiveness and peace.' He appealed especially to the young: 'Do not follow those leaders who train you in the ways of killing. Love life. Respect life – in yourselves and in others.' He warned the Irish and the world: 'The ideology and the methods of violence have become an international problem of the utmost gravity. The longer the violence continues in Ireland, the more acute will the danger become that this beloved land will become yet one more theatre of international terrorism.'

John Paul appealed to religious leaders of every kind to unite in crushing violence. He told a gathering of non-Catholic clergy and theologians: 'All Christians must join together in opposing violence in any form and all assaults against the human person. . . . We must all be ministers of reconciliation.' At the Marian shrine of Knock on 30 September 1979 he prayed: 'Teach us that evil means can never lead to a good end. That all human life is sacred. That murder is murder no matter what the motive or end.' That same evening, dining with the Irish Catholic bishops in the Dominican convent at Cabra, he begged them to uphold the law. 'Faith and social ethics', he pleaded, 'demand from us respect for the established state authorities. This respect also finds its expression in individual acts of mediation.' The bishops were 'spokesmen for the moral order. This order is superior to force and violence. In this superiority of the moral order is expressed all the dignity of men and nations.'[22]

John Paul has returned again and again to the theme of violence. He sees violence as the antithesis of truth, as well as of love. There is, in his analysis, an organic and causative connection between murder and lies. Violence is caused by anti-truth, and especially by the twisting of words out of their true meaning and the manipulation of the media. To describe a government with which you disagree as a form of 'systemic violence', and then use this formulation as a moral justification for employing violence yourself to overthrow it, is a hideous distortion of truth, a form of 'anti-truth' (one of his favourite expressions). The constant portrayal of violence, and especially of terrorist activities, on television is also a form of anti-truth. But the worst form of anti-truth is the notion that violence can be constructive and enjoy moral authority. In a message for the World Day of Peace in December 1979, John Paul warned: 'The idea is spreading that the individual, and humanity as a whole, achieves progress principally through violent struggle.' This was a lie. 'Violence flourishes in lies and needs lies.' So 'restoring peace means, in the first place, calling by their proper names acts of violence in all their forms. Murder must be called by its proper name. Murder is murder. Political or ideological motives do not change its nature. On the contrary, they are degraded by it.' To renounce violence, he continued, did not mean keeping silence in the face of injustice. Injustice must be exposed, in respect for truth. But injustice must not be denounced in a manner likely to provoke violence, 'the cost of which is often paid by the victims of the injustice'. It was, said John Paul, 'one of the big lies' which poison society that issues of social justice could be presented in absolute terms of good and evil, and the better qualities of one's opponents ignored 'for the sake of condemning them more comprehensively'. Truth 'follows a different path'. It 'never throws away a chance of peace'.[23]

John Paul returned to Latin America at the end of June 1980, when he visited Brazil, now the largest Catholic territory in the world, with 100 million Catholics and 330 bishops. With this in mind he became the first pope to learn Portuguese, and he spoke the language throughout his visit. He placed himself firmly behind the Brazilian hierarchy, both in their opposition to unauthorized and quasi-political forms of evangelism, and in their sharp and frequently voiced criticism of social conditions. Visiting the President, João Figueiredo, he immediately raised the issue of human rights in Brazil, which has a semi-authoritarian regime.[24] His support for the bishops repudiated the government view that they are 'unrepresentative' of Brazilian Catholicism. He went out of his way, in São Paulo, to endorse the archbishop, Cardinal Evaristo Arns, whom the government particularly disliked, and emphasized: 'I speak in the name of Christ, in the name of the church – in the name of the whole church.'[25] Much of his time was spent addressing Brazil's business and ruling classes. He begged them to be poor in spirit, to acquire the spirit of the poor by opening their hearts to them, to recognize that 'human dignity is more important than all the wealth of the world', to place full employment and the right to work at the very centre of their economic policies.[26]

But he also spoke to the poor and to the workers. On 2 July, visiting one of the Rio *favelas* or slums, the Favela Vidigal, he took off his gold ring and gave it to the local priest, for the destitute. He told 150,000 workers in a São Paulo stadium: 'Power must never be used to protect the interests of one group to the detriment of the others. But equally the class struggle is not the path to social order; it brings with it the risk of reversing the roles of those who engage in it, and creating new situations of injustice.' He referred to 'the dignity of work, the nobility of work'. Work, he told them, 'is a discipline in which the personality is strengthened'. As men and Christians, they imprinted their own dignity on their work, however humble and insignificant it was. To the Christian, work is not a symbol of degradation and exploitation. It associates him with God in creation: 'You are collaborators with God in the work of creation – carry on, with the sweat of your brow, yes – but above all with the rightful pride of being created in the image of God himself. Carry on the dynamism contained in the command given by God to the first man, to populate the earth and subdue it.' Work makes man not only a co-creator but in a sense a co-redeemer; 'Everything that is painful, heavy, mortifying and crucifying in the monotony of everyday work allows man to associate himself with Christ on the cross in the work of redemption.'[27]

John Paul strove on this visit to lift notions of economic activity and social categories out of the sterile context of class-warfare and violent confrontation, and to place them in the new context of his own Christian humanism. He exhorted the Brazilian bishops to follow him on this alternative path of social evangelism. Talking to them at Fortaleza on 10 July 1980, he praised the close interest they took in what he called 'urgent temporal questions'. The Brazilian bishops, he said warmly, projected 'an image of poverty and simplicity, of complete dedication, of closeness to your people and presence in their lives and problems'. Brazil was 'a radically Catholic nation' with 'a special vocation' in the world. Their calling, he said, absolutely forbade them from taking sides in politics or submitting to 'any ideology or secular system'. There could be no argument about that. 'But it does not prohibit you – rather it calls you – to be near and at the service of all men and women, especially the weakest and most needy.' A social pastorate was the church's right and duty, and 'It is the bishops' function to prepare and propose such a pastoral social programme'.

Laying down guidelines for such a programme, John Paul asked them to note especially: 'The bold reforms that are necessary are not designed solely to collectivize the means of production, particularly if this means concentrating them in the hands of the state, which then becomes the only source of capital. These reforms ought to have the goal of enabling all to have access to property, since property, in some respects, constitutes the indispensable condition for man's liberty and creativity, enabling him to rise out of obscurity and alienation.'[28]

In social matters, John Paul has repeatedly emphasized, the role of the church is not an activist one, it is an educational one. Ordaining seventy-four priests at Rio on 2 July 1980, he told them: 'You are not doctors or social workers, you are not politicians or trade unionists.' Still less are priests freedom-fighters or chaplains to terrorists. They are teachers and ministers of the Gospel. Their immediate allegiance is to their bishops and the *magisterium*; their ultimate loyalty is to the Word itself and to Him who gave it – not to parties or ideologies or systems. In his preaching of a social

Gospel, and especially in his dealing with Latin America, John Paul has been anxious to halt and reverse the secularizing process among the clergy set in motion by the spread of radical ideologies and, instead, to re-sanctify their ideas and activities by the spread of his new Christian humanism. The church must never lose itself in the two-dimensional world of politics; it must always introduce the divine dimension, which creates new illuminations and per-spectives of human conflict, replaces hate with love, determinism with conversion, violence with reconciliation.

The vehemence and consistency of John Paul's teaching, its manifest fair-mindedness and freedom from taint of any ideology or political flavour, is gradually having its effect on the church in Latin America. John Paul II is a patient man: he realizes it will take time to reverse secular notions which have established themselves in the minds of some clergy. Thus, in Nicaragua, Catholic priests were allowed to serve as ministers in the new, radical Sandanista regime when it assumed power after the collapse of the Somoza dictatorship. In 1980 the Nicaraguan bishops asked the priests to resign. They appealed to the Vatican. The Vatican replied that the Nicaraguan church should arrange its own affairs in this respect, with the priests resigning when they could be conveniently re-placed. In June 1981 the bishops declared the priest-ministers 'in open rebellion'. Misplaced zeal is an inescapable characteristic of a living faith, as the church has been discovering, and rediscover-ing, for two millennia. In the Church of Mercy in Nicaragua's capital, Managua, the parish priest has built a new altar in the shape of a barricade. The stations of the cross he has hung up show Jesus in the clothes of a left-wing revolutionary, being ill-treated by right-wing soldiers wearing National Guard uniforms.[29]

John Paul knows that these childish gestures continue to be made. He is not a man to order altars to be torn down, or pictures pitched on to the fire: he leaves that to the totalitarian atheists. He has laid down the rules of conduct. He has assured himself of the general loyalty of the hierarchies in Latin America. He has sown the seed of his Christian humanism. It will, he feels confident, work its way into the minds of good and earnest priests. That altar, those stations of the cross, will in due course be replaced, voluntarily.

In September 1981, in the encyclical *Laborem Exercens*, John Paul set out the argument behind his social theory which casts the church in the role of teacher, rather than fighter. There is, he argues, no inherent conflict between capital and labour. Capital is only the accumulated product of human work. It has rights in so far as labour has rights: there is no irreconcilable conflict of rights. Human labour creates capital 'by producing a whole collection of increasingly perfect instruments for work'. The Marxist notion of class warfare, springing deterministically from the structure of the production process, must therefore be false. It is based on a false image which presents capital and labour as two impersonal forces. In fact capital-labour is a single, accumulating, above all human, entity, God-directed in accordance with the command of the Book of Genesis: 'Be fruitful and multiply, and fill the earth and subdue it.' That is the correct image, 'a consistent image, one that is humanistic as well as theological'.[30] By its teaching the church can replace the distorted, materialistic image with the true humanistic one of Catholic Christianity.

Laborem Exercens, however, argues throughout that materialism is not an error of the Marxists alone. In some respects John Paul is less disturbed by the secularization brought about by radical politics – which springs from fervour – than by the secularization brought about by Western materialism – which springs from lack of fervour. If the greatest evil of the age, especially in the collectivized world, is totalitarian atheism, and if its rival, especially in the developing world, is the politics of violence, a third master evil of our times, which flourishes mightily in the wealthy West, is the betrayal of spiritual values by stealth, especially by those pledged to uphold them.

6

Secularization
by Stealth

JOHN PAUL II undoubtedly sees in the liberal societies of the West the reserves of strength on which free, Christian man can call to defend himself, if need be, against the brutal physical pressure of totalitarian atheism. In Western liberalism, too, he recognizes the spirit of tolerance which is the natural guarantor of religious freedom, and the habit of debate which is the best answer to the appalling thirst for violence which threatens to take over the radical movement in the poorer countries and among the underprivileged everywhere. John Paul is a friend and admirer of the West; he is also among its fiercest and most profound critics. He believes the West can destroy itself and, in doing so, place the Catholic Church, indeed the whole of Christianity, in terrible danger. He voiced these fears with particular sorrow and urgency when he visited the United States in October 1979.

It is one of John Paul's axioms that, for human beings, the denial or absence of spirituality – that is, materialism – is not a neutral condition, but actively destructive. It is a gangrene, a process of mortification. In the materialism of the West he detects the aroma of guilt, one of the most corrosive of human emotions, itself springing from fear and adumbrating death. He has remarked in *Dives in Misericordia* that the hallmarks of Western society were 'guilt, uneasiness and remorse', because it was a society aware of its fundamental defects. 'We live against a background of gigantic remorse', he wrote, because 'wealthy and surfeited people', indeed whole societies, lived side by side with shortage and destitution, real and growing hunger, caused by the 'defective machinery of the world' which produced 'radical injustice'.[1]

In Ireland, on his way to the United States, he paused between his denunciations of violence to beg Ireland not to fall victim to the materialism which 'until now has been alien to Irish society'. It must not allow itself to be duped by the campaign of 'false pretences' waged about 'sexual freedom, the sacredness of life, the indissolubility of marriage, the true purpose of human sexuality, the proper evaluation of the material goods progress offers us'. 'All Christians', he told representatives of the Irish Protestants, 'must stand together to defend spiritual and moral values against the assaults of materialism and licence.' Speaking to young Irish Catholics, he asked what use political freedom was if they became prisoners of their own material selfishness: 'The life of pleasure is the new slavery.'[2]

Throughout his American visit (especially in his address at Yankee Stadium on 2 October 1979) he preached against the double selfishness of Western materialism: the habit of absorbing a disproportionate share of the world's limited resources, of treating the poorer countries as the rich man treated Lazarus,[3] and the tendency to judge all human relationships by the standards of personal hedonism. Such self-regard produced spiritual death, perhaps actual death.

There is, it should be noted, a gloomy side to John Paul, which tends to come to the fore when he contemplates the West. He has a puritanical hatred of consumerism, which he scrutinizes suspiciously for the *memento mori*: he looks for the grinning skull in Arcadia. In a remarkable homily preached at Turin on 13 April 1980, reflecting on his American trip, he argued: 'Progress, which has been brought about by generations of men with such labour, with the waste of so much energy and at such a cost, contains in its complexity a powerful element of.death. It conceals, even, a gigantic potential for death.' Was not the consumer's world merely the other side of the coin of nuclear weapons? Even while sating himself, 'modern man is afraid'. So: 'This orientation of enormous progress, which has become the central characteristic of our civilization, might it not become the beginning of the wholesale and planned death of man? Those terrible death-camps, of which some of those still alive carry traces on their very bodies, are they not also a presage and anticipation of this death of man?' Man was guilty because he was killing God in his mind, and fearful because he felt he was succeeding. The 'death of God' notion filled man with secret terror. Why? 'Precisely because man, who makes God die, knows he will not find a decisive restraint against killing man too. That curb is God. The ultimate reason why man should respect and protect the life of human beings lies in God himself.'⁴

In John Paul's analysis, the complexity of the relationship between God and man lies at the very heart of Christianity. In a sense it is a family relationship, almost a love-hate relationship, at all events marked by extreme tension. Man needs God in that he feels instinctively that the withdrawal of God presages his own self-assassination. But at the same time he feels impelled to challenge God, driven by his own pride and audacity, to echo the defiant words we find in the Old Testament: 'I will not serve, *Non serviam*.'⁵ In his 1976 Lenten series, *Sign of Contradiction*, John Paul wrote powerfully of man's temptation to turn away from God towards the world, 'a terrain where human pride seeks not the glory of God but its own satisfaction. The world is a territory over which the struggle between Man and God takes place, where the created being defies his creator. This is the great drama of history, myth and civilization.'⁶ Secularization is a kind of perverted religion of this defiant side of man, ranging over the whole spectrum of human behaviour and becoming 'a sort of counter-Revelation'.

Can man embark on such a disastrous course without an external agent of evil leading him on? John Paul thinks not. The false notion, common among both Western and Marxist humanists, that the worship of God de-humanizes and emasculates man, he traces back to the tempting voice of Satan in the third chapter of Genesis: 'In the day ye eat thereof, then your eyes shall be opened, and ye shall be as gods, knowing good and evil.' Man thinks this voice comes from within himself, and so it does in one sense; but it is also a voice from outside. Besides man's undoubted capacity for self-destruction, John Paul sees a great objective force of evil roaming creation, whose most diabolical strategy is to convince its victims that it does not exist: 'Might not the ultimate temptation, a temptation *sui generis*, consist in precisely this, that man should be persuaded into believing himself alone?' But man is not alone: neither God nor the Evil One is a figment of his imagination.

Not only is man not alone in creation: there is an organic link between the sacral and the human. John Paul advances a line of argument which, in our times, has been forcefully expressed by such theologians as Karl Rahner, but which goes back at least to Pascal, that without God man would gradually cease to be human and would become merely a very clever animal. Man owes his humanity to the notion of God, and if this notion disappears from his thoughts and his vocabulary, the humanity would disappear too.

The argument also applies even when the notion of God – belief in God – is retained but the believers deliberately minimize the importance of the sacred elements in their life and worship. This process has been taking place in all the Christian churches, in varying degrees, over the past few decades. It came to the Catholic Church late, but it has been proceeding very rapidly since the end of the Council. It is sometimes, rather euphemistically, referred to as 'de-mythologizing'. John Paul prefers the word 'de-sacralizing'. The process applies both to the presentation of the mysteries of religious belief and to the impingement of those beliefs on daily life. Until very recently almost all human activities had a sacral context, whether it was a harvest festival or a 'churching' after successful childbirth. Gradually this context is being withdrawn, dismantled, soon to be forgotten. A sense of awe and mystery is dispersed, and with it vanishes an important restraint on our animal natures. The phrase 'Is nothing sacred?' has a double meaning: 'Is nothing holy?' but also 'Is nothing to be respected?' Where nothing is sacred, what is entitled to respect?

It is John Paul's belief that de-sacralization must lead, sooner rather than later, to de-humanization. The process applies especially to the whole world of sexual relations and intimate human values. The need for the sacral in sex is an important part of John Paul's attitude to human rights and it is absolutely central to his theory of Christian humanism. In *Dives in Misericordia* he argues strongly that the person for whom the sacred is unimportant must suffer moral decay even though he keeps up, for a time, a façade of non-religious ethics. When absolute or fundamental values, resting on a sacral notion of natural moral law, are abandoned in favour of moral relativism, or even the complete suspension of moral law represented by modern 'permissiveness', there is a danger, as he puts it, of 'a purely utilitarian relationship between individual and individual'.[7] It is at this point that de-humanization occurs, because each individual tends increasingly to see the other not as a person but as an object, to be made use of or exploited. Altruism disappears, the humanity of the other is no longer considered, a quasi-animal relationship develops, and as it does so the humanity of the exploiter diminishes too. We end with two exceptionally ingenious animals which are, because ingenious, exceptionally destructive.

As a Christian humanist, John Paul sees the span of life as an inseparable continuum. Conception, birth, marriage, procreation, death are all contingent on each other. None can be isolated, treated separately. De-sacralize one, the process spreads to all. The Pope sees modern attitudes to abortion as the sinister index of the de-humanizing process, and as a clear demonstration of the way in which scrapping sacral sanctions and attitudes leads to a growing disrespect for life. Of course, no one who has spent most of his life within the gruesome penumbra of Auschwitz, who comes from a country where an alien force carried out the most extensive and systematic – and, by its own logic, utilitarian – assault on the human person in history, can remain unemotional about the extinction of unborn life. John Paul is emotional on the subject of abortion. It must be added, however, that he is also being entirely rational and consistent in identifying mass abortion as an example, *par excellence*, of the de-humanizing process. For the fearsome scenes now being enacted in hospitals and clinics all over the world could not conceivably be tolerated without denying the foetus his or her humanity. Equally, the men who organized the burning of six million people in ovens – four million of them in Auschwitz itself – were able, because they had escaped from the restraints of the sacral, to deny the humanity of those they destroyed. The analogy between the abortion clinic and the death camp becomes more menacing the more frequently it is raised; and for a Pole from Cracow it is impossible not to raise it.

Hence John Paul has condemned abortion repeatedly and everywhere, and in a way which places it at the centre of his structure of human rights and Christian humanism. It is not, and it cannot be, for John Paul a peripheral issue: it goes to the heart of his moral beliefs. When he said mass in Washington, in front of the Capitol, on 7 October 1979, he insisted:

If a person's right to life is violated at the moment in which he is first conceived in his mother's womb, an indirect blow is struck also at the whole of the moral order, which serves to ensure the inviolable goods of man. Among those goods life occupies the first place. The church defends the right to life not only in regard to the majesty of the Creator, who is the first giver of this life, but in respect, too, of the essential good of the human person.

The right to life was all-embracing and equally valid and sacred 'from the moment of conception through all its subsequent stages'.[8]

Indeed, as John Paul put the point in an address to journalists early in his pontificate, the rights of man begin with the rights of the child, and the rights of the child begin with conception. A child, he said, has a right to live. It has a right to be reared in a family, so that a parent who deprives a child of the first by abortion or the second by divorce is like the government of a state which permits no human rights. The child also has a right to the truth; that is, to a decent education in ethics, which itself depends on freedom and plurality in the schools. But these subsequent rights are meaningless without the right to live in the first place. Deprive a child of that and you automatically deprive him or her of the others. We must respect this right, then, 'for the honour of our civilization'.[9]

The reference to honour is characteristic. Auschwitz was a calamitous dishonour to European civilization. Abortion besmirches our culture. It is a disgrace - that is the word he frequently uses, and he says it with passion. On 21 September 1980, marking the six-hundredth anniversary of the death of St Catherine, patroness of Italy, he thundered: 'Every attack on a child in its mother's womb is a great blow to conscience. It is a great disgrace. It is a great sorrow.'[10] And abortion is not merely an assault on the individual foetus: it undermines the solidarity and mutually protective nature of the family. 'If', he has argued, 'children know their parents can kill one of them - and if they already have killed one of them - that is a tragic diminution of family stability.'

It is when John Paul talks and writes about the family that the value of his pastoral experience becomes manifest. The assumption that a priest is debarred from analysing and commenting on the problems of human sexuality by his celibacy is invalid. A parish priest is likely to acquire, with experience, as extensive a knowledge of sex both in and out of marriage as most doctors in general practice; and a bishop of many years' standing will have had to deal with every variety of marital disaster. A pope may have led a sheltered existence. Paul VI, for instance, was shielded by ill health from many human contacts in youth and early manhood. He never held a parish; he lacked pastoral experience altogether until, late in life, he acquired the splendid metropolitan benefice of Milan. He was designated for a high ecclesiastical career from a very early age; one might almost say he was born to be pope.

John Paul, by contrast, had no such advantages or disabilities. His vocation came late. He had girl friends. He experienced the normal emotional relationships of a virile and exceptionally gifted and intelligent young man. After recognizing his vocation, he embraced chastity. But as a priest and bishop he had more than thirty years' experience in big parishes and in one of the world's most populous archdioceses. There can be little he does not know about human frailty – and resilience. He has always had a particular interest in the family, not least because his own was so shattered by misfortune. He regards it as the greatest of human institutions, which possesses divine sanction more palpably than any other. It is sacral, sanctified. His experience as a minister of religion under an atheistic totalitarian state has made it seem especially precious. The Polish life of the family was an arcane, protected area which the Communist state found it difficult to enter and impossible to destroy. The more the sterile horror from without pressed upon it, the more the family linked arms in self-defence, rejoicing in its friendship and warm fecundity. How could such a marvellous human construct commit suicide by de-sacralizing itself? Must it not, rather, reinforce its integrity by every means at its command?

As a priest, still more as a bishop, John Paul worked for family survival. In Cracow he created a Family Institute which became a key element in his pastoral experience. He placed in charge of it a woman psychiatrist, who had survived the horrors of Ravensbrück concentration camp and had herself been a victim of medical 'experiments' by Nazi doctors. There were then many such in

Poland (most are now dead), living testimony to a 'utilitarian' view of human material, another reason why John Paul personally detests abortion. In Cracow he had many doctors among his friends. But the Family Institute gave him a special insight not only into the medical aspects of sex – the burden of repeated pregnancies, venereal disease, miscarriages, physical incompatibility, the menopause, impotence – but also the impact of poverty, desertion, wife-beating, alcoholism, illegitimacy and chronic illness and debility.

Some of the knowledge thus acquired went into the book *Love and Responsibility*, in which he combined his pastoral experiences with his philosophical and ethical speculations on man as a procreative creature. As we have seen, this book had a bearing on Paul VI's encyclical *Humanae Vitae* condemning contraception. When the encyclical appeared in 1968, John Paul reissued the book, supporting Paul VI's ruling. The condemnation of the contraceptive pill, which then so outraged liberal opinion, now begins to seem less obscurantist as medical evidence of long-term effects accumulates. John Paul would argue that this was foreseeable from the start. The body of a healthy young woman has an almost irresistible urge to create life. To attempt to frustrate this process by the clumsy ingestion of a chemical concentrate is tantamount to an assault upon one of the body's most sensitive and fundamental functional systems. How could there not be disastrous side-effects?

The truth is that, as our experience of contraception on a global scale accumulates, the attitude of the Catholic Church begins to seem less obscurantist and more clear-sighted. All forms of artificial contraception are unsatisfactory for one reason or another. The 'natural' or rhythm method, which the church sanctions, is unsatisfactory too. The church does not deny it; it merely says it is not morally wrong. As a scientific problem, contraception is unsolved; perhaps it is insoluble. But it is a mistake to say Catholicism does not have a solution. It does: self-restraint. John Paul would argue that restraint in sex is part of the sacral approach. It is a tribute that men and women of honour, of culture, are willing to pay as their contribution to preserving marriage as a beneficent force in society. The point was made by a great Protestant poet. The whole of civilization, wrote W. B. Yeats, 'is an exercise in self-restraint'.

Restraining the self, the ego, is a way in which one partner recognizes the personality of the other, refuses to see him or her as an object to be used, rejects the utilitarian and restores the sacral. The mutual recognition of, and respect for, personality is of the very essence of Christian humanism. That is why John Paul was entirely consistent in October 1980 when he said that a man who lusted after his wife in his heart committed adultery. The degradation of the wife into a lust-object is destructive of marriage and therefore invalidates the moral legitimacy of the act, which becomes sinful.

The reverential and sacral approach to marriage and sex is reflected in some of John Paul's imaginative works, such as his play *The Goldsmith's Shop* (1960) which dates from the same time as *Love and Responsibility*. Both are, in effect, meditations on the sacrament of marriage. Taken in conjunction with the series of homilies John Paul gave in Rome in the course of 1980, reflecting on the story of Adam and Eve in Genesis, they represent the first attempt by a pope to produce a mature theory of sex in the light of modern knowledge.

Long before the Second Vatican Council changed the Catholic perspective on marriage, John Paul had already placed conjugal love (including the enjoyment of sex) on a par with procreation as the object of matrimony; in short he had refused to endorse the church's traditional order of marital objectives. But he has been careful to point out that the prolonged avoidance of birth by the 'natural' method is as morally inadmissible as artificial contraception.[11] He denies the possibility of total sexual freedom (even within marriage), believing it to be a contradiction in terms. For John Paul freedom is indissolubly linked with, is a function of, responsibility. Only the responsible person is truly free. In this respect he sees a close parallel between public affairs and sexual behaviour. He opposes determinism in sex as hotly as he opposes it in politics, and for the same reason. To say that a person is impelled towards sexual activity, or a certain form of sexual activity, is to insult his humanity and to deny his free will just as surely as to insist that men's political opinions and behaviour are determined by modes of production and membership of a class. In both cases man is humiliatingly presented as the helpless subject or slave of material forces.

It follows naturally from John Paul's anti-determinism that he cannot countenance forms of sexual deviance such as homosexuality. He has no sympathy with the view that homosexuality is a compulsion of nature. There is no compulsion of nature. That is what free will is all about. He sympathizes with the homosexual in the same way as he sympathizes with any other man or woman separated from the supposed goal of physical satisfaction by the invisible frontier of the moral law. The frontier may be crossed, but that is sin, and the frontier remains no matter how many times it is violated.

John Paul has repeatedly set his face against any blurring of definitions and distinctions in sexual matters. In this field more than most, he feels, confusion is the enemy of truth, clear language and logic. He seems to have little time for the ancient and hallowed Christian notion, so strongly favoured by some of the early doctors of the church, such as St Jerome, that the body is nothing more than a temporary lodging for the soul.[12] In his view, the body has great importance in itself, and all its functions, not least those which differentiate the sexes, are parts of God's design. The distinctions between male and female are therefore of great significance and cannot be brushed aside by the crudities of modern unisex theology. 'Maleness and femaleness are fundamental categories,' he remarked during one of his 1980 Wednesday homilies, 'and they are not interchangeable.'[13] This insistence reinforces his rejection of homosexuality as a morally acceptable form of conduct. But, more important, it confirms his view that men and women have radically different, though complementary, roles to perform in God's design.

John Paul's attitude to women has been variously criticized as 'sexist', 'Polish', traditionalist and reactionary. Speaking to 5,000 Italian women on 29 April 1979, he defended the record of Christianity in this field. Jesus, in his attitudes to women, was 'bold and surprising' in contrast to 'the standards of the day, when woman was considered in pagan culture to be merely an object of pleasure, of possession and of labour, and in Judaism was subordinated and humiliated'.[14] Why were there no women apostles? He quoted the passage in St Luke which lists the group of women standing immediately 'after the twelve' as assisting in Jesus's ministry.[15] He insisted that the role of a housewife was 'not a humiliation but a consecration ... almost a mission'. In the Christian life, he argues, the importance of a calling is not to be judged by secular criteria but by the readiness, intensity and wholeheartedness of the response. It was the decision of Providence that women should not be called as apostles, and therefore as priests. But in the devotional life of the church women have always been outstanding. Lack of holy orders was no obstacle to the exercise of influence by such notable women as St Catherine of Siena or St Teresa of Avila, and the entire calendar of male saints pales beside the lustre cast by the immaculate Blessed Virgin, Queen of Heaven (and Poland).

John Paul's intense devotion to the Virgin Mary serves, paradoxically, to inflame still further the animosity towards him of certain Catholic women's rights activists who are campaigning for the ordination of women. This was one of the issues most frequently thrust in front of the Pope's nose during his American visit. The leader of the Catholic women demanding the right to the priesthood, Rosemary Radford Ruether, has described the feeling of male priests for feminists as 'gut hatred' and denounced their use of the eucharist as a 'power instrument'. Neither expression is likely to undermine the resolution of a man like John Paul; quite the contrary. Nor is he impressed by the argument that, in the decade since the Council, over 50,000 American women have left the religious orders.[16] That, he would say, is more likely to be due to a relaxation of traditional rules and standards, than to their maintenance. Men and women, he argues, are called to many forms of service in the church. Priesthood is one of them. But the essence of all service is fidelity. He told American nuns in the great basilica of the Immaculate Conception in Washington: 'Faithfulness in Christ, especially in religious life, can never be separated from faithfulness to the church.'

It was on this occasion that a leading Catholic woman militant, Sister Theresa Kane, the then President of the Leadership Conference of Women Religious, made a personal protest to the Pope. She wore secular clothing, thus defying his plainly expressed wish that all nuns wear their habit, and she insisted on reading out a strident demand that the church 'respond by providing the possibility of all persons being included in all ministries of our church'.

It was not clear whether John Paul grasped her point at the time (his English was not then always adequate to cope with unforeseen incidents). He patted her head in a vague gesture of approbation or dismissal. Afterwards an order of American nuns bought space in the *Washington Post* to apologize to the Pope for the 'public rudeness shown him'.[17]

Just over a year later, during his visit to West Germany in November 1980, John Paul was publicly attacked by women militants for visiting the tomb of Albertus Magnus in Cologne, on the grounds that Albertus slandered women; and in Munich he was denounced by a Catholic 'youth leader', Barbara Engl, for 'clinging fearfully to tradition' – a peculiarly inept formulation, fearfulness being about the last emotion one would associate with John Paul.[18] His view of the work best done by women in the church is certainly traditional, but it is honestly arrived at and wholly consistent with his humanistic philosophy. He does not believe the sexes are equal, because he believes they are different, but he does not place them in any order of merit or value. In this as in all major issues he is very much his own man; clamour, especially sloganized clamour, is unlikely to deflect him in the course he has chosen.

Indeed, one of his principal purposes in visiting the United States so soon in his pontificate was to make it unmistakably clear that the church was not engaged in a continuing and radical revision of its fundamental positions. He was anxious to kill any false hopes entertained by the liberal fringe. Much more important, he wanted to reassure the vast majority of the faithful, and especially of the rank-and-file priesthood, that the essentials of the church's dogmatic and moral theology, its canon law, and its internal disciplinary system, were not matters for argument but for obedience.

The reassurance had become painfully necessary because the church in the United States, once ultra-loyalist, even docile, in its allegiance to Rome, had become disoriented by the Council and its aftermath – and of course by the secular radicalism unleashed during the 1960s, of which America had been the principal victim. In the last years of Paul VI the American church had appeared leaderless and subject to a spreading moral anarchy. Not only ordinary Catholics but priests and even bishops had been bewildered and frightened at the wholesale abandonment of traditional Catholic attitudes by what appeared to be official or quasi-official bodies. One example was the publication entitled *Human Sexuality: New Directions in Catholic Thought*, described as 'A study commissioned by the Catholic Theological Society of America'. This advocated a permissive or tolerant attitude to activities hitherto regarded as sinful virtually without reservation, such as masturbation, fetishism, transvestism, use of 'sex clinics', various operations for changing sex, use of pornography, fornication when practised by 'involuntary singles', 'divorced singles' and widows, and sexual acts between homosexuals ('a homosexual engaging in homosexual acts in good conscience has the same rights of conscience and the same rights to the sacraments as a married couple practising birth control in good conscience').

John Paul was determined to show that there was no possibility, at present or in the future, that Rome would endorse do-it-yourself moral theology or accept any significant relaxation in the rules by which it ordered its affairs. He did not go to seek a show-down with the heterodox and the rebels. That has never been, and is not, his way. His massive certitude and overwhelming benevolent strength sweep aside the need for threats or any shrillness of tone. He is a divine juggernaut, but one more anxious to help everyone aboard than to crush those in his path. He made it clear, however, in public discourse and still more in private colloquy, that rebels would no longer find a sympathetic ear in Rome, while conservatives could henceforth rely on undeviating support there.

The result was that, alongside the overwhelmingly favourable response John Paul evoked among millions of American Catholics (and non-Catholics), there was a steady stream of critical venom of a type which no previous pope had ever received from any section of the American Catholic community. John Paul was compared to Jim Jones, leader of the mass-suicidal Jonestown cult. He was accused of 'lack of sensitivity', or 'pious and moralistic reassertions' of traditional doctrine which 'shocked' and 'perplexed' the faithful. He was called a 'pious, pharisaical, autocratic, woman-hating white whiskers', supporting the 'injustice, phony trials, machinations, hypocrisy and witch-hunts' of the Vatican, allowing Rome to become 'dominated by an atmosphere of bullying and secretiveness and ecclesiastical power-plays'. He was told to 'take off his long dress' and 'assimilate Küng's masterpiece, *On Being a Christian*'. He was 'a new Torquemada of the Tiber', determined to force the church into a 'Procrustean bed modelled after the conservative Polish church'. He should 'listen and learn', show 'more sensitivity and less dogma'. He had 'set the ecumenical movement back a hundred years, and that's conservative', encouraged 'the crazies', turned the church into 'a giant hypocrisy'. He was nothing more than 'an impatient, energetic conservative determined to reinforce traditional dogma', a 'wizard of Castel Gandolfo', a 'paid star in show-business', a man whose greatest failure was 'a lack of sympathy and understanding of human problems'. Some of this abuse came from ex-priests and their wives or mistresses; but some of it was from sections of the Catholic press, Catholic authors, priests in good standing and even teachers at Catholic universities.[19]

Pope John Paul has never reacted to this type of abuse. He has a stable and well-adjusted personality, disinclined to take notice of malice. One of his former professors, Father Rozycki, recalls an occasion when, as vicar-capitular, he was in virtual charge of the Cracow archdiocese: 'He gave the best parish at his disposal to a priest who had made vicious, personal attacks on him.... The campaign against Wojtyla organized by this priest became so serious that I considered it my duty to inform Bishop Wojtyla about it for his own good. If he had not taken the matter in hand, he would probably not have become archbishop, or cardinal, or pope.'[20] Public criticism of the pope of a personal nature by Catholics would have been almost unthinkable twenty years ago. Today, in John Paul's view, it is to be expected. He will ignore it so long as he is persuaded it does not damage his office. But the best reply, of course, is to maintain the course he has set; and this he certainly has done.

Throughout 1980 John Paul continued his occasional reflections on marriage and sexual conduct, inspired by biblical texts, which he delivered on Wednesdays. They serve to refute the notion that, in such matters, he is an obscurantist or an unthinking traditionalist. Nothing illustrates better the originality of his mind and his freedom both from emotional conservatism and liberal cliché-response. Commenting on Genesis 2:25: 'And they were both naked, the man and his wife, and were not ashamed', John Paul told his audience:

The exchange of the gift of the person constitutes the real source of the experience of innocence. We can say that interior innocence, that is, righteousness of intention, in the exchange of the gifts consists in recipro-cal 'acceptance' of the other. In this way mutual giving creates the communion of persons. The opposite of this 'acceptance' or 'welcoming' of the other human being as a gift would be a privation of the gift itself and therefore a changing and even a reduction of the other to an 'object for myself' – an object of lust, for example. This extorting of the gift from the woman by the man, or vice versa, and reducing him or her in one's mind to a mere object, marks exactly the beginning of shame,

which of course we get in Genesis 3:1, when the figleaf makes its appearance.[21]

John Paul has also taken a series of practical steps to reinforce the Catholic Church's traditional view of marriage as an indissol-uble, monogamous union. In the spring of 1980, during a pastoral visit to a group of African countries, he brought firmly to an end rumours, which had circulated in the last years of Paul VI, that the church, as part of a programme of 'africanization', would give its blessing to some forms of polygamous marriage. Monogamy, he said, was not a European invention, imposed on Africans by the process of colonialism. It was God-given, God-ordained, and the church had no option in the matter but to enforce it with all its spiritual power. It was noted that two of the African leaders whom John Paul met on his tour, Presidents Mobutu and Houphouët-Boigny, found it politic to get married just before the pontifical visit. When this was drawn to the Pope's attention, he drily termed it 'the first fruits of my pastoral visit to Africa'.[22]

In Rome, John Paul conducted a review of the procedures which, in canon law, examine possible impediments to existing marriages, which may invalidate them and allow church courts to annul the union. There had been suggestions that, under Paul VI, annulments had become easier to obtain – they had certainly increased in num-ber – and John Paul satisfied himself that there would be no further relaxation in the church's traditional reluctance to declare a marriage null, particularly where children have been born to the union.

As the first climax of his campaign to restabilize Catholic moral theology, especially in the whole area revolving around sex and the family, John Paul held a general synod on the family. It took place in Rome from 26 September to 25 October 1980. In the United States he had been menaced and abused by the extreme wing of Catholic liberalism when he reasserted traditional doctrine. In Rome he had to counter the more plausible case of what might be called its 'responsible' wing. Those who wished the church to relax its ruling on artificial contraception, and the admission of divorced people to the sacraments, had done a good deal of homework. They produced statistics. Thus an American prelate, Archbishop Quinn, put forward evidence showing that Catholics in the United States did not, in practice, observe the papal ban on contraceptives. Figures collected by the National Pastoral Congress for England and Wales, held at Liverpool in May 1980, were also placed in evidence. There was an eloquent speech from Cardinal Basil Hume, Archbishop of Westminster, who argued that Catholics using contraceptives 'just cannot accept that the use of artificial means of contraception in some circumstances is *intrinsice inhonestum*, as the latter has been generally understood'. Archbishop Derek Worlock of Liverpool sought to convey the feeling of the pastoral congress by putting the case for those who were divorced and remarried: 'Is this spirit of repentance and desire for sacramental strength to be for ever frustrated? Can they be told only that they must reject their new responsibilities as a necessary condition for forgiveness and restoration to sacramental life?'

These speeches were gleefully reported, but they do not seem to have represented the general view of the synod. That was more faithfully conveyed by John Paul himself, on Sunday 12 October, when he chose to stress the positive importance of the family's spirituality, rather than the currently fashionable reasons for undermining its durability and integrity. It is a curious fact that the church was slow to admit matrimony as a sacrament, the first recorded acknowledgement being by Archbishop Hincmar of Rheims, who died in 882; and not until the age of St Thomas Aquinas did the experts teach that it conferred grace. In the last century, however, papal teaching has placed growing stress on the spiritual importance of the Christian family, and John Paul has now pushed it to the very centre of the Christian apostolate.[23] The purpose of the sacrament of marriage, he told the synod, 'is to construct with living cells the body of Christ which is the church'. Christian marriage is 'impregnated by grace ... a way of evangelical life, a search for the face of the Lord, a school of Christian charity'.[24]

The early proceedings of the synod, including the speeches of the liberals, received wide publicity. Once the synod began to discuss and vote on the actual propositions before it, however, a veil of privacy descended. John Paul was very assiduous in attending the sessions; he took copious notes; he held lunch-time meetings with members every day. He made his views abundantly clear. His central position is worth stressing because it is one of the keys to his pontificate. Of course the church has the duty of sympathy for those who find the demands of the Christian life too onerous. But its primary responsibility is to the truth and to the great body of the Christian faithful who expect and rely upon the church to uphold it. The silent, faithful majority must be able to draw from the synod, as he put it,

... the conviction, the confidence and the certainty that it is a right and duty of the church to cultivate and carry out her doctrine in pastoral guidance on marriage and the family. The church does not intend to impose this doctrine and guidance on anyone, but is ready to propose them freely and to safeguard them as a reference point which cannot be renounced for those who style themselves Catholics and who wish to belong to the ecclesial community.[25]

That is the essential John-Pauline message: the church is not a compulsory society, it is not totalitarian; it is a voluntary society, but one with rules, which are precise, clear, binding and unchangeable.

The synod affirmed by vote some forty-three propositions on marriage which, in effect, restated Catholic orthodoxy on every point. In his homily at the end of the meeting, John Paul noted that it had restated 'the indissolubility of marriage' by 'not admitting to Eucharistic Communion those who have divorced and have, against the rule, attempted another marriage'; that it had 'openly confirmed the validity and clear truth' of Paul VI's *Humanae Vitae*, banning artificial contraceptives, which he praised as a 'prophetic message, profound and relevant to today's conditions'; and that it had refused to countenance casuistic devices to get round the rules, 'as if there were in divine law various levels or forms of precept for various persons and conditions'. The law was the law was the law. As for women, he said, the synod had recognized woman's 'dignity and vocation as a daughter of God, as a wife, and as a mother'; and it had asked that 'human society be so constituted that women should not be forced to engage in external work', so that 'the mother might devote herself fully to the family'.[26]

The synod was thus an unconditional victory for the forces within the church which John Paul purposes to uphold, and it was a striking example of the granitic resolve he brings to the task. It was greeted with pain and anger by some sections of the liberal wing.[27] But most progressive clerics were stunned into unaccustomed silence by the magnitude of the papal triumph. They were also unnerved by what they began to see, for the first time, as the total integrity of the Pope's position, the way in which all his teachings, on human rights and dignity, on materialism, on violence, on justice and mercy, on the various forms of Christian service – such as marriage – all locked into the basic philosophical machinery of his Christian humanism. What they were up against was not a mere traditionalist, like Paul VI, hanging on to such positions as, in his uncertainty and irresolution, he felt he might succeed in defending, but a sturdy and positive campaigner, with a clear and consistent view of the world, rooted in the Bible and the Fathers, in the *magisterium* and the Schoolmen, but reshaped and burnished to meet all the assaults of the modern age, and prepared to carry the action into the enemy camp. This pope was not much interested in tactics, and timely concessions, and skilful fudging of issues. He did not care greatly for statistics, which might prove anything or nothing. What he cared about was the truth. As he put it when he dismissed the members of the synod, 'No one can exercise charity other than in truth.' It might appear to be charitable to admit divorced persons to the sacraments, or concede to practising homosexuals a legitimate moral status, or permit married couples to use contraceptives. But the truth had first claim on the church. If charity conflicted with truth, it was not charity at all, but indulgence, weakness, false compromise, treason to God.

It has been, then, a salient purpose of John Paul, in combating the materialism of the West, to make it clear that the moral teaching of the church is not, as it were, up for auction. The era of experiment and doubt is over. The era of certitude has recommenced. But that message has to be conveyed at every level of the church, and in the first place to its own clergy. We now turn to the fourth great evil confronting the reinvigorated papacy: the erosion of discipline and morale within the ecclesiastical community itself.

7

Imperilled Certitudes

JOHN PAUL II is a man of his age in the providential sense. He brings to the 1980s the precious gift which is most needful and welcome to it: certitude. A Polish friend shrewdly observed of him: 'You sense that he is secure, and that makes you feel secure too.'[1] One of the tasks John Paul has undertaken is to convey this feeling of security not just to individuals through personal contact – valuable though that is – but to hundreds, to thousands of millions, on a truly world-wide scale. After the restless experimentation of the 1960s, after the breakdown and disillusionment of the 1970s, how to base the new realism of the 1980s on a firm foundation of reassurance, the rediscovery of ancient truth, the reassertion of fundamental values, the redefinition of what is good and what is evil, not relatively but absolutely, always and everywhere?

It might seem an impossible task for one man. But of course John Paul has at his command a matchless instrument, which might have been expressly fashioned for this purpose. It came into his hands just in time. There was a moment, in the mid-1970s, when the Roman Catholic Church seemed in real danger of inflicting grievous injury on itself, to the point of destroying those characteristics which are its greatest strengths: its self-confidence, its internal order, its unchangeability. With the coming of John Paul that moment passed. The damage has now been contained. It is being repaired. The instrument is being fashioned for service again. It is much required.

No human institution in history has placed so much stress on continuity and authority as the Catholic Church. Some of the churches of Rome go back to the early fourth century, at which

time the bishops of the city were already associated with a centralized, disciplined and magisterial presentation of Christianity. In a
number of fundamental respects, the way the papacy sees the
church and the world has not changed since the time of Pope
Gregory the Great in the late sixth century. The tone of voice, the
institutional cadence we hear in Gregory's 854 surviving letters –
as, for instance, in his instruction to St Augustine of Canterbury to
undertake his expedition to convert the English – is not very
different from the Maundy Thursday letter which John Paul II
addressed to his bishops in 1979.[2] The atmosphere of stability and
order radiated by the papal archives, which perhaps date as a
concept from the time of Constantine when the popes first occupied
the Lateran, is awesome.[3] The prevailing sentiment of papal Rome
has always been, for more than 1500 years, serenity of conviction.
If security is to be found in any organ of earthly government, it is
to be found there. And if that calm certitude affronts the mind of
the twentieth century, it finds a grateful response in the
twentieth-century heart.

The security of Catholicism is indissolubly linked to the claims
of the Holy See, and it is on those claims that John Paul has based
his restoration. These claims are formidable and, by human standards, audacious. The 1870 constitution on the papacy, *Pastor
Aeternus*, contains, among other anathemas, the following:

> If anyone says that the Roman Pontiff has only the office of inspection
> or direction, but not the full and supreme power of jurisdiction over the
> whole church, not only in matters that pertain to faith and morals, but
> also in matters that pertain to the discipline and government of the church
> throughout the whole world; or if anyone says he has only a more
> important part and not the complete fullness of the supreme power; or if
> anyone says that this power is not ordinary or immediate over each and
> every church or over each and every faithful shepherd or member, let him
> be anathema.[4]

This remains the formal position of the church, in whole and in
detail, and if John Paul were asked if he assented to this constitution, he would of course say that he did.

He does, however, in presenting the doctrine of infallibility, use
a collective rather than a personal form of expression. This is made
desirable, though not essential, by the dogmatic constitution *Lumen*

Gentium of the Second Vatican Council (24 November 1964). This reaffirmed papal infallibility ('And all this teaching about the institution, the perpetuity, the meaning and the reason for the sacred primacy of the Roman Pontiff and of his infallible *magisterium*, this sacred council again proposes to be firmly believed by all the faithful'), but further asserted that 'the order of bishops, which succeeds to the college of apostles and gives this apostolic body continued existence, is also the subject of full and supreme power over the universal church, provided we understand this body together with its head the Roman Pontiff'.[5] What this means is that the pope is infallible (when speaking *ex cathedra* on faith and morals) even without the bishops; the bishops are not infallible without the pope; but in practice the two will act together.

John Paul argues that this collective quality, exercised by the church as a whole, should be regarded not so much as a 'power' as 'a gift and service'. In his letter to the German episcopal conference, dated 15 May 1980, he sees freedom from error in faith and moral teaching as an essential, indeed inevitable, consequence of Christ's decision to set up a church on earth. He asked: 'When Christ endowed the church with everything needed to carry out the mission entrusted to her, could he have withheld from her that gift of certainty about the truth she professed and proclaimed?' Belief in infallibility is no more than an expression of confidence in Christ's love for the church he created: 'We cannot fail to profess it if we believe in the love with which Christ loved his church and loves her incessantly.' It is not a question of recognizing truth in a man but truth in Christ. 'Infallibility as a whole, and especially for the one who participates in a special way in the infallibility of the church [himself], is essentially and exclusively a condition of the service which he must discharge in this church. "Power", in fact, cannot be understood and exercised anywhere, much less in the church, but as service.' 'The truth about the infallibility of the church', he admits, 'may seem a less central truth' and occupy 'a lower position in the hierarchy of truths' than those revealed by God and professed by the church. None the less, it is essential because it is 'the key to that certainty with which the faith is professed and proclaimed, as well as to the life and behaviour of the faithful'. He then adds the clinching argument: 'For if that essential foundation is shaken or destroyed, even the most elementary truths of our faith begin at once to disintegrate.'[6]

Infallibility, then, is a truth of last resort, a sort of ultimate deterrent to error, rarely to be used, more valuable as a potency than an actuality, its very existence rather than its exploitation forming a guarantee and seal of truth in what the church tells us and how it conducts itself. But it is also a manifestation of divinity in the church. As John Paul told the Puebla conference: 'It is unity around the Gospel, the Body and Blood of the Lamb, and Peter living in his successors, all of which are different signs, but all of them important signs, of the presence of Jesus among us.' Infallibility was thus one way in which the church's essential unity was divinely guaranteed. (This passage, it is interesting to note, evoked from Hans Küng the comment: 'Near blasphemy.')[7]

While it is impossible to see the church splitting so long as the doctrine of infallibility is resolutely upheld, normal authority is administered through the bishops: just as Peter 'lives in his successors', so the apostles live in them. From the moment he became pope, John Paul has never missed an opportunity to uphold episcopal authority and to insist that the hierarchical form of government must receive the full and wholehearted support of every member of the church. The pope governs through the bishops and, within his diocese, the bishop is church government. Anybody seeking to evade episcopal control will receive no sympathy from John Paul, as he has repeatedly made clear. Collectively, the bishops form an important part of the central government of the church. It seems to me very likely that, in about ten years' time, when he judges the restoration of the church to be nearing completion, John Paul will summon another General Council to debate, register and approve his work, and to lay down guidelines for the church in the twenty-first century.

In the meantime he makes full use of the system of episcopal synods. As established by Paul VI in 1965, the synod can take several forms. It can be a general assembly, of patriarchs, archbishops and bishops elected by national episcopal conferences, plus ten representatives from the religious orders (all male). In case of urgency, a synod can be called consisting simply of the chairmen of each episcopal conference plus three representatives from the orders. An alternative is for the pope to summon a meeting of the full college of cardinals, which includes all the principal archbishops in the world, plus the curial heads of departments. The Pope used this device in November 1979 when he wanted to consult the most senior clergy about the church's finances. In addition, he can call a regional synod from a particular area or country, consisting of the bishops of the area plus appropriate curial cardinals and his own appointed nominees. John Paul chose this method to deal with difficulties in the Dutch church, which we shall examine in the next chapter.

General synods, normally held every three years, are the most weighty of these gatherings, and have been systematically tackling all the principal areas of the church's activity: revision of canon law (1967), collegiality (1969), the priestly ministry (1971), evangelization (1974), the catechism (1977), the family (1980). The *motu proprio* or personal instruction of Paul VI which set up the system on 15 September 1965 states that such general synods are to be held 'to inform and give advice' to the pope (though in certain circumstances the synod might also be given 'deliberative power'; such a case has not yet occurred).

As the pope decides whether and when to call such synods, where they shall sit, determines the agenda, presides (if he wishes), prorogues and dissolves them, and decides whether he will accept or ignore their conclusions, it has been asserted that they have failed in their purpose, which was to embody the collegiate principle in the central government of the church. But this is to misunderstand how the church functions and what it is supposed to be doing. The church is not a secular body ruled by a government with material aims which can be secured by a choice between empirical means. That, indeed, lends itself to the notion of sovereign assemblies and direct representation, with all the apparatus of votes and majorities. But the church is quite different. It is concerned not with choices but with truth. There is only one truth, divinely revealed. Therefore the church is an autocracy tempered by consensus. The synod is not a parliament seeking a majority, but a mirror, as it were, in which the autocracy sees the consensus for which it speaks. Pope and synod interact. They influence each other. They represent different aspects of the workings of the Holy

Spirit. In their complementarity they are creative, and it is now difficult to see the church functioning without this partnership, which has established itself with great success in little over a decade.

One might say that John Paul himself, as leader of the church, is essentially the product of the synodal system, that he would not have become pope without it. Thus the collegiate principle has established itself. There is no more enthusiastic supporter of the synod than John Paul, who sees it as a practical means to associate large numbers of bishops with the central direction of the church, and to prevent the emergence of any constitutional fissure between the central and local government of the church, between bishops and pope. It is a much more efficient and accurate way of discovering the mind of the church than a series of devolved legislative assemblies, which in the Anglican Church, for example, have produced frustration tempered by sedatives.

The image of John Paul as a Polish steamroller flattening the bishops beneath his triumphalist progress is misconceived. If there is, indeed, any flattening that needs doing, John Paul expects the bishops to do it. He has called them 'the architects of unity'. They are the superstructure of church government, of which the pope is no more than the pinnacle, albeit a formidable one. All his statements on the subject, and his actions, confirm that he regards the bishops, under the leadership of the pope, as the church's ruling body – as he puts it, 'with Peter and under Peter'.[8] In a meeting with the French bishops at Issy-les-Moulineaux, 1 June 1980, he made it clear that he sees the episcopate as the mainstream, unifying force in Catholicism. On the one hand, he said, there were the 'progressivists'. They were 'always eager to adapt even the very content of faith'. As a result the faithful were 'bewildered'. 'They are obsessed by "advancing",' he said. 'But towards what do they "advance" when all is said and done?' On the other hand there were the 'integralists'. They 'shut themselves up in a particular period of the church' – the Tridentine period, in effect – and reject the church's need to change and grow. That, by implication, is to deny that 'the spirit of God is at work in the church today'. The bishops, with their broad, collegiate wisdom and prudence, are there to ensure that neither force deflects the church from its true path or damages its self-confidence and morale.[9] In this continuing, historical task, the bishops have the right to ask from Catholics 'faithfulness, fidelity and discipline, all harmonized by love'. Even the humblest Catholic has the right to participate in the governing structure of the church from parish upwards; and all the faithful – they are not called that by chance – have the corresponding duty to witness their faith by promptness and loyalty in obeying the lawful commands of their pastors and doing what they are called upon to perform.

If the government of the church revolves around the bishops, the health of the faith ultimately depends on the quality of the priesthood. John Paul is a priest's pope. Wherever he goes, it is on the serried ranks of the priests who come to greet him that he casts the fondest and most watchful eye. In Paris in 1980 he told young French people in the Parc des Princes: 'I've been pope for nearly two years, a bishop for over twenty years, but for me the most important thing is still the fact that I am a priest.' To John Paul a prelate who becomes separated from the duties of the priesthood is a man doomed to progressive spiritual starvation, for the priest is the prime agent of evangelization, and the chief minister of the sacraments. John Paul has striven, as pope, to cling to his pastorate, to administer the sacraments as often as possible. That is why he takes so close an interest in his own diocese and its central parishes, in his ancient cathedral of St John Lateran, and in the inner workings of his pontifical basilica, St Peter's. From time to time he hears confessions there. Thus, on Good Friday 1981 he replaced, for an hour or two, one of the regular multilingual confessors in St Peter's, and heard confessions in German, Hungarian, Italian and Spanish.[10]

At the heart of the John-Pauline restoration of Catholicism is the absolute distinction he draws between clergy and laity, between priest and people. The notion of a special priestly order to administer the sacraments does not go back to the earliest Christian times. It seems to have been developed in its most assertive form by the Roman church, from the fourth century onwards, and became closely associated with the centrality of the mass in Latin worship. It is thus one of the great characteristic features of Roman Catholicism, and by choosing to emphasize its importance John Paul shows, once again, that he is above all a Catholic pope.

In his eyes the priest is an elect person, specially singled out for the honour and privilege of his calling, for service and, if so appointed, for sacrifice. The priest is not an ordinary man. To illustrate this point, John Paul cites the remarkable story of Blessed Maximilian Kolbe. Kolbe was a very active Franciscan priest whose friary at Niepokalanow in Poland, which he created from 1927 onwards, was one of the largest in the world, virtually self-supporting, the centre of a Catholic publishing empire. In February 1941 he was arrested by the Nazis, for organizing a shelter for refugees (including Jews), and in May found himself in Auschwitz. There, he earned the love and respect of other inmates for what one of them, also a priest, called his 'radiant holiness'; he also attracted the peculiar venom of the Nazi guards and suffered atrocious punishment. That was by no means unusual: some 166 priests were murdered in this terrible camp.

What distinguished Kolbe's death was its voluntary nature. In July 1941 a prisoner was reported escaped, and ten men were selected to die as a reprisal, in a windowless underground chamber called the bunker, where they were simply locked in and left to die, without food or water. One of the ten men, Franciszek Gajowniczek, shouted in despair: 'My wife, my children – I shall never see them again.' Father Kolbe then stepped forward and offered to take his place. The SS officer in charge, Fritsch, accepted, but asked: 'Who are you?' Kolbe replied: 'I am a Catholic priest.' The condemned men were in the bunker for over a fortnight, dying one by one, while Kolbe led them in increasingly faint prayers and hymns. Eventually, he and three other survivors were killed by injections of carbolic acid.[11]

There are carefully recorded eye-witness testimonies to Kolbe's heroic piety, suffering and death, and after 1945 the cause of his canonization was pressed vigorously. John Paul, as Archbishop of Cracow, took a leading part in the Kolbe movement and was present when he was beatified in Rome on 17 October 1971. On that occasion he noted the simple pride with which Fr Kolbe gave his calling as an explanation of his sacrifice: 'Who are you?' 'I am a Catholic priest.' He commented: 'At a time when so many priests all over the world are fussing about their "identity", Father Max-imilian Kolbe gives the answer, not with theological argument, but with his own life and death.' He continued: 'The nightmare memory of the concentration camps is slowly fading. The young know scarcely anything about them. ... But the survivors of that period know only too well that under a totalitarian system the human person is degraded, humiliated and mocked. Against that background only hatred can flourish. A survivor once said to me: "I hate them, because they taught me to hate." ' Fr Kolbe did not hate, and he held up his priesthood as an emblem of love's survival even in that fearsome place. Thus the 'Golgotha of the modern world', as John Paul terms it, was sanctified by the death of a martyr.

That Kolbe will be canonized in due course seems certain. The Pope regards him as one of the great saints of modern times, indeed a peculiarly modern saint. When he revisited Auschwitz as pope, in June 1979, he went to Kolbe's cell – Number 18 in the Death Block, Block 11 – and prayed in it, while outside stood the man with ten children, Franciszek Gajowniczek, whose life Kolbe saved. Later John Paul said mass at Birkenau, part of the Auschwitz complex, assisted by 150 priests who had once been prisoners in the camp, and a congregation of many thousands, wearing their old convict suits. The fact of Auschwitz, huge, hideous and in-effaceable, is something John Paul carries round with him, as an indication of the limitless depravity to which men descend under a totalitarian atheism. The burden is lightened by the Kolbe story, and by its testimony to the special grace and strength conveyed by the priestly vow: 'Who are you?' 'I am a Catholic priest.'

To convey his sense of the importance of the priesthood, John Paul addressed to all the priests of the Catholic faith, on Maundy Thursday 1979, a customary letter in which he set out with great care, eloquence and even passion his own elevated idea of priest-hood. From its opening, adapted from St Augustine, 'For you I am a bishop, with you I am a priest', it is a very characteristic John-Pauline work.[12] It presents the priestly self-discipline and sacrifice unambiguously – John Paul will never allow concessions in the demands made on a priest – it glories in the privileges attached to the priestly vocation, quoting Gregory the Great: 'The supreme art is the direction of souls.' But it also dwells on what, for want of a better expression, might be termed the spiritual glamour of the priesthood:

Dear brothers: you who have borne 'the burden and heat of the day', who have put your hand to the plough and do not turn back, and perhaps even more those of you who are doubtful of the meaning of your vocation or of the value of your service: think of the places where people anxiously await a priest, and where for many years, feeling the lack of such a priest, they do not cease to hope for his presence. And sometimes it happens that they meet in an abandoned shrine, and place on the altar a stole which they still keep, and recite all the prayers of the eucharistic liturgy; and then at the moment that corresponds to the transubstantiation a deep silence comes down upon them, a silence sometimes broken by a sob – so ardently do they desire to hear the words that only a priest can efficaciously utter.

In essence, however, the letter was a restatement of the traditional Catholic view of the priesthood. As such it was received with consternation among the ultra-liberals. The fact that it brought comfort and reassurance to the great majority of priests, who feared the progressive erosion of their special calling, attracted less publicity. John Paul denied he was saying anything new or unusual. During his visit to Poland in June 1979, he commented on the letter's reception:

Here and there it has been suggested that the Pope was trying to impose the Polish model of priesthood on the whole world. But these were isolated voices, looking for something that was not there. For the most part the letter was received with satisfaction as a very simple, clear and at the same time brotherly statement of affairs. . . . There can be no conceptual gaps, no imprecision. We need to know from the very start where we stand, what it is we rely on. Occasionally concerned voices were raised, concerned about whether the church could survive this vision of priesthood in today's secularized world. But I left Poland in the deep conviction that it was *only* with this vision of priesthood that the church would survive.[13]

This notion of a spiritual counter-attack against secularism, of the need not for concessions but, on the contrary, for a spiritual heroism of the type for which Kolbe provided an example, inspires John Paul's determination to uphold the priestly disciplines in all their rigour and durability. It is his belief that the sacrament of ordination, which gives a human being such power over words in the mass, changes him permanently. As he puts it in his letter, it 'imprints on our soul the mark of an indelible character'. This being so, the renunciation of orders, the repudiating of vows freely taken in receiving them, is abhorrent. In Philadelphia in October 1979, he told a meeting of priests' councils: 'Priesthood is for ever. *Tu es sacerdos in aeternum.* We do not return the gift once given.'

Under Paul VI very large numbers of priests were permitted to renounce their vows and to leave the ministry without in any way sacrificing their status as communicating Catholics; in many cases, in fact, without relinquishing their posts in Catholic schools and universities. This liberal policy was a mistake. Many of these former priests became active and in a few cases malevolent propagandists against Catholic discipline and traditional moral teaching, often using the Catholic press as a platform. The loss of priests imposed greater burdens on those who remained loyal, and the idea that vows were no longer or necessarily perpetual – and the priesthood a mere temporary arrangement – unsettled many of the younger clergy and embittered some of their elders. The drain of priests caused by a misplaced charity was perhaps the chief cause of the catastrophic fall in morale among the clergy which marked the last years of Paul VI. Since the election of John Paul II the stream of laicizations has dwindled to a trickle, and it is evident that the policy has been changed, if not exactly reversed. New 'norms' have been prepared for judging applications, of which about 4,000 have been made; and only hard and exceptional cases will now be considered.

John Paul hopes that by ending the scandal of mass laicization he will reaffirm the awesome solemnity of ordination in the eyes of young seminarians, restabilize the clergy and restore the universal respect priests until recently enjoyed among the laity. To this end he misses few opportunities to emphasize the gulf which separates the priest from the layman. He has instructed the American hierarchy, for instance, to stop the unauthorized practice of layfolk distributing Holy Communion, or any lay intrusion in the specifically hieratic administration of certain sacraments. He has been obliged to clear up confusion created by the imprudent wording of one or two Council documents. As he pointed out in his 1976 Lenten series, the so-called doctrine of the common priesthood of all, which the Council enunciated, was not intended to blur the distinction between the clergy and laity but, rather, to draw attention to the 'enormous wealth of lay vocations within the church'.[14] It is absurd, in John Paul's view, to pretend that there is no or little difference between the laity, however conscientious, and those who have taken vows of lifetime service wholly and exclusively to God. There is, he thinks, a very great difference and it ought to be a visual one. Talking to seminarians at Maynooth in Ireland, he urged them: 'Do not hesitate to be recognizable, identifiable, in the streets as men who have consecrated their lives to God. . . . Do not help the trend towards "taking God off the street" by adopting secular modes of dress and behaviour yourselves!'[15]

John Paul thinks a priest should have a distinctive if modest pride in his priesthood and seek to emphasize it by his 'specialness' in the world. Clerical dress is the outward sign; the inner reality is his active dedication to service, of which celibacy is a necessary component. John Paul is anxious to stress that the debate within the church on celibacy is now closed. He made it clear in his 1976 series that he thought Paul VI was right to withdraw the topic from the Council. It had been exhaustively, even exhaustingly, discussed. It was dealt with in the encyclical *Sacerdotalis Caelibatus*, and again at the 1971 synod.

Nevertheless, in his letter to priests of 1979, John Paul did put the case for celibacy again, and with his own characteristic originality and rigour. His Christian humanism does not allow for limited commitments, part-time roles, demi-enthusiasms. A human being, to be a Christian, must undertake service in his life, and that service cannot be half-hearted, incomplete or conditional. Properly conceived, marriage is a central and onerous form of Christian service, a 'gift of the spirit', which involves its own dedication, fidelity and single-mindedness. It is a full and complete form of Christian service. Priesthood is a different, though complementary, form of service, with its own comprehensive demands of concentration and fidelity. Regarded as service, they are mutually exclusive. How can a marriage realize its Christian fulfilment if the husband and father is dedicated to his role as a priest? How, *a fortiori*, can a priest fulfil his special vow of total and lifelong service to the ministry of God's word, if he has conflicting commitments to a quite different set of duties? The combination must devalue both. No doubt all things are possible to a superman, but Catholicism is not about supermen; it is a practical, utilitarian religion designed to give countless millions of ordinary, fallible creatures their best possible chance to pass safely through the narrow gate into eternity.

John Paul dismisses the idea that celibacy infringes a man's humanity. It is a renunciation, as Christ put it, 'for the sake of the kingdom of heaven'[16] and thus an eschatological sign. But it is also a gift, a treasure: there is a positive value in celibacy which all good priests experience and which John Paul himself, it is plain, appreciates at its full value. It has, as he put it in his letter, 'a great social meaning'. Dedication for service means becoming 'a man for others'. A husband, by marriage, becomes 'a man for others' in the radius of his own family. But the priest, 'by renouncing this fatherhood proper to married men, seeks another fatherhood' to 'children of his spirit, people entrusted to his solicitude by the Good Shepherd. These people are many, more numerous than an ordinary human family can embrace.' This pastoral vocation of priests is extensive; it is of a missionary character. Each individual in the priest's purview, John Paul notes, 'expects attention, care and love'. Therefore, John Paul concludes, 'the heart of the priest, in order that it may be available for this service, must be free' – and celibacy is a sign of that freedom.[17]

The reaffirmation of sacerdotal celibacy, by word and action, is one of the principal ways in which John Paul has brought home to everyone, inside and outside the church, that the period of drift and uncertainty in its fortunes is now definitely over. The celibacy rule will be upheld, now and for ever, in all its sacramental intransigence. The assurance is given especially to the clergy themselves, who now know exactly where they stand and what they can expect. John Paul has given them back the stability and certitude and concentration of their lives.

But the celibacy ruling is also a blazing sign, plain for all to see, and reaching to a much wider multitude, that the Roman Catholic Church has recovered its nerve. There will be no yielding to pressure groups, however vociferous. The standard of conduct and self-sacrifice demanded of its chosen ministers will not be lowered. Nervous and agitated hands will not be permitted to dilute the essence of Latin Christianity, that potent concentrate distilled over two millennia, which has provided spiritual intoxication for the élite and daily comfort for grateful millions over a huge arc of human history. For John Paul has grasped the salient truth of Catholic sociology. The people of the Catholic faith value it not because it is yielding but because it is inflexible; not because it is open-minded but because it is sure; not because it is adaptive and protean but because it is always, everywhere, the same. It is the one fixed point in a changing world; and if it changes itself (as from time to time it must), such transformations must be as imperceptible as a glacier's, moving with majestic gravity along a path preordained by its own nature. Catholicism has the time-scale not of fashion but of geology.

The insight and principles John Paul brought to the celibacy issue he has been applying in other fields. He has been plainly disturbed, even baffled, by the problem of the liturgy. The liturgical edifice of Latin Christianity, in its unified Tridentine form, was once one of the most precious and complex manifestations of the human spirit which our civilization has been able to devise. It was art, ethics, philosophy, history and worship in one; and also a self-ordering of the kind necessary to civilized self-restraint. Its Latinity gave it both geographical ubiquity and historical continuance, so that words spoken in Rome in late antiquity had the same meaning and significance when uttered near the summits of the Andes in the twentieth century.

There is no evidence that, when John XXIII called his Council, he had any intention of adopting a vernacular liturgy or introducing any other fundamental changes. Nor did Paul VI ever clearly announce that he favoured a liturgical revolution. Yet that is precisely what occurred in the decade 1965-75. Many busy and eager hands tore at the ancient fabric. Heavy ecclesiastical flywheels moved slowly: little wheels spun in destructive fury. Committees assembled, dispersed, reconvened in endless series. There seems to have been no master plan and no central, guiding spirit. By the time the incense cleared, all that was left of the Tridentine liturgy was a beautiful ruin, amid the scattered stones and charred embers of which there arose the plebeian cacophony of homespun services, to the music of adolescent toys. The object was supposedly to secure greater participation in the services by the laity, and a greater understanding of what was said and done at them. But the result was misunderstanding for the young, confusion for the middle-aged and heartbreak for the old. There was also an increasing fall in attendance. Latin largely disappeared, and with it went what Coleridge called 'the willing suspension of disbelief' which a hieratic or arcane language brings to the contemplation of the necessarily mysterious. Some much-loved services, like the evening exposition of the Blessed Sacrament known as Benediction, vanished entirely. Uniformity receded. The physical clutter of centuries of religiosity was reduced, but in widely varying degrees. A Catholic traveller no longer knew what to expect, or whether he would understand it.

Such upheavals had occurred before: in the fourth century, for instance, when the Christian clergy, newly endowed with the strength of secular power, demolished the temples of pagan antiquity; or in the sixteenth, when the Reformers of northern Europe destroyed much of the religious art of the late Middle Ages in the name of expelling superstition. There was a bitter paradox in the fact that, under Paul VI, priests, on the instructions of their bishops, cast on to the flames the very emblems of devotion which their predecessors, during Reformation and Counter-Reformation, had fought and even died to defend.[18]

John Paul cannot and has not attempted to reverse these lamentable events. What he has done is to limit the extent of the damage by insisting that diocesan bishops enforce the new liturgical rules, such as they are, and that unauthorized experiments cease. He has thus ended some grievous abuses, particularly in the United States. He has also given limited encouragement to the revival of Latin services, to the extent of making permission to hold them simpler and easier to obtain. But he seems to recognize that Latin, as a universal liturgical language, is now a lost cause.

Where John Paul has been able to provide more reassurance is by his insistence that the church will not rashly embark on further experiments, notably in the field known as 'inculturation', that is, the attempt to reflect non-European cultures in the Catholic liturgy, and indeed over a much wider range of practices and even beliefs. This is a delicate issue. Next to Latin America, Africa poses the most serious regional problem for the church. In both areas the Catholic population is increasing fast – in Africa the church is making converts in large numbers – and therefore in relative importance within the church's global composition. But in Latin America the cultural conflict with European Catholicism is not of great importance. In Africa it could be worked up into a major issue by those anxious to present Christianity as a form of colonialism. During his African tour in the late spring of 1980, John Paul had to face this dilemma. At the interdiocesan centre at Kinshasa in Zaire, he gave his blessing to the idea of 'inculturation', as well he might, since the whole of St Paul's evangelical mission to the Gentiles can be presented as a case of 'inculturation', in which a Hebraic message was represented in Hellenic terms. But he added that it 'requires a great deal of theological lucidity, spiritual discernment, wisdom and prudence' – and, not least, time.[19]

The Pope recognizes that Africa is moving through a period of intense post-colonial sensitivity, which by God's grace will not last indefinitely, and at the end of which sensible decisions can be taken in a calmer atmosphere. He reasons, no doubt rightly, that the cultural colouration of Catholicism, which is not so much European as Mediterranean and even Middle Eastern, is one of its great strengths and attractions, even, or perhaps especially, to Africans. To seek to dilute it, by ill-considered ventures into 'africanization', undertaken through motives of guilt and fear – the worst possible counsellors – would be a formula for shameful disaster, worse even than the changes in the liturgy, which at their boldest did not impinge on matters of faith. That the church must expect and even tolerate some degree of 'popular religion' in black Africa is unarguable. But the process must be contained at this spontaneous level, and the future left to time and providence to clarify. So the Pope has ruled.

A different but related dilemma confronts the church over the ecumenical movement. Over this issue different popes have pursued varying tactics, strategies even; it has now a long history and has generated successive archaeological layers of policy.[20] To some extent the movement has acquired its own momentum and it has certainly created its own lobby within the church. In the West the issue is seen primarily in terms of a Protestant–Catholic dialogue. But for the Vatican it is far more complicated. It is at the centre of a multiple process of theological diplomacy in which concessions to one interlocutor may be seen as further intransigence by another.

So far as the Anglicans are concerned, much of the detailed work on what are regarded as the three principal areas in dispute, the definition of the eucharist, which includes the conflict between transubstantiation and consubstantiation, the ministry, including the recognition of Anglican orders, and authority, which incorporates claims to infallibility, has been completed. The difficulties are not insurmountable. The problem lies elsewhere. Though John Paul is well disposed to the ecumenists, and takes every opportunity to meet other Christian leaders (as at Accra on 9 May 1980, when he talked to Dr Runcie, Archbishop of Canterbury), he is painfully aware that he is not negotiating with a stable partner. The Anglican church is changing as fast, if not faster, than Roman Catholicism during the worst period of Paul VI's pontificate. There is no sign of this process ending, or of any real determination among the Anglicans of wanting it to end. As John Paul sees it, Anglicanism is suffering from the same nervous sickness which afflicted Catholicism when he inherited it, but has not yet had the courage to call in a doctor. For Rome, in the process of recovery, there is no great advantage in acquiring a new, exceptionally volatile and contagious partner.

In any case, the recovery of Catholicism must have priority. It is now getting back its old courage and assurance, but the process will take time. John Paul had some shrewd things to say on this point when he wrote a letter to the German episcopal conference on 15 May 1980.[21] How, he asked, can one church negotiate with another effectively if its own affairs are not in order and it is not wholly clear about its own beliefs? And who or what is to clarify those beliefs unless it be authority? He wrote: 'Only a church deeply consolidated in the faith can be a church of authentic dialogue.' Again: 'Only a mature faith can be an effective advocate to true religious freedom, freedom of conscience and all human rights.' In order to engage in the adventurous course indicated by the Council, the faithful must have special confidence in the Holy Spirit and its activity. How does that manifest itself in Roman Catholicism? Why, through the *magisterium* and the doctrine of infallibility. But these are precisely points at issue.

In his letter John Paul quoted the Council decree on ecumenism, *Unitatis Redintegratio*, and noted as 'significant' that it did not speak of 'compromise' but of 'meeting in a still more mature fullness of Christian truth'. In John Paul's view it is not so much a question of the churches moving towards one another as of moving forward on complementary trajectories which at some stage must meet. That may prove to be a very long business. In the meantime, he told the German bishops, 'Nothing is so foreign to the spirit of ecumenism as a false irenicism which harms the purity of Catholic doctrine and obscures its genuine and certain meaning.' The best foundations for ecumenism, he insisted, were 'certainty of the faith' and 'confidence in the power of Christ'.

For the foreseeable future, John Paul clearly places more substantial hopes in the parallel negotiations with the Eastern Orthodox churches. He knows much more about these communities. They are more stable entities. They are not being buffeted by a secularizing wind and by conflicting eddies of internal turbulence. Moreover, the Roman church already has a kind of bridge to the Eastern churches in the shape of the Uniates, of which John Paul has much experience, a bridge which offers the kind of practical opportunities he relishes.

The Russian Uniates, as we have already noted, were forcibly reunified with the Russian Orthodox Church, by a decree of Stalin, in the late 1940s. Its bishops were imprisoned; the church continued to assert its independence, and links with Rome, living an underground existence. In 1963 John XXIII secured the release from prison of the senior prelate, Archbishop Josef Slipyi, who was brought to Rome and made a cardinal. He proved, as the Russians had already discovered, an awkward piece on the ecclesiastical chessboard. As head of the Ukrainian church, which has many emigrant adherents throughout the world, notably in North America, he used the title of patriarch. Paul VI refused to yield it to him. It is not in the interests of Rome to envenom its dealings with the existing patriarchates of the Orthodox Church, already complicated enough, by acknowledging the existence of another, which they do not recognize. Moreover, the Uniates were themselves divided on the issue. John Paul resolved to settle this problem, at least. On 12 November 1979 he consecrated Miroslav Lubarchivsky as Ukrainian Metropolitan of Philadelphia, in the United States. One of Lubarchivsky's many merits, in the Pope's eyes, was that he was opposed to the creation of a new patriarchate. Four months later, John Paul summoned a four-day synod of the Ukrainian bishops, which opened on 24 March 1980. Its chief object was to appoint an assistant bishop to the very elderly Slipyi, with right of succession as Major Archbishop (as it is termed) when Slipyi died. The proceedings were secret. Cardinal Slipyi did not prove easy to persuade. But John Paul was able to negotiate with him, and the other bishops, in their own tongue. At all events, the synod ended with John Paul's choice endorsed: Lubarchivsky was chosen as the future Major Archbishop. A serious and potentially intractable problem was thus neatly disposed of.

In the meantime, John Paul had been pressing forward with his own eastern contacts and plans. On 28 November 1979 he began the least agreeable of his foreign journeys, to Turkey. The Turkish government betrayed no enthusiasm for his visit, and received him in Ankara with purely formal honours as a head of state. The Turkish people showed indifference or hostile curiosity, an ominous harbinger of the near-fatal attempt on his life in May 1981. But it was not the aim of the visit to charm the Turks. John Paul toured Ephesus, where the Virgin Mary was first proclaimed Theotokos, or bearer of God. His chief object, however, was to call on Patriarch Dimitrios of Constantinople (Istanbul), whom he heard celebrate the liturgy of St John Chrysostom, on 30 November.

In the Eastern church authority is dispersed. The four ancient patriarchates of Constantinople, Alexandria, Antioch and Jerusalem, and the later patriarchates of Russia, Georgia, Serbia, Bulgaria and Rumania, are all self-governing, or autocephalous as they are known. Other Orthodox churches of the East, and expatriate churches (there are three million Orthodox in the United States alone), also enjoy autonomy. But the Patriarch of Constantinople is accorded an honorary primacy and is known as the Ecumenical Patriarch. He cannot 'deliver' Orthodoxy. But he can speak on its behalf, to a certain extent, and he is the only safe point of departure for an exploration of the eastern labyrinth.[22]

John Paul and Patriarch Dimitrios signed a joint declaration on 30 November, the feast of St Andrew, Peter's brother, who is said to have died at Patras in AD 60. This declaration set up a bilateral committee for theological dialogue, which six months later held its first sessions in Patmos and Rhodes (29 May to 4 June 1980). The issues in dispute between Latins and Greeks are varied. The Western use of unleavened bread in Holy Communion, according to strictly traditional Orthodox teaching, has been held to invalidate the sacrament; but this is no longer significant. The chief theological dispute centres around the expression *Filioque*, 'and the Son', which the Latins seem to have begun adding to the Creed from the Third Council of Toledo (AD 589) onwards, and which expresses the double procession of the Holy Ghost, 'from the Father and the Son'.[23] The Eastern objection is that *Filioque* undermines the notion of a single fount of divinity in the Godhead, thus making it more difficult to reconcile the already delicately balanced doctrine of the Trinity with the basic concept of monotheism.

The *Filioque* dispute, however, is to some extent a historical problem. Some aspects of it which aroused passionate anger from the ninth century onwards have now been cleared up by modern scholarship. At least as important, when the crucial breach occurred in AD 1054, and more important when unsuccessful attempts were made to heal the schism at Lyons (1274), and Florence (1438-9), were the claims of the see of Rome to an overriding authority. This, too, is an historical argument, but it is emphatically not an academic one. Rome is a centralized church; Orthodoxy a devolved one. The origins of this bifurcation go back about 1500 years.

It is at this point in the argument that John Paul considers it useful to return to the problem of Christian unity as a whole. He regards it as significant that the effective breach with Orthodoxy occurred immediately prior to the rapid and thrustful development of Roman canon law in the closing decades of the eleventh century – the 'Hildebrandine Reformation'. The two developments were clearly connected. The emergence of Rome as the court of final appeal in a centralized system of church law was, of course, the foundation of the papal triumphalism of the later Middle Ages, which itself was a major causative factor in the Protestant Reformation. It is arguable, then, that the Reformation was in some sense a consequence of the schism with Orthodoxy. If, therefore, unity is to be sought in a spirit of historical logic, it is well to begin at the beginning, and heal the breach with Constantinople first. Only thereafter will it be profitable to seek a final accord with Canterbury and the other Protestant communions.

This accords with other considerations John Paul has in mind, both tactical and strategic. Although it is true that in the twentieth century Anglicans and Orthodox had warmer relations with each other than either body has had with Rome, this is more a reflection of their common fear of Roman dogmatic imperialism than of any identity of views. Doctrinally, Orthodoxy and Protestantism are very far apart. In Greek eyes, the Latin church is Protestantism, and the Reformed churches are mere non-conformist offshoots of the original schismatic trunk. If, *mirabile dictu*, Rome were to conclude first a successful reunion with Canterbury, the likelihood - the certainty, almost - is that such an accord would make progress with Constantinople more difficult. That is one reason why Rome will not even contemplate the notion of women priests, and fears Anglican and Lutheran compromises on this issue, for it knows the Orthodox churches are strongly and unanimously opposed to such a reform. More important, however, is Rome's belief that healing the schism with Orthodoxy will, in practical terms, prove more easily attainable than any deal with the Protestant West. Prudence, then, dictates that it should have priority, more particularly since the compromises on Rome's assertion of its primacy and authority needful for any agreement with Orthodoxy would be highly relevant for subsequent negotiations with Protestantism, to which of course the Orthodox churches would be a party, and possibly a persuasive one.

Finally, John Paul himself cannot fail to see ecumenism in its political and geographical dimension, and in both respects the arguments for taking the Eastern option first are conclusive. The evil of totalitarian atheism is the greatest of the perils Rome faces, and it is embodied in the Soviet Union. The Catholic Church, in confronting this evil, has been inhibited all along by the divisions within the Christianity of Eastern Europe, and in particular by the subservience of Russian Orthodoxy to the Marxist-Leninist state. That subservience springs from weakness; and the weakness would undoubtedly be cured by reunification with the vigour and assertiveness of Rome. John Paul believes that Russian Orthodoxy is a slumbering giant, which might be roused by the sacral kiss of brotherhood from Rome. Who knows? It might be too much to hope that the revival of Russian Orthodoxy would break up the totalitarian atheism from within. But certainly it would undermine the negotiating position of the Soviet power with all the Christian churches throughout Eastern Europe, and strengthen the cause of religion everywhere.

These are distant prospects. But a vigorous, ambitious pope in his early sixties is right to contemplate them, and allow for them in his immediate moves. That explains why John Paul does not, at present, hold out hopes for decisive progress in negotiating with the Protestant churches. It also helps to explain his evident anxiety to master and subdue any heterodox tendencies in his own camp. For John Paul cannot allow any intemperate Latin theologians to alarm his Orthodox interlocutors or, *per contra*, encourage them to raise their terms. Thus we turn to the last of the five evils which threaten Rome's well-being, the anti-truth within.

8

The Shadow of Heresy

THOUGH JOHN PAUL II is not, technically, a theologian, he is a philosopher of religion and is certainly better equipped than any other modern pope to engage with the theologians on their own ground. That is just as well, for the Roman Catholic Church, having long been shielded from the impact of modern adventurist theology, is now being forced to examine its claims and, once and for all, to entertain them, or reject them decisively. There is a crisis in Catholic theology, and John Paul is necessarily at the still centre of it.

That Rome was for long cut off from theological developments, as from historical study of the Bible and related fields, was due to its general policy of self-imposed isolation which began in 1648. Rome did not like, or accept, the Treaty of Westphalia, which in effect acknowledged the fact of the Reformation. Thereafter it tended to reject the modern world as the realm of anti-Christ and to lock itself into its own fortress, of which the pope's great castle of Sant'Angelo, guarding the Vatican, was a brooding symbol. The drawbridge was briefly lowered in the first phase of Pius IX's pontificate, then raised in panic as the 1848 revolutions swept Europe. Pio Nono became an exalted reactionary, a spiritual isolationist. His rejection of the new Italian state confirmed the policy of sealing off contact with the world, as if it were a kind of plague; and his new triumphalism, epitomized by the dogma of infallibility, seemed to downgrade theology into a closed science, at best the ancillary of pontifical lucubrations. Catholicism acquired an 'official' theology, concerned merely to defend established positions and interpretations.

But experimental theology continued, as it were, underground, occasionally rising to the surface and inviting suppression. Around the turn of the twentieth century, the 'Modernist' movement emerged, with Friedrich von Hügel and George Tyrrell as its leading exponents. Its object was precisely to bring the Catholic tradition into closer touch with modern philosophy and the historical, physical and social sciences, and it was for this very reason that Pius x determined to crush it. His encyclical *Pascendi* and his decree *Lamentabili* (both in 1907) outlawed the movement as 'the synthesis of all the heresies'. Three years later a *motu proprio, Sacrorum Antistitum*, imposed an 'anti-modernist oath' not only on suspect clergy (who were excommunicated if they declined to swear it) but on all candidates for ordination in major orders and those appointed to teaching posts in Catholic institutions.

Between the wars, then, Catholic theology was a high-risk profession, and few outstanding theologians were not, at some time in their careers, regarded as suspect or actively curbed. Original work continued none the less, in Germany in the 1920s, and, after the rise of Hitler, in France, chiefly in Paris and Lyons, under the name of 'engaged theology' (i.e. engaged in the world). The Dominicans took the lead, but some Jesuits were also involved. They had to fight a continual battle with the Holy Office to get their work published and authorized, and to keep their teaching posts. In 1942 the most important of them, the Dominican Fr Chenu, was removed from his post as Rector of the Dominican house of studies in Paris. A manifesto he wrote, demanding pluralism in theology (as opposed to the form of Thomism which was virtually the only one taught in Catholic seminaries), was put on the *Index Librorum Prohibitorum*. His leading pupil, Yves Congar, also suffered. Among the Jesuits, in addition to the German, Karl Rahner, there were Henri de Lubac and Jean Daniélou, both from the Jesuit house in Lyons. All were in trouble from time to time. But they, or sympathetic colleagues, always managed to cling on to a number of teaching posts, the real key to eventual success in Catholic theology. Thus their pupils multiplied. So did their books. Even in the period immediately following Pius XII's encyclical *Humani Generis* (1950), the last general attempt to discipline theological innovation, these inexhaustibly prolific men continued to publish. Scarcely one has a bibliography of less than a thousand items. They may have been discountenanced but they were certainly never silenced.

With the Second Vatican Council their day of triumph arrived. They surged out of their metaphorical catacombs to take possession of the kingdom. They by no means monopolized the ranks of the Council's *periti*, or theological experts, but they made the most noise. And their voices were heeded. Of all the theologians, Congar had the most influence on the Council documents. Honours accrued. Daniélou became a cardinal, de Lubac was invited by Paul VI to concelebrate with him at the end of the Council. Their pupils took the best jobs in the Catholic institutes. Their works became part of the mainstream of Catholic teaching.[1]

The impulse behind the new theology was that the church should leave its citadel and reach out into the world. That, indeed, was the whole aim of the Council. But what exactly did reaching out into the world mean? How far should it go? How was it reconciled with Christ's emphatic statement that 'my kingdom is not of this world'? The difficulty arose in part from the stunning suddenness with which the Council enveloped the church. The coming of modern theology to Catholicism had been delayed by papal obstruction for more than half a century. Now it came in one tremendous onslaught. It was as though the forces of change, having been dammed up by ever more desperate barriers – becoming increasingly indignant and self-righteous in the process – were suddenly unleashed as the dam broke, and swept down with tempestuous fury on the smiling valley of Catholic complacency, destroying all the familiar landmarks.

This was the scene which confronted John Paul when he emerged from the conclave. Theology had lurched out of control. The church, having in good faith stretched out the hand to the world, seemed in danger of being enveloped in its rough embrace and crushed to death. But John Paul was not inclined to panic. He has mixed with intellectuals all his adult life. He is one. He takes them seriously. He does not take them too seriously. He rejected the notion of a frontal counter-attack on the lines of *Pascendi* or *Humani Generis*. He did not and does not want to silence discussion or inhibit publication. He is himself an inveterate discussor and prolific author. No one who has lived under first a Nazi then a

Soviet tyranny, and who has battled with a secular censor for a quarter of a century, who has seen his own pastoral letters and articles cut, and had his books seized at the frontier, can ever be anything but sympathetic to freedom of speech and the press.

That is the starting-point of John Paul's approach to theology. There must be freedom of inquiry and publication. Some of the church's most self-destructive mistakes, he has argued, arose from the denial of this freedom in the past. Since becoming pope he has shown himself determined to erase the stigma of Galileo's recantation from the church's record. On the hundredth anniversary of Einstein's birth, he called for an inquiry into the Galileo case and told the Pontifical Academy of Sciences: 'The greatness of Galileo is now recognized by all. We cannot deny that he suffered terribly at the hands of the church and of church bodies.' He added: 'Just as religion needs religious liberty, so science legitimately claims freedom of research.' Research must be free of any 'international servitude or intellectual colonialism'.[2]

Indeed, John Paul argues energetically that there has been a reversal of alliances, and that the church is now ranged firmly in the ranks of intellectual freedom. During his visit to Germany in November 1980, he gave a talk on 'Science and Faith' to university teachers and students in Cologne cathedral, and asserted:

In the past, defenders of modern science fought against the church with the slogans Reason, Freedom and Progress. Today, in view of the crisis about the meaning of science, the multiple threats to its freedom and the doubts in many minds about progress, the battlefronts have been inverted. Today it is the church that takes up the defence. The defence of reason and science, which she recognizes as being able to attain truth . . . of the freedom of science, through which it has its dignity as a human and personal good, and of progress in the service of a humanity which must have it to safeguard its existence and its self-respect.[3]

John Paul, then, sees no conflict, but rather an alliance, between science and Christianity. Further: he believes that all forms of speculative or empirical inquiry serve to reinforce rather than reduce faith. It is one of his most fundamental convictions that God and truth are inseparable. Pursue one, you find the other; deny one, you injure the other. He believes that God is expressed in all discovery, and his favourite quotation from the Old Testament occurs in that enchanting poem King David dedicated to his Master of Music: 'If I ascend up into heaven, thou art there: if I make my bed in hell, behold thou art there. If I take the wings of the morning, and dwell in the uttermost parts of the sea; even there shall thy hand lead me, and thy right hand shall hold me.'[4]

God and his truth are ubiquitous, waiting to be discovered. The entire universe, real and speculative, is the legitimate subject of intellectual inquiry. That is the right of man. But, as always in John Paul's thinking, rights are accompanied by responsibilities. And theology being the queen of sciences, the responsibilities which rest on theologians are the heaviest. Respecting truth means respecting and fearing God. John Paul again quotes the psalmist: 'The fear of the Lord is the beginning of wisdom.'[5] This creative fear of the Lord is expressed by theologians in respect for the bishops, who may not possess their skills in the science but are depositories of God's truth and regents of his authority. As John Paul put it, at Fortaleza in Brazil: 'The true theologian knows, by a supernatural instinct, that it belongs to the bishops to watch over his activity for the sake of the people of God.'[6] Episcopal concern was admonitory; it was also a form of liberation. John Paul, as an intellectual, knows that the worst form of intellectual slavery today is subservience to prevailing fashions. Hence, he told the Irish students at Maynooth, by teaching in conformity with the college of bishops, the theologian could escape this debilitating bondage.[7]

Intellectual fashion is one form, and an important form, of anti-truth. Here we come to the nub of the problem, as John Paul sees it. If God and truth are ubiquitous, so likewise are Satan and anti-truth. Theologians, of all people, must be aware of a huge, protean and hyperactive agency of evil in the world. The fourth talk of John Paul's 1976 Lenten series was devoted to this topic: it is a brilliant exposition of the nature of evil, especially intellectual evil.[8] Satan, the 'spirit of evil', is the Anti-Word. The beginning of evil is the assault on truth. The first sin, of Adam, was preceded by the first lie, Satan's, and its unthinking repetition by Eve. The metaphor of Genesis teaches that anti-truth is the cause of active evil. Lying is the prolegomenon, the foreword, to the encyclopaedia of evil. Hitler and Stalin began by lies and then proceeded on their course of physical destruction: anti-truth was the plinth on which the monstrous superstructures of Auschwitz and the Gulag were erected.

John Paul's perception of Satan and anti-truth has been shaped by the mystic current in Christian thought. In his 1976 Lenten series, John Paul drew attention to the mystical theory of knowledge, first elaborated by St Bonaventure (1217–74), the Franciscan theologian known to the church as 'the Seraphic Doctor'. In his *Itinerarium Mentis in Deum* (the journey of the mind to God), Bonaventure discusses the various ways in which knowledge, intuitive as well as rational, draws the soul to God. It is characteristic of John Paul that he used this sermon on Bonaventure to denounce structuralism, which argues that ideas are not autonomous but the mere product of institutional structures. Structuralism is a form of the moral relativism which stands in polar opposition to the absolute values of his Christian humanism, and on this occasion he castigated it as the anti-itinerary, leading men further away from truth. It was, he said, worse than agnosticism or atheistic positivism since it 'calls in question thought itself and casts doubt on the subject and the very meaning of knowledge'. Structuralism produced the 'anti-theology' of the 'death of God', arguing that God died out of human thought with the decay of the supporting structures which had 'created' Him in the first place.[9] By contrast, in Bonaventure the image of God leads ultimately to His presence; one might almost call it a 'birth of God' theology.

Bonaventure's mystical theory of knowledge served as a prelude to the work of St John of the Cross who, as we have already noted, has been a formative influence on John Paul for many years. The appeal St John holds for the Pope is significant in a number of ways. First, he was an unusual, not to say a heterodox, figure. For most of his active career he was in trouble with the church authorities, and one of his greatest works was actually written in an ecclesiastical prison in Toledo in 1578. He and his associate St Teresa drew many of their ideas from the early sixteenth-century *Alumbrados* or Illuminists, who were heretics, and from a Franciscan work which was already on the Index when they used it.[10] The work of St John hovered close to the frontiers of orthodoxy, as of course do most great religious movements. In a sense nothing seems further from John Paul, that pillar of sound doctrine, until we remember that the pope he most resembles, Innocent III, was also able to patronize and learn from what were, in those days, marginal forms of Christianity – the first Dominicans and Franciscans – while putting down manifest heresy with great resolution.

The second attraction of St John for John Paul is that he was a poet: indeed to many he is Spain's greatest poet. Nor is his poetry in the margin of his theology. St John is attempting to show how an ordinary mortal apprehends a being beyond the reach of human understanding and feeling (yet none the less loving). As with St Bonaventure, the soul makes a voyage. First comes the 'night of the senses' when the soul, detached from all 'sensible' devotion, begins to exist in a state of pure faith. Then follows the 'night of the spirit', accompanied by intense suffering, which prepares the soul for union with God. St John's descriptions of this process, *The Ascent of Mount Carmel* (describing the first stage) and *The Dark Night of the Soul* (the second), are in fact no more than commentaries on his poem *En Una Noche Oscura*.[11] This use of poetry to express theological concepts which prose cannot fully illuminate has a powerful appeal to the poet in John Paul. Indeed it is clear that he, too, can make points in a poem which leave him floundering in philosophical jargon when he puts them in formal ecclesiastical language.

However, the principal appeal of St John of the Cross for John Paul lies in his concept of faith, which was the aspect of the poet's work which first attracted him. According to St John, faith, to which theology is the key, is an arena of titanic struggle between God and Satan. Satan attempts to destroy the good by creating a simulacrum of God, by impersonation. He seeks to reduce man's two principal defences against evil: faith and humility.[12] Faith sets before us the realm of God; humility is a just appreciation of our status within it as dependent creatures. In St John, God and Satan, truth and anti-truth, are expressed in terms of illuminism: 'The light of faith is darkness for Satan'; 'The white robe of faith so dazzles Satan that he cannot even see the soul it adorns'.[13] That is why any undermining of faith, especially by those charged with formulating it (the theologians) and, above all, by those charged with teaching its formulation (professors of theology), is so devastating a dereliction of duty.

What makes matters worse, says St John, is that Satan is often at his most cunning and effective among those on the road to holiness. 'In attacking souls moving generously towards God', he appeals to the pretext of good. Unless the soul relies on pure faith, Satan will succeed, for he is brilliant at dissimulating error. Once deception is accomplished, pride takes over – pride in error – and thus it becomes 'impossible to undeceive them'.[14] That is why Satan is 'the sworn enemy of humility'. He 'lurks like a dangerous animal in the shadow of good works, from which we conceive a dangerous admiration for ourselves'. The slightest failure in humility opens the door to him. All that is not built upon pure faith, and does not help us to greater love of God, can become 'riches of iniquity unto injustice'. It is not the beginner but the experienced, the learned, those with long records of public service to God who are the chosen victims of Satan: the more we receive, the more we run the risk of foundering in pride.[15] Failure of faith almost always arises from lack of humility. Pride destroys faith, and pride is the *déformation professionnelle* of the theologian.

The mechanism of the fall is the same even in the most spiritually sophisticated and learned persons. At the root there is always excessive self-confidence, a rash reliance on one's own chosen path, a refusal to submit to the judgement of him who holds God's place (the ecclesiastical superior), an awareness of being favoured by God in terms of insight, intelligence and acquired merit. From that moment on, all kinds of intellectual confusion are possible, the soul is disorientated. The point to which St John returns time and again is that Satan is a superb counterfeiter. He destroys souls by persuading them they are doing good; he is expert at mixing truth with lies, even at promoting good for his long-term purposes, 'for there is no evil spirit who is not prepared to suffer something for his own honour' (an *aperçu* which could have come only from a Spanish poet-theologian). The greatest triumph of Satan is to persuade clever and holy men that he no longer exists. Thus he 'causes the ruin of a great multitude of religious who set out on the life of perfection'. The only reliable defences, what St John calls 'the three cautions', are the three simplest and least sophisticated of virtues: faith, humility and obedience.[16]

From this analysis two points follow, which John Paul has very much in mind when dealing with theologians. First, for the theologian humility is the pre-eminent virtue. That is one reason why John Paul commends Aquinas, the greatest of them. Lack of egoism was at the heart of his system. As John Paul told the Eighth International Thomist Congress in September 1980, St Thomas was the 'true pioneer of modern scientific realism' because he believed philosophy was not 'a subjective system put together at the pleasure of the philosopher but must be the faithful reflection of the order of things in the human mind'.[17] Again, when John Paul went to the Angelicum, his old college in Rome, for the hundredth anniversary of Leo XIII's encyclical, *Aeterni Patris*, making the Thomist theology pre-eminent,[18] he drew attention to Aquinas's 'sincere, total and lifelong acceptance of the teaching office of the church, to whose judgement he submitted all his works both during his life and on the point of death'. On his deathbed, John Paul said, Aquinas renewed his complete submission of mind and heart to divine revelation, and he added: 'How beneficial it would be for the church of God if today too all Catholic philosophers and theologians followed the example of the *Doctor Communis Ecclesiae*.'[19]

That is the spirit in which John Paul expects theologians to behave. It is not, alas, the way in which they customarily do behave, least of all if they are within the orbit of German theology. Broadly speaking, theological systems revolve around the relative importance and status attributed to God and man. Hebraic theology exalted God and debased man. Hellenic theology tended to narrow the gap by stressing man's potential, even the possibility of *apotheosis*. The earliest Christians, with their God-made-Man, offered a bridge between the two systems which St Paul actually constructed: but the synthesis left unresolved many problems of theological presentation, especially the person of Christ as a historical figure. Modern German theologians have tended to err in the direction of Hellenism.

This new Prometheanism is, in one sense, easy to forgive, for theologians have felt bound to answer the challenges levelled at

Christianity by Ludwig Feuerbach, the founder of modern atheism and, indirectly, of atheistic totalitarianism. Feuerbach argues that the debasing of man is essential to organized religion: 'To enrich God, man must become poor; that God may be all, man must be nothing. The emptier life is, the fuller, the more concrete is God. ... Only the poor man has a rich God.'[20] The answer to Feuerbach given by Karl Rahner, the most influential of modern Catholic theologians, is that the contradistinction is false: 'The autonomy of the creature does not grow in inverse but in direct proportion to the degree of the creature's dependence on, and belonging to, God.' The upward ascent of man is a function of his realizing the potentiality of God within him, so that Prometheus is not an atheist but a Christian.

John Paul is in sympathy with this approach. It accords with his idea of Christian humanism. Indeed, it springs from the same intellectual root, for John Paul's philosophy is much influenced by Martin Heidegger, whose seminars Rahner attended and who provided his introduction to the Thomist philosophy of religion. It is important to grasp that John Paul, unlike his predecessors Pius XII and Paul VI, is not intellectually out of sympathy with the school of those theologians he has been obliged to subdue. Quite the contrary.

The difficulty, as historians are constantly forced to observe in recording religious dispute, is that theology is a very emotional business. It can possess a man, almost like a disease – what the great Reformer, Philip Melanchthon, referred to sadly on his deathbed as *rabies theologorum*, lamenting that the Germans were so prone to catch it. Whether a theologian remains orthodox or topples over into catastrophic error is often not so much a matter of intellectual necessity as of temperament – or, to put it less charitably, of moral weakness. The stress on humility as the golden theological virtue springs from this fact. Fr Rahner is a case in point. His theological writing is distinguished by great penetration, marred by sombre obscurities, and morally elevated by genuine diffidence. He accords with Etienne Gilson's definition of a major theologian: a combination of audacity with intellectual modesty.

But every theologian is different, and this is one reason why John Paul has dealt with them individually. To a great extent the problem has been posed by the attitude of the media. Thus the case of the French Dominican, Jacques Pohier, whose book *Quand je dis Dieu* was condemned in April 1979 for 'a number of errors and dangerous affirmations', attracted little attention. By contrast, the troubles of another Dominican, the Flemish scholar Edward Schillebeeckx, who teaches theology at the Catholic University of Nijmegen, have been sensationalized. In one sense that is right, for it raises important issues. Official Catholic theology, of the Thomist kind, has tended to be highly rational and theoretical. All 'modern' theologies have inclined towards what is termed 'praxis', that is action or practical application in the real world. The so-called Dutch school is a notable example of this tendency. Its philosophical inspiration comes from quarters very familiar to John Paul: the world of existentialism and phenomenology. But Fr Schillebeeckx has not looked to Heidegger for his religious philosophy, getting it rather from the neo-Marxists of the Frankfurt school, such as Jürgen Habermas. His praxis has a distinct inclination to the left.

For such theologians, anxious that their work should provide positive guides for collective action in this world, there is an almost irresistible tendency to project backwards into Christ's mission some of their own political values and, more important, to stress his manhood at the expense of his Godhead. So we find here. Schillebeeckx has been engaged on a trilogy of books dealing with the historical Jesus, the Christ of the early church and the total impact and meaning of Christianity. He has complained that the church authorities were not willing to wait until the project was complete and judge it as a whole. But in that case he should have waited himself and published it all simultaneously. The church is bound to consider the cases of Christian souls who may have been misled by the first volume and died before the third was published. That was why he was summoned to Rome in December 1979 to answer questions about his first volume, published in 1974.[21]

In this book, *Jesus*, he argues that there is no gap between what Jesus said about himself and his presentation by the church: the historical Jesus existed and he was the Messiah. But the interpretation leading up to the definitive Councils of Nicaea and Chalcedon was one-sided and based largely on St John's Gospel (the most emphatic in emphasizing Jesus's divinity), as opposed to the three synoptic Gospels. He then presents the case for re-opening the pre-Nicaean debate, and the last part of the book is an introduction to this design, to be concerned with the kingdom of God in this world 'and the praxis that goes with it'.[22] Schillebeeckx has said: 'I do not deny that Jesus is God, but want to assert that he is also man, something that has been overlooked. It is precisely as man that he is important to us. But when you say that, you are suspect.'[23] Yes; but what sort of man? Schillebeeckx has argued that the first Christians, in the New Testament accounts (especially the synoptics), constructed their christology out of their own practical experience and knowledge. We should do likewise. Every man his own christologist! Naturally, the way we see Christ will not be exactly the same as it was for those who composed the New Testament or formulated the creeds. Thus the road is opened to liberation theology or any other 'theology of praxis'.

The dangers of such an approach may be more apparent than real. But they have to be taken seriously. What becomes of the principle of revelation, which is fundamental to Christian doctrine? What limits are to be imposed on the Christs of our imagining? Is there to be a communist Jesus, a fascist Jesus, a capitalist Jesus? Where, if anywhere, is there a role for the *magisterium*? There is nothing specifically Catholic in Schillebeeckx's analysis. His books are works of systematic theology, but it would not be easy to discover, from internal evidence alone, where his allegiance lay. Yet he teaches Catholic doctrine at a Catholic university. It is not surprising that the authorities in Rome, at the Congregation of the Faith, who are specifically charged with satisfying themselves about the purity of doctrine taught in the church's institutions, wished to raise questions and request explanations. More surprising is Schillebeeckx's reluctance to provide them. Where was the spirit of St Thomas Aquinas? He has frequently asked for 'dialogue' with non-Catholics. Why did he disdain dialogue with his own church?

The case of Father Hans Küng is more dramatic because he is a robust, hugely self-confident and combative figure, who at times seems to see himself, in his relations with John Paul, as Prometheus outwitting Zeus or Martin Luther defying Leo x. Certainly there is a Protestant spirit about him. He won his doctorate of theology at Paris, and founded his reputation by an attempt to reconcile Catholic teaching with the Protestant doctrine of justification, as presented by Karl Barth. This work, *Justification* (1957), it has been said, led to Rome's opening a file on Küng, which was added to when he published a book written immediately after John XXIII called the Council. Nevertheless, Küng was appointed a Professor of Theology at the University of Tübingen in 1962, and John XXIII made him an official *peritus* at the Council in 1962; in 1963 he was translated to a new chair of Dogmatic and Ecumenical Theology and made director of a specially created Institute of Ecumenical Research. He became the centre of the international *Concilium* pressure group, with its own magazine and affiliates. In short, Küng emerged as a real power in the church. He was an indulged child of the sixties.

Küng has never confined himself to theology but has written about every aspect of the church, publishing a steady stream of books, magazine and newspaper articles, interviews and press statements, and making use of all the resources of modern mass communications, Catholic and secular, to propagate his views. His relations with the ecclesiastical authorities in Germany, and with the central power in Rome, have been tense and acrimonious for nearly a quarter of a century.

In 1963 the Holy Office opened proceedings against Küng's book *Structures of the Church* (1962). These were halted the next year, thanks to the intervention of the soft-hearted Jesuit ecumenist, Cardinal Augustine Bea. In 1965 Küng received a warning from Cardinal Ottaviani, head of the Office, and had an unsatisfactory audience with Paul VI. In 1967 a decree of the Congregation for the Doctrine of the Faith (as the Holy Office had been re-named by Paul VI in 1966) stipulated that further dissemination of *Structures* should cease until talks had been held in Rome. Küng ignored this ruling. In May the following year he was summoned to Rome, but declined to go; protracted negotiations ensued about a meeting. In May 1970 a Küng statement on mixed marriages led to his first public censure by the German episcopal conference. In July he published a still more controversial work, *Infallible? An Inquiry*, which provoked, the following January, a hearing before two German bishops and two theological experts in Stuttgart. Their report was the foundation for a statement on 8 February 1971 by the German episcopal conference condemning the book, followed two weeks later by a condemnation by a doctrinal commission in Rome. In 1975 the German bishops and the Doctrinal Congregation concluded their proceedings against *Structures* and *Infallible?*, and the German bishops also made their first statement condemning a new Küng book, *On Being a Christian*. During the years 1976-8 Küng conducted a number of negotiations with Cardinal Seper and Archbishop Hamer of the Doctrinal Congregation, with the German doctrinal commission, and with Cardinal Höffner of Cologne, president of the German episcopal conference.[24]

All these events were given the widest possible publicity and became episodes in a continuing saga, a sort of theological soap opera, presented by Küng and his admirers as one man's struggle for freedom of expression against the intolerant machinery of Roman authoritarianism. Against this background, Küng became a best seller. It was crucial to his appeal to a wide audience that he was not just an ordinary theologian but an officially accredited Catholic theologian locked in struggle with repressive superiors. That gave his conflicts the drama of rebellion. Küng has compared theology to an investigation, and contrasted his own, free-lance inquiries as 'a private detective', with the official, police-like inquiries of the church. But the truth is that throughout the 1960s and 1970s, Küng was an official theologian himself, indeed a highly privileged one. Without this official status, it is most improbable that his work would have found a large audience, for its intrinsic merit is not striking.

John Paul inherited what was, therefore, a long-standing problem, indeed a continuing one, for Küng too has a prodigious output – at John Paul's accession, the Küng bibliography already listed 382 items.[25] Küng envenomed matters by keeping up, in public, a sort of running critical commentary on John Paul's actions, culminating in a violent attack on the Pope in October 1979, which received world-wide publicity in the *New York Times*, the *Frankfurter Allgemeine Zeitung*, *Le Monde* and other leading journals. There is no reason to think these personal assaults have influenced John Paul's handling of the Küng case. What concerned him, as it concerned the Doctrinal Congregation, was Küng's perception of the truth, the manner in which he presented it, and its effect on the faithful.

On the first point, Küng is, like Schillebeeckx, concerned with praxis and stresses the manhood of Christ. In *On Being a Christian*, the best-known of his books, he asked: 'Can we have less of a Christology in the classical manner, speculatively or dogmatically "from above" but – without disputing the legitimacy of the older Christology – more of a historical Christology from "below", in the light of the concrete Jesus, more suited to modern man?'[26] Here is another invitation to do-it-yourself dogmatic theology. Yet Küng is inconsistent, for elsewhere he denounces loose, populist presentations of Jesus's Godhead. He denies that Jesus is 'simply God'. The child who points to a crucifix and says, 'That is God, hanging on the cross,' is the victim, according to Küng, of a misunderstanding, 'an irresponsible dilution, superficiality, simplification and even a heretical one-sidedness of the well-thought-out and secure teaching of the early councils'. Such misrepresentations were heretical. Thus: '"God in human form" is Monophysitism. "God suffering on the cross" is Patripassianism.'[27] But according to these criteria, Küng himself sometimes gives the impression of being an Arian. The reader does not derive from Küng's writings that he accepts the divinity of Christ, that is to say the central doctrine of the incarnation, as it has been commonly understood by Catholics, whether theologians or simple communicants, over many centuries.

Secondly, the spirit in which Küng presents his thoughts has more in common with a Protestant approach than a Catholic one. The point was made in an article on Küng by Walter von Löwenich, the Protestant Professor Emeritus in Church History at Erlangen, in 1971. Referring to the *felix inconsequentia* or happy lack of logic in Protestant theology, he noted: 'Officially one clung to the old doctrinal formulations, while modern theologians were left to find their own way in their divergences from these credal statements. In my view this compromise was, despite its confusion, the right one for the situation. It looks as if something similar is now happening in contemporary Catholicism.' He concluded: 'Evidently there can today no longer be an unequivocal answer to the question: What is Catholic?'[28]

John Paul, however, is determined that the Catholic Church will never settle for such confusion, will never agree to parallel sets of beliefs - one in the official formularies, another in the changing and divergent teaching of theologians. That is not what Catholicism is about. Moreover, John Paul believes there is, and must be, an unequivocal answer to the question 'What is Catholic?' Therein lies his case against Küng.

Finally, it will be apparent that Küng also lacks the spirit of St Thomas Aquinas. That is an understatement. His statements reveal the man. 'My inquiry into infallibility gave rise to the greatest debate among Catholic theologians since Vatican II.' 'The more gentle notes of my previous works had not aroused those in responsible positions in the church, so I had to sound the alarm.... There are cases, and this is one of them, where it is expedient to engage in polemics.' 'I can always be convinced by reasons, but I am still waiting for them.' 'I am possessed by a boundless intellectual curiosity that can never be satiated.' 'I cannot understand why the German bishops' conference has now issued its third statement against a book that, according to the witness of countless men and women, both clergy and laity, has done so much to help them with regard to their faith and life as Christians.' 'What may perhaps distinguish me from others is simply that I am looking for a clear, honest and consistent solution.'[29] In his many public statements and in his dealings with the ecclesiastical authorities, Küng has contrived to give an impression of personal arrogance, intellectual intransigence and contumacy to recognized authority. These are not, in John Paul's view, acceptable characteristics in an official Catholic theologian.

On 15 December 1979, the Doctrinal Congregation concluded its hearing into the case of Fr Schillebeeckx and, the same day, issued a condemnation of Fr Küng's teachings. John Paul had an engagement at the Gregorian University, and took the opportunity to underline the centrality of defined dogma and the *magisterium* in the presentation of the Catholic faith. Early in 1980, the German bishops withdrew Küng's licence to teach Catholic theology at Tübingen, though this did not prevent him from continuing to direct the Institute for Ecumenical Research. To John Paul this seemed a fair solution. No one is seeking to silence Küng. He is simply no longer recognized as a teacher of specifically Catholic doctrine. In a letter dated 15 May 1980, John Paul commended the German bishops for their decision. His letter was a cool and detached argument, seeking to strip the affair of its overwrought emotions. It was absurd, he said, for a man to wish to teach Catholic theology if he does not agree with it. 'Does a theologian who no longer accepts completely the doctrine of the church still have the right to teach in the name of the church, and on the basis of a special mission received from her? Can he himself still wish to do so, if some dogmas of the church are contrary to his personal convictions? And under these circumstances can the church, in this case her competent authority, continue to oblige him to do so?' For Küng to continue in his official role would thus be a lie. Hence: 'The decision of the Congregation for the Doctrine of the Faith, taken in common agreement with the German episcopal conference, is the result of the honest and responsible answer to the above questions.'[30]

In his anger at the decision, Küng compared himself with the Soviet dissident Andrei Sakharov, who had just been exiled to Gorki, and to Galileo. He also claimed that John Paul infringed his human rights, which in other contexts the Pope had hotly defended. But Küng was not forced to recant, like Galileo, nor restrained, like Sakharov. As the church sees it, he was merely prevented from acting under false pretences. As for human rights, do not university students and readers have rights too? When he visited Germany later in the year, John Paul told a meeting at Fulda that the church as a community and Catholics as individuals had the right to know that their inherited certainties would not in any way be weakened.

John Paul is well aware that these certainties cannot be protected merely by depriving heterodox theologians of their teaching authority. It is sometimes necessary to give authoritative, general guidance in areas where doubts have arisen. Thus on 17 May 1979 he authorized Cardinal Seper, Prefect of the Doctrinal Congregation, to publish an official letter on the church's eschatological teaching, which could be seen as a warning to experimental theologians. This reaffirmed a broadly traditional view of the Four Last Things. Resurrection must be understood as referring to 'the whole person; for the elect it is nothing other than the extension to human beings of the resurrection of Christ itself'. On hell, the church 'believes that there will be eternal punishment for the sinner, who will be deprived of the sight of God, and that this punishment will have a repercussion on the whole being of the sinner'. The Catholic doctrine of purgatory was also reasserted. On eternal life, the letter continued, 'Neither Scripture nor theology provides sufficient light for a proper picture of life after death.' But Christians were required to believe in a 'fundamental continuity' and must be aware of the 'radical break' which none the less occurs, when the 'economy of faith' (this life) is replaced by 'the economy of fullness of life' (the next).[31]

John Paul believes that such *aides-mémoires* are helpful from time to time. But in general the faith must be left in the hands of the bishops, who since the earliest times have been the prime custodians and teachers of dogma; indeed the phrase *ex cathedra* (from the episcopal chair; hence, cathedral) applies both in its origins and in its present usage primarily to them. That was one reason why the German bishops were left to play the decisive role in the Küng affair. Hence, when the bishops themselves are in confusion, the church faces a real crisis, and extraordinary measures are required.

In January 1979 Cardinal Jan Willebrands, the Dutch primate, told John Paul that the Dutch episcopate were hopelessly divided over a number of aspects of pastoral theology. Four out of the seven were determined progressives; two were equally determined traditionalists. Willebrands himself had tried to mediate, but had failed. In March that year John Paul summoned all of them separately to Rome, and had an individual interview with each. This, too, proved ineffective. Thereupon John Paul called a synod of the Dutch bishops, to be held in Rome in January 1980; it was, as he termed it in his opening homily, 'an unprecedented event'.

The synod met 14–31 January 1980 and concluded its business in an atmosphere of concord and general relief. One reason may have been the successful observance of confidentiality. As John Paul, commending the need for secrecy, told observers: 'I am sure you will understand that the church, like all families, at least on certain occasions, needs to have moments of exchange, discussion and decision which take place in intimacy and discretion, to enable the participants to be free, and to respect people and situations.' Another, perhaps weightier, reason was that John Paul gave the synod his close personal supervision. As he noted in his closing homily, he had kept them under his eagle eye: 'I was able to be with you and take part in most of the assemblies in the mornings and in the afternoons.' He had warned them at the outset: 'To be a pastor and a bishop of souls, that means keeping the word. *Keeping the truth.*' He reminded them 'in all seriousness' of Jesus's saying: 'If a man loves me, he will keep my words. ... He that loveth me not keepeth not my sayings.'[32]

The Dutch bishops took this admonition to heart. They closed ranks around a set of forty-six propositions which broadly confirmed the traditional practice of the church, reinforcing the authority of bishops over priests and of priests over laity. Clause 3 read: 'Neither bishops nor priests are the delegates of the faithful.' Other propositions directed that 'pastoral workers' (who may be married men and women and who in the Netherlands sometimes perform the tasks of curates) were not to carry out the duties of priests, deprecated unauthorized changes in the liturgy, ecumenical gestures or intercommunion without permission, the employment of ex-priests in teaching theology, and the failure to assert Catholic doctrine in education. Proposition 21 stated that the bishops were 'unanimous in their desire to follow faithfully the decisions of the popes and to maintain the rule of celibacy'.[33] The Dutch bishops left Rome full of praise for John Paul's *tour de force*.

There is a limit, however, to which even a strong-minded pope is able or would wish to impose doctrinal uniformity. John Paul is an original and adventurous man. So long as he is pope no theologian, and no enterprising bishop, need avoid innovation or adventure, provided he is in good faith. What John Paul was concerned to do, particularly in the first years of his pontificate, was to get everyone to recognize doctrinal confusion for the great and fundamental evil it is, and to insist that the ancient rulings and procedures were still in force, and must be obeyed. This he certainly achieved. Indeed it can truthfully be said that, on all the five great evils facing the church and humanity, John Paul was able early in his mission to sound the tocsin and to alert the defences.

To what extent was this purely a personal achievement of an

exceptionally vigorous and single-minded man? Or was John Paul simply drawing on the vast spiritual, moral and physical resources which any successor of St Peter has at his immediate disposal, if he chooses to use them? The question is important, and it became of immediate and melancholy relevance on 13 May 1981 when John Paul, during his regular Wednesday audience in St Peter's Square, was shot by a Turkish assassin. His wound was severe and painful and might have been fatal. It must have raised in many minds doubts about the durability of the John-Pauline restoration. We must now turn, therefore, to the longer-term aspects of John Paul's programme, and examine the agencies, human and divine, which are there to assist in making his work permanent.

Part Three

SOURCES OF AUTHORITY

9

Human Instruments

FOR A WORLD-WIDE ORGANIZATION, in contact with 750 million people, the Catholic Church has an extraordinarily small central base. The papal state consists only of the 109 acres of the Vatican City, most of which is taken up by the basilica of St Peter's and the Vatican gardens and museums, plus a number of extraterritorial enclaves within and outside Rome. John Paul possesses few of the physical instruments of government. Paul VI abolished the papal gendarmerie and the Noble and Palatine Guards. Only a hundred or so Swiss guards are left. There is a daily newspaper, a powerful radio station run by the Jesuits and a printing house. The pope has his own bank and mints his own coins. There is a small railway system for goods and a helicopter pad. But in most other respects the state, which has about 450 actual citizens, is a legal and constitutional device to guarantee the sovereignty of the papal absolutism, rather than a physical entity.

This is an enormous advantage. The old papal states, which once embraced most of central Italy, had been a chronic embarrassment to the papacy during the last two centuries of their existence, before they were swallowed up by the new Italian state in 1870. The pope got all the odium for their feeble and often corrupt administration without any of the benefits of real power. Now he gets the best of both worlds: the prestige and status of a state, with virtually none of its problems. Above all, in an age of expanding welfare expectations and human rights, including the right to housing, education and full employment, he does not have to look after people. From the window of his private apartments in the Vatican palace, John Paul can gaze over the city of Rome, with its appalling crime rate, its political and financial scandals, its housing shortages, its quasi-bankrupt treasury, its crumbling health and transport systems, and reflect: 'My kingdom is not of this world.' It is a comforting thought.

As a result, the central administration is still very small. The curia was reformed by Sixtus v in 1588 and again by Pius x in 1908, but until very recently it retained many of the characteristics of a court of the *ancien régime*, indeed of a medieval *curia regis*. The Second Vatican Council asked that the curia be 'reorganized and modernized', chosen on 'a more representative basis', with the co-option of 'more bishops, especially diocesan bishops', and 'lay people of virtue, knowledge and experience'.[1] Paul vi, by no means averse to tinkering, responded with his apostolic constitution, *Regimini Ecclesiae Universae*. The result, as with all modern 're-forms' of administration, was expansion.

There is here an element of paradox, indeed of irony. John XXIII had no respect for bureaucrats. Asked how many people worked in the Vatican he replied: 'About half of them.' He did not love the curia, which he felt had persecuted him. His prudent solution was to leave it severely alone. The progressives of the Council lacked his wisdom. They thought the power of the curia was too great and they insisted on changes. As a result, in addition to the traditional Congregations, or ministries, for the Bishops, for the Clergy, for the Doctrine of the Faith, for the Religious Orders, for the Oriental Churches, the Sacraments, the Missions and Religious Education, sixteen new bodies were created: Secretariats for Non-Christians, for Non-Believers, the Council for the Laity, for Justice and Peace, and so on. These new departments constitute what is called the 'new curia'. Actually, it is the old curia writ trendily. Only one of the sixteen, the Secretariat for Christian Unity, carries much influence. But the number of curialists has trebled, from 1,322 just before the Council to 3,150 in the last year of Paul vi, with a corresponding expansion in bureaucratic power.[2]

All the same, the Vatican government remains a comparatively small operation, well adapted to the exercise of a personal autocracy. It is possible for John Paul to know personally, and meet periodically, all his officials down to the purely clerical level. The advantages of this domestic scale are obvious. Hence he has not sought to change the curia. Quite the contrary: he has taken steps to stabilize it and consolidate its morale. He has rightly recognized that the notion of a clash of interests between the pope himself, on the one hand, and 'the curia' as an entity on the other, is misleading, though it has often been employed by those who comment on Vatican affairs. What is undoubtedly true is that, if a pope is uncertain about his own views and policies, or fails to articulate them clearly, senior members of the curia will tend to impose their own ideas, on the basis of a collective bureaucratic consensus. This occasionally happened under John XXIII, who was sometimes diffident about putting forward his own views in areas where he felt he lacked experience. It happened increasingly during the last years of Paul VI, though not on issues about which he cared deeply. It might well have happened under John Paul I, though it is remarkable how often a humble man learns to trust his instincts under the weight of divine autocracy. Naturally, a weak pope would produce an assertive curia. But a pope with a strong personality, clear views and industrious habits – and there is no doubt that John Paul II possesses all three – has not the slightest difficulty in getting the curia to carry out his policies. The curia, like most bureaucracies, welcomes determined leadership.

John Paul has understood these matters very well. His curial policy has thus been conservative. The election of the first non-Italian pope in 450 years was not followed by a self-conscious 'internationalization' of the court. Nor was there a sudden influx of Poles, as some had feared. Some changes were made inevitable when Cardinal Jean Villot, the Frenchman who had served Paul VI as Secretary of State, or chief minister, died in March 1979. In the first week in May John Paul announced a reconstruction. It left things much as they were.[3] Villot's post went to Cardinal Agostino Casaroli, who had been in charge of the Council for Public Affairs (in effect the papal Foreign Minister), and has been closely associated with Vatican *Ostpolitik*. Casaroli was himself succeeded by his own deputy, Archbishop Achille Silvestrini, who had been involved in the religious liberty aspects of the Helsinki accords. A second foreign affairs post went to an archbishop of Lithuanian descent, Mgr Andryss Backio, specializing in matters affecting the Soviet Union. The job of *sostituto*, or deputy, at the Secretariat of State was entrusted to a non-Italian, the Spanish Mgr Eduardo

Martínez Somolo, formerly Apostolic Nuncio in Colombia. This post, which traditionally had involved keeping in touch with Italian domestic politics, had been the power base of Cardinal Benelli. The fact that it went to a Spanish-speaking diplomat with close links with Latin America emphasized a new order of priorities, but one which had already been formed before John Paul's election. The former *sostituto*, Cardinal Giuseppe Caprio, was placed in charge of finance. The Italians, indeed, did not lose ground in the changes, since one of John Paul's earliest decisions was to replace the American Cardinal Wright, Prefect of the Congregation for the Clergy, by a conservative Italian, Cardinal Oddi.[4]

The following month, on 30 June 1979, John Paul held a consistory at which he created fifteen new cardinals. One of these was *in pectore* (that is, his name was not revealed but locked in the pope's breast), and he is presumably an ecclesiastic behind the Iron Curtain. But of the other fourteen no fewer than six were Italian, the remainder coming from Poland (two), France, Canada, Vietnam, Ireland, Japan and Mexico. Thus the European preponderance within the college, and the Italian paramountcy within that preponderance, were actually reinforced.

The rearrangement of the curia and the consistory were intended to be reassuring to the curialists. But in the following month, July 1979, John Paul went further. At a general audience he went out of his way to express his confidence in the curia, and his gratitude for its services.[5] Moreover, on a number of occasions he has issued quiet warnings that any attempt to drive a wedge between his person and the curia would be ill received as well as futile. Thus on 10 July 1980, when he spoke to the Brazilian bishops in Fortaleza, he called for 'unity with the pope' expressed in 'acceptance of his word'. This obedience, he emphasized, was expected 'not only when he speaks personally, but also when he speaks through the institutions which collaborate with him in the pastoral government of the church and speak in his name, with his approval, if not with his mandate'.[6] John Paul has been quick to dispel any illusion that important rulings by the curia, especially in exercising discipline or in reinforcing traditional practices, have been or can be made without his authority. He is not the kind of man to allow subordinates to place him in an embarrassing position. Nor is he the kind of man to hide behind them when something unpleasant has to be done. He is the master. The curia is the servant. There is a general identity of views between them, but the relationship remains hierarchical. That is how the curialists prefer it, and under John Paul they have become a happier band of brothers. That has been an important element in John Paul's restoration.

John Paul turned to the vexed problem of the Vatican's finances in the summer of 1979. The following November he summoned all the cardinals to Rome to outline the problem to them and seek their advice and consent. Vatican finance is complicated, but for some time its main structure has been perfectly well known.[7] In essentials it is the same as that administered by the Church Commissioners and the other financial organs of Anglicanism: a combination of investment and property income plus fluctuating donations from the faithful. The investments were based on the financial part of the settlement made with the Italian government in 1929. In the last part of Pius XII's reign the church was well advised by Cardinal Francis Spellman of New York and his Wall Street experts, and its reserves flourished during the long, post-war bull market.[8] At the end of the 1960s it was reasonably prosperous, with large and remunerative investments in Italy and overseas.[9] Like virtually all investment funds, the Vatican performed much less well in the 1970s. In addition, some very serious mistakes were made. Like his old master, Pius XII, Paul VI had a weakness for taking advice from unofficial sources. The Vatican was first the beneficiary, then the victim, of the financial schemes of Michele Sindona, whose downfall was effectively accomplished in 1974, the year when so many fragile financial empires collapsed.[10] The Vatican's losses were heavy. Thereafter, the unofficial advisers were pushed into the background. John Paul made clear his preference for old-fashioned, if unspectacular, methods when he placed all the financial threads in the hands of Giuseppe Caprio, an experienced financial official who had been by-passed by the investment adventurism of the early 1970s.

But risky ventures are not the main cause of the Vatican's cash problems. Like every other government in the world, it expanded its activities in the 1960s and early 1970s. It does not have a welfare state to finance, but it still has three times as many public servants to pay as in the early 1960s, with a smaller investment income (allowing for inflation) than it had then. Unlike secular governments, it does not possess a natural tax base. The result is a deficit. John Paul told the assembled cardinals that the deficit for 1979 was £8.5 million and that it would rise to £9.5 million in 1980. Proposals were adopted for a simplification of the Vatican's various financial agencies, which were announced by the Pope in January 1981.

Such administrative changes, however, make only a marginal difference in the long run. They help to avoid errors, but they do not in themselves generate wealth. In the modern world, where religious institutions can no longer expect munificent private endowments, ecclesiastical finance is increasingly influenced by what might be termed charismatic fund-raising. Money is collected from countless individuals by the successful projection of a faith around a central pastoral figure. The phenomenon is most familiar in the United States, but it is to be found everywhere. Indeed it has always been a characteristic of organized religion. In the Catholic Church it has taken various forms, notably Peter's Pence, contributions to the Holy See from outlying areas, such as England and Poland.[11] Catholicism, with its emphasis on the person of the pope, is peculiarly well suited to this form of voluntary offering, and John Paul II with his expansive, outgoing personality, and his love of crowds, is exceptionally well qualified to arouse the enthusiasm and generosity of the faithful. In fact contributions to Rome from all over the world have substantially increased since he was elected. His overseas visits have, of course, further stimulated this flow of cash. They are not in themselves designed to raise money; indeed they are expensive to mount and thus a further drain on central funds in the first instance. But they produce a pattern of support from which the Vatican is a decisive beneficiary.

John Paul II's spectacular foreign visits have been his most obvious personal contribution to the renewed health and popularity of the papacy. This represents a remarkable switch in Vatican strategy. Pius IX responded to the loss of his papal states by making the most of his role as 'the prisoner in the Vatican', surrounded by a hostile secular power. He could not, or would not, travel at all, so the faithful responded by travelling to him, the new railways making such mass pilgrimages possible and cheap. This strategy of im-

mobility was maintained until the death of Pius XII. It accorded
well with the fortress mentality of the church's view of the world,
but it was already becoming out of date when John XXIII decided
to let down the drawbridge. John began to travel in Italy, but it
was his successor Paul VI who took the decisive step when he flew
to the Holy Land in 1964. He followed this with other overseas
visits, to India, the United Nations, to Fatima in Portugal, to
Bogotá, to Uganda, to the Philippines and Australia. But Pope Paul
was evidently not at ease in this high-pressure international pastorate, and the programme of travel petered out after 1970.

John Paul II has from the start grasped the important fact, to
which history bears abundant witness, that evangelism is largely
shaped by the means of communication. He has noted, for instance,
the extraordinary resurgence of Islam since cheap jet travel made
it possible for tens of millions of ordinary Moslems to go on
pilgrimage to Mecca and become *hajis*. The combination of the jet
and the helicopter gives the Pope, in his view, the physical means
to exercise a pastoral care over his global see in the same way as
bishops carry out periodic visitations over their dioceses. But a
papal visit is not only a visitation. It is also an exercise in the
decentralization of government, what he has termed 'collegiality in
action'. And, finally, the Pope also travels as a pilgrim, to all the
manifestations of God's action in the world. His journeys, he told
the curia in June 1980, were 'an authentic pilgrimage to the sanc-
tuary of the living people of God'.[12]

John Paul has made regular large-scale travel a normal and even
an essential part of papal duties. Defending this programme, a
Brazilian bishop pointed out that in Latin America, as in Asia and
Africa, 'the poor cannot afford to travel'. There has been criticism
too, which John Paul answered in June 1980: 'Many people say
that the Pope is travelling too much and at too frequent intervals.
Speaking from the human point of view, they are right. But it is
providence that guides me, and sometimes it suggests that we do
certain things to excess.'[13] On a practical basis, the question was
whether John Paul's tours were a sensible investment of his time
and energy. The figures seemed to suggest they were. In his first
three years in office, John Paul's overseas services and appearances
were attended by over 100 million people, more than one-seventh

of the entire world-wide Catholic community. Of course, the great gatherings his presence assembled, some of three million or more – among the largest concentrations of human beings in the history of mankind – raised fearful problems of security, which naturally seem more serious after the near-successful attempt on his life. The papal travels are exhausting and sometimes rugged. During the visit to Zaire, the press of the million-strong crowd in Kinshasa was so great that nine Africans were trampled to death. In Nagasaki in 1981, hundreds of thousands of Japanese attended a three-hour open-air service in sub-zero temperatures: nine communicants broke bones slipping on the ice and 466 were treated for exposure.[14] John Paul has not always heeded prudent counsels when making his plans. He is not the first pope to quote St Paul with relish: 'Divine folly is wiser than the wisdom of man . . . to shame the wise, God has chosen what the world counts folly.'[15]

This personal evangelism has been undertaken not merely because it is a type of activity at which John Paul is superbly gifted and which he manifestly enjoys. Each expedition has had its own particular purpose. There is the overall, long-term aim of re-inforcing success (as in Poland), or of encouraging a struggling church under pressure (Brazil) or of trying to break new ground (the Far East). It is one of John Paul's cherished objectives to recreate the dynamism of the church's missionary effort in East Asia. In Tokyo, in the spring of 1981, he appeared on television to answer questions from young people in slow but intelligible Japanese. From Manila he sent greetings 'to the brothers and sisters of the church in China', at the same time dispatching his Secretary of State, Cardinal Casaroli, to Hong Kong to see the elderly Jesuit bishop, Mgr Dominic Tang Yiming, who was released from a Chinese prison in 1980 after serving twenty-two years as an 'agent of Western imperialism'. Three months later, in June 1981, John Paul made Mgr Tang Archbishop of Canton, as a further step towards re-establishing contact with the 2.5 million Catholics of China.[16] One of the most useful consequences of papal travel is a continuing awareness of the strengths and weaknesses of Catholicism over the whole global spread, so that resources can be switched, as required, from one theatre to another.

The efficient allocation of resources requires, of course, a world-

wide framework of uniformity and discipline. John Paul has been
anxious to create a genuinely international church whose priests
and nuns regard overseas service as normal and welcome, and who
are trained to perform it. But, while allowing for local circumstances, the growth of knowledge and the individual insight, an
international church must teach the same Gospel: truth is indivi-
sible. That is why John Paul hastened the publication of the
constitution *Sapientia Christiana*, drawn up by Cardinal Gabriel-
Marie Garrone and the Congregation for Catholic Education,
which defines the *magisterium* with regard to what it terms 'a just
liberty in teaching and investigating'. At his general audience on
18 July 1979 John Paul referred to this document which applies in
particular to the 125 or more Catholic centres of higher ecclesiastical studies – sixteen in Rome (the 'Pontifical Roman Academies'),
forty-seven Catholic universities created by the Holy See throughout the world, and thirty-four theological faculties in state universities.[17] 'To proclaim the Gospel, to teach,' he said, 'means
encountering the living human being, man's thought, which continually seeks the truth in a different way and in new fields. Man
is always asking questions. To find the true answer, precise,
persuasive and in conformity with reality, he is prepared to
undertake difficult and tedious researches. This thirst for truth is
one of the undeniable expressions of the human spirit.'[18]

John Paul has made it clear that he regards a general uniformity
of teaching and discipline in the church's centres of higher education as indispensable to the creation of an expanding international
force of loyal and dedicated senior clergy. Equally if not more
important is the Vatican's own foreign service of nuncios and
apostolic delegates, who report directly to the pope. These ninety
or so overseas missions have a double role. They represent the
Vatican as a state to the government where they are accredited, and
they are the eyes and ears and voice of the pope in his dealings with
the local Catholic hierarchies.

The system of nuncios, which replaced the earlier system of
papal legates, has always been regarded as an expression of the
international power of the papacy, especially over local churches,
and above all of the pope's right to appoint bishops and other
senior clergy. Hence medieval and renaissance governments sought

fiercely to restrict papal legations and, when they signed concordats, insisted on limiting their activities. There are still a number of informal agreements (for instance in Poland) between the state and the Vatican governing the selection of the hierarchy. But criticism of the system now tends to come rather from local Catholic liberals than from the secular authorities. During the Council there were demands that the system be scrapped; or that nuncios be selected from among, or even appointed by, the local bishops. These demands have been repeated from time to time, notably by Fathers Küng, Schillebeeckx and their supporters just before the August 1978 conclave.

Neither Paul VI nor, still less, John Paul II has yielded to these pressures. In 1969 Paul VI published a pontifical letter or *motu proprio* setting out the duties and powers of these papal representatives.[19] Two years after John Paul's election, a papal diplomat was allowed to publish a semi-authoritative commentary on this document, with the endorsement of two powerful former curialists, Cardinal Benelli and Cardinal Salvatore Pappalardo.[20] The effect was to reaffirm the authority of the pope in the detailed direction of all local churches, and to re-emphasize the role of the nuncios and delegates in communicating this authority.

As the *motu proprio* stated, and as the commentary stressed, 'the authority which the pope exercises over the entire church is one that is full, supreme, universal, ordinary and immediate'. These carefully chosen words were a reminder that the pope's commands extend to all the details of Catholic life, doctrinal, moral and liturgical, that they cannot be challenged by anybody, however august, within the church, that they apply everywhere, that they radiate from the routine discharge of his office, and that they must be obeyed promptly and without argument.

Nuncios and delegates do not normally compete with the functions of local bishops or interfere in them. But they attend the opening sessions of episcopal conferences and all further sessions if so instructed by the pope. They are channels of verbal and written communication between the pope and senior Vatican officials on the one hand, and local bishops on the other. Perhaps most important of all, they advise the pope on episcopal appointments. The right of local episcopal conferences to propose to the pope the names of candidates for vacancies is defined in another *motu proprio*.[21] This is complicated by local traditions and arrangements. Thus in the provinces of England and Wales, the cathedral canons of the vacant see prepare a list of possible candidates, which is discussed by the bishops of the province under their metropolitan and forwarded to Rome. But such local lists, as the commentary points out, are 'not binding in the sense that, in specific cases, the nuncio is entitled to propose as candidates additional names which are not actually on the list'. The pope, indeed, can and sometimes does produce a completely new name himself. Quite apart from the desire to produce the best bishops, there is in fact an important principle at stake in reasserting the nuncio's role in episcopal appointments. It is John Paul's view that the choice of bishops should be governed by universalist rather than by local considerations. The chief criterion is not what local opinion, real or imaginary, wants. It is the well-being of the whole church. Hence it is not desirable that nuncios should always, or even usually, be local bishops. They are not the representatives of the localities to the pope: they are the representatives of the pope to the localities. They stand for the unifying rather than the devolutionary principle. And, in the last resort, they represent the undoubted and comprehensive juridical power of the Holy See. John Paul has coined a phrase for himself: 'A centipede whose legs are the legates.' The centipede may move slowly, even awkwardly; but it has many legs and it covers all the ground.

Other organizations which cover all the ground, and which are at John Paul's service in assisting the unifying process, are the religious orders, and especially the Jesuits. The Society of Jesus, formally established by Paul III's bull *Regimini Militantis Ecclesiae* in 1540, is bound by a special vow of obedience to be completely at the pope's disposal anywhere in the world.[22] By means of the *Spiritual Exercises* devised by St Ignatius Loyola, their founder, Jesuits have traditionally displayed the most impressive discipline and *espirit de corps* of any of the church's orders. But they are also the most elaborately educated, with a high proportion of scholars and scientists, the most politically conscious and the most committed to a mission 'in the world', especially among the mighty. They are therefore controversial and combative, and sometimes an embarrassment to the Holy See. Indeed in 1773 Clement xiv yielded to secular pressures and suppressed the society, though it was reconstituted by the reinvigorated papacy in 1814. Thereafter it expanded steadily, especially in the long pontificate of Pius xii, reaching its apogee shortly after his death, in the early 1960s. At that time the Jesuits numbered 36,000 with 12,000 teachers in higher education, and had been responsible for the intellectual formation of more than one in four of the college of cardinals and nearly a third of the episcopate as a whole. Under Pius xii, who was profoundly and intimately influenced by Jesuit methods (even his housekeeper came from a Jesuit-formed order of nuns), the Society was the intellectual mortar that kept the whole vast edifice of the church upright and weather-proof.[23]

Even at that period, however, the Jesuits had their liberal and conservative wings. The Belgian Fr Jean-Baptiste Janssens, Jesuit General from 1946, loyally enforced Pius xii's anti-dissenting encyclical *Humani Generis*, from 1950 onwards. Leading Jesuits like Teilhard de Chardin, Riccardo Lombardi, Karl Rahner, Stanislas Lyonnet, Courtney Murray and Gonzalo Arroyo were disciplined or leant upon. One celebrated Jesuit intellectual, Hans Urs von Balthasar, actually left the Society as a result. All the same, at the Jesuit-run Gregorian University in Rome students were encouraged to 'explore in depth' the 'errors' of philosophers like Marx and Sartre and Protestant theologians like Karl Barth. Some of the rebels of the 1960s and 1970s, like Küng, were the products of this approach, and to begin with Küng was defended by his old Jesuit teachers, though Rahner repudiated him in 1970. The Jesuits did not cut an impressive figure at the Council. They disagreed in public, their conservative wing failed to put up an effective rear-guard action and their liberal wing was upstaged by the Dominicans. In the middle of the Council Janssens died. In 1965 a general congregation in Rome elected a youngish liberal from Spain, Pedro Arrupe. In the spirit of the 1960s, he promptly retired the senior conservatives at the Jesuit headquarters and set about introducing a 'reform'.

The result has been a tragedy. There can be no doubt that the division among the Jesuits and the decline of the Society's morale were among the principal reasons why the church was in such an enfeebled state at John Paul's accession. As we have already noted, the fall in Jesuit numbers during the 1970s was precipitous – even higher than among the Catholic clergy as a whole – and it was most striking in what had hitherto been the expanding areas, the United States, Latin America, Spain and the Netherlands. Jesuits in their thirties and forties left in battalions. Some of those who remained became extremists and troublemakers, and sought to turn Jesuit houses, including important training establishments, into nests of subversion and heterodoxy. In the United States, a Jesuit priest, Daniel Berrigan, became publicly associated with ultra-radical politics, liturgical adventurism, married priests, the ordination of women, the legitimation of contraceptives and the burning of draft-cards, for which last he went to gaol. In Uruguay, the Jesuit priest Juan Segundo was one of the originators of 'liberation theology'. Canada produced its own ultra-liberal Jesuit, Bernard Lonergen, Chile the Allende partisan Gonzalo Arroyo, who fled to Europe to start 'Christians for Socialism', Argentina a left-wing organ, *El Criterio*, and a group called 'Priests for the Third World', Mexico a Jesuit pressure group called 'Priests for the People'. Jesuit university chaplains provided some of the worst cases. There were unseemly personal disputes between Jesuit dogmatic and moral theologians. Some long-established Jesuit publications, famous for their dependable scholarship, fell into the hands of rabid editorial committees and became notorious for their political polemics and questionable theology.

Arrupe proved reluctant to discipline his erring members. The old Jesuit houses of correction had been abolished. The usual 'punishment' in the 1970s was to send a rebel on holiday. Arrupe was repeatedly rebuked by Paul VI, who urged him to call a general congregation to bring the mutinous to order or expel them. But the meeting, held in 1974, was a failure and Paul VI had to intervene and wind it up.[24] John Paul has clearly been defeated, so far, by the problems of the Jesuits. On 21 September 1979 he summoned Arrupe to an audience and urged him to take further measures to control his dissidents. Arrupe responded by sending an admonitory letter to all Jesuits, dated 19 October 1979. Some individual acts of discipline were carried out. One American Jesuit, William Callaghan, was forbidden to advocate the ordination of women.

Another, Robert Drinan, was obliged to vacate his seat in Congress. But these measures were carried out with little enthusiasm, and Arrupe did not conceal that he was acting on papal orders. John Paul declined to accept his resignation, however, and told him that a further general congregation 'would not be opportune at this time'. In August 1981, however, Arrupe suffered a stroke. John Paul responded, two months later, by appointing the elderly conservative, Father Paolo Dezza, as his personal delegate, to prepare a general congregation 'to be called in due time' and meanwhile to 'superintend the government of the society until the election of a new superior general'.

The vacuum left by the contraction of the Jesuits, and the decline of their ability or willingness to sustain Catholic orthodoxy, has to some extent been filled by the expanding international institute of layfolk, Opus Dei. It was founded in Madrid in 1928 by a Spanish priest, José María Escrivá de Balaguer y Albas, and was formally registered as the Sacerdotal Society of the Holy Cross and Opus Dei. It retains a very Spanish flavour and a Tridentine, Counter-Reformationary religious culture. Escrivá, who died in 1975, was convinced, just as Ignatius Loyola and St John of the Cross were, that the church had become infected with decay. As he put it, 'There is an authentic rottenness. At times it seems as if the Mystical Body of Christ were a decomposing corpse which stinks.' The object of the Opus Dei is to counter this process, by the exemplary lives of its members and by their influence within the counsels of the church and in leading secular institutions, including governments. Like the sixteenth-century Jesuits it seeks to form the characters and views of youth, whom it assiduously recruits, and it runs a large number of student hostels, as well as the University of Navarre in Pamplona. It was originally confined to laymen, but a women's section was established in 1930 and from 1943 it added a section for priests. By the early 1980s it was operating in eighty-seven countries with a total membership of over 72,000 of whom about 2 per cent were priests.

If Germany tends to produce noisy, heterodox theologians, Spain seems to specialize in controversial religious orders. Opus Dei has been the most successful Catholic movement of the twentieth century, and it has aroused intense suspicion and jealousy, not least within the church itself. Like the Dominicans, another order of Spanish origin, it is accused of fanatical doctrinal zeal and intolerance. As with the Jesuits, before their recent radicalization, Opus Dei is said to be ultra-conservative and to have exercised enormous political influence, particularly in Spain and above all during the late 1960s and early 1970s. It is also accused of educational imperialism, and fights running battles with Catholic chaplains in some universities. Like the reformed Carmelites of St John of the Cross and St Teresa of Avila, it is said to subject young recruits to intolerable mental conditioning and excessive physical rigour, including the use of self-inflicted corporal chastisement.[25] Like the medieval Benedictines, it is accused of possessing incalculable wealth. From time to time a former recruit 'defects' and makes damaging statements about the internal affairs of the institute, rather as in the early years of this century the testimony of 'escaped nuns' was published by the Protestant Truth Society and similar bodies. Opus Dei documents are 'disclosed' and become the basis for sensational newspaper articles.[26] Like other Catholic religious organizations, Opus Dei keeps its internal affairs confidential and is thus described as 'secretive'. In fact the many and extensive investigations into its aims, structure and methods have revealed very little that is damaging and nothing which was not also applicable to many Catholic orders of priests, monks, friars and nuns, especially in the training of recruits. Every accusation that has been hurled at it was also made, at one time or another, about the Jesuits, and usually with better reason. The truth is that Opus Dei has all the virtues and all the blemishes of any other well-organized, successful, zealous and self-confident religious movement. It believes wholeheartedly that it is doing God's work and is therefore tireless and none too scrupulous in pressing its claim for recognition, privileges and freedom of action.

Opus Dei has set its heart on two objectives in particular. The first is the beatification, and eventually canonization, of its founder. Such a campaign, of course, is absolutely routine for any Catholic body. The second aim is to get its status as a secular institute, conferred by Pius XII in 1950, raised to the level of what is termed a 'personal prelature'. This also is a familiar tactic of an ambitious order. If Opus Dei had its way, it would no longer be supervised by the Congregation for Religious and Secular Institutes and would be assigned to the Congregation of Bishops. It would have its own bishop, would cease to come under the control of the diocesan bishops and episcopal conferences of the countries where it operates, and would in effect (like the Jesuits) report directly to the pope. As Jesuit history has shown, there are enormous advantages in such a relationship for both parties.

It testifies to the shrewd long-sightedness of John Paul that he has grasped this point. Over the past quarter century he has had many dealings with Opus Dei members in different countries. He knows a lot about its work and on balance he strongly approves of it. It was his custom, when a cardinal, to give a talk at the Opus Dei centre whenever he visited Rome. He reveres the memory of Escrivá, whose aims and activities were so similar, in many respects, to those of Fr Maximilian Kolbe. In his view, Escrivá had the right combination: a robust adherence to the traditional dogmas and moral standards of Catholicism, together with the missionary zeal to apply them in the modern world. It is the formula to which John Paul's mind constantly returns: not the secularizing of the church, but the sacralizing of the world. The fact that Opus Dei is essentially a lay organization is, for him, not a source of suspicion but an obvious and practical advantage. He believes, like most senior Catholic prelates with knowledge of the subject, that Opus Dei's political influence, even in Spain, has been exaggerated. But in so far as it exists, he welcomes it. Has it not always been one of the aims of Holy Church to raise the voice of spiritual wisdom among the seats of the mighty?

Just before the August 1978 conclave opened, Cardinal Wojtyla, as he then was, included among his devotional exercises in Rome a visit to Escrivá's tomb, to say prayers. Shortly after becoming pope he wrote a letter to Opus Dei, dated 15 November 1978, on the occasion of its fiftieth anniversary; he congratulated it on its work and expressed the opinion that its status must be resolved. At his first Christmas as pope he presented every member of the Secretariat of State with a copy of an address he had delivered at the Opus Dei centre. On 19 August 1979 he told 300 members of Opus Dei gathered in Rome: 'Yours is truly a great ideal which anticipated the theology of the laity that later characterized the church of the Council.' None of this suggests that John Paul intends to advance the institutional interests of Opus Dei in the same way as Pius XII advanced the interests of the Jesuits. Popes have been traditionally wary of accepting the claims of new religious bodies for special treatment. They like evidence over a long period that the Holy Spirit is at work. But, on the face of it, Opus Dei appears to be the kind of instrument John Paul needs to assist him in carrying through his restoration on a permanent basis: orthodox, loyal, dedicated, superbly organized and disciplined, ubiquitous and youthful.

The fact that Opus Dei has many enemies, has been the object of a liberal campaign in the media, and is widely presented as obscurantist and reactionary, will not deter John Paul from judging it, and employing it, strictly on its deserts. One virtue he does not lack is moral courage, including the courage to stand out against the conventional wisdom. He is rightly suspicious of fashion, especially in religious matters. He detects in Opus Dei some highly unfashionable merits. That is in itself high commendation to him. If some of the criticism rubs off on him, he will bear it with fortitude.

We come here to a central aspect of John Paul's character and mission. In using the structure of the church, and especially the charismatic appeal of the papacy itself, to promote the restoration of Catholic morale, John Paul has not scorned exploiting his own popularity. Far from it. It is, as he would say, a gift of God. But the Catholic Church has not survived and flourished over two millennia by being popular. It has survived because what it taught was true. The quest for popularity, as opposed to the quest for truth, is bound to fail. Indeed John Paul would argue that it has been precisely the quest for popularity among those of little faith, by relaxing moral standards and obfuscating plain dogmas, which has decisively failed in recent years. In doing so it has inflicted grievous damage on a church which, in the past, had never hesitated to court unpopularity. Roman Catholicism is not a market-research religion. It is not in business to count heads or take votes. In its sacred economy, quantitative principles do not apply. Dogma and morals are not susceptible to guidance by opinion polls. The truth is paramount and it must be the naked truth, presented without cosmetics and exercises in public relations.

One aspect of this truth is that the Roman Catholic Church is a divine as well as a human institution. Its human instruments are important, and John Paul has already indicated that he intends to make shrewd use of them in his pontifical ministry. But the church is primarily sustained by the divine agency. John Paul's leadership is above all an assertion of this fact. His restoration of the church depends indeed on many carefully judged human dispositions, but it depends most of all on the affirmation and worship of God.

10

Divine Agency

THE CHRISTIAN HUMANISM of Pope John Paul II is, you might say, a broad church. It does not lay down a special road to God, for it presumes there are many. Indeed it hints that the Christian soul may take two or more simultaneously. John Paul is a hard-reading intellectual who cannot bear being without a book within easy reach or in his pocket. But that pocket will also contain a rosary and probably a holy medal. The prayers which spring to his lips spontaneously are simple ones. As he was being carried to hospital after the assassination attempt in May 1981, it was the Hail Mary, in Polish, which he whispered, over and over again.

Being an existentialist of a kind, John Paul is reconciled to the contradictions in man, a creature in which intellect and emotions, idealism and carnality, good and evil struggle constantly for mastery. It is characteristic of this internal bifurcation that the existentialist analysis, for example, may lead either to stoical despair or to God. Like Pascal, John Paul regards man as having free will yet somehow programmed in spirit. 'We have the power of resisting grace,' Pascal wrote, 'nevertheless God forms within us the motives of our will and effectively disposes of our hearts.'[1] John Paul not only rejects but positively hates determinism. Like all those who have been influenced by existentialism, he is concerned to affirm the reality of human freedom and responsibility against every scientific or philosophical or indeed religious theory (such as Calvinism) which denies them. Yet he agrees with Pascal that human freedom cannot be absolute – it is limited by desire – and therefore there is no necessary conflict between human freedom and divine grace. To Pascal, an 'autonomy' which means remoteness from

God is not freedom but a form of bondage; and that is a thought constantly in John Paul's sayings.[2]

Above all, John Paul shares Pascal's astonishment at man's divided nature: 'What a chimera is man! What a novelty! What a monster, what a chaos, what a contradiction, what a prodigy! Judge of all things, imbecile worm of the earth; depository of truth, a sink of uncertainty and error; the pride and refuge of the universe!'[3] The thoughts expressed in this famous passage from Pascal would occur spontaneously to one who watched at close quarters the crime of Auschwitz and the way in which the human spirit rose above its atrocities. To quote Pascal again: 'The greatness and wretchedness of man are so evident that the true religion must necessarily teach us both that there is in man some great source of nobility and a great source of wretchedness. It must then give us a reason for these astonishing contradictions.'[4] That, John Paul would argue, is precisely the programme of Christian humanism.

This humanism of belief is at root an optimistic creed. That is what makes it such a striking contrast to the atheistic alternatives, of left or right. To Heidegger, on the right, man's personal existence was a unique and transcendent possibility, rooted in immediate temporal relationships, which achieves authenticity in the capacity to face nothingness, by living itself out in the full acceptance of death.[5] Sartre, holding that belief in God is irreconcilable with belief in human freedom, moves along similar lines. The huge anxiety of man arises from his need to create his own values and his lack of certainty that he is on the right track. How miserable it is to have to face life without divine support! 'It is distressing that God does not exist. ... Man, with no support and no aid, is condemned every moment to invent man.'[6] The only solace is what Sartre calls 'total engagement', moral action which gives a man solidarity with lovers of freedom against its enemies.[7]

To John Paul, the stoical heroism of Heidegger and Sartre, which is nothing more than a defiant gesture in a framework of disbelief, becomes meaningful only when it is recognized that the impulse behind it is, precisely, the urge towards God. It is conveyed in Tertullian's luminous phrase *anima naturaliter Christiana*, a soul which is Christian from its origin and is created by or derived from the inescapability of the word 'God'. This notion of Christian humanism has been developed most effectively by Karl Rahner, to whom John Paul is obviously indebted no less than to Pascal. The existence of the word and concept 'God', Rahner argues, is the only thing which brings man face to face with the single whole of reality and the single whole of his own existence in it. If that word 'God' did not exist, those wholes would not exist either. We would be conscious only of the separate fragments of reality and of our lives, like the lesser creatures. If God disappeared, man would become less self-conscious. As Rahner puts it: 'Man would have forgotten the totality and its ground, ... would have forgotten that he had forgotten. ... He would have ceased being a man. He would have regressed to the level of a clever animal.' The race might survive in a biological sense, even retain its technology, but it 'would die a collective death and regress back into a colony of unusually resourceful animals'.[8]

This is the origin of John Paul's notion that the death of God would involve the death of man, that man's existence and God's are inextricably entangled. All human experience, properly understood, is experience of God, and therefore to confess belief in God is to embark on the quest for truth and meaning, and the freedom men find in God and God alone. The essence of Christian humanism is that man is driven by some interior force to realize his full personality; that the force is from God, in the form of grace; and that the realization is towards God, through the incarnation of his Son.

These are complex thoughts to present to a mass audience. One of the problems which confronts the modern church is how to democratize its new theology. Of course this particular difficulty has arisen many times before. It is partly a matter of language. In the early church, for instance, trinitarian concepts and christology were developed in Greek and imperfectly presented in Latin: that was one reason why the Latin and the Greek churches drifted apart. Existential theology was developed mainly in German and it is not easy for Anglo-Saxons or Latins to follow, even when they are comparatively well educated. Rahner, for instance, has felt obliged to defend his own obscurity by observing: 'True theology is precisely a reflection of the fact that there is only one who reconciles truths, who integrates them into his own truth: God,

who has promised us that his truth will one day be our happiness.'
He adds: 'The Christian has less "ultimate" answers which
he could throw off with a "now the matter's clear" than anyone
else.'[9]

That may be so, but it is not an explanation that the supreme
pontiff of a church of 750 million souls can regard as sufficient.
Catholicism has always sought to illuminate its presentation of
theological mysteries with signs and symbols, metaphors and par-
ables. That is why a man like John Paul parts company with
theologians such as Rahner (and Küng) when they rule out the
validity of what they term 'naïve theism'. Rahner, for instance, is
fond of remarking that such a theist believes in a God as illusory as
the one in which atheists refuse to believe – a naïve God he defines
as one 'who operates and functions as an individual existent alongside of other existents and who would thus, as it were, be a member
of the larger household of all reality'. In fact most Christians have
always believed in such a God and always will. It is not for
theologians to censor the pictures which divine grace places in the
minds of ordinary men. Rahner's argument indeed leads him to the
absurd paradox that this kind of theism, the demotic theology of
the masses, is concealed atheism and vice versa, 'and in the sense
ultimately no one can say of himself whether he believes in God or
not'. Such a line of inquiry is profitless.

It is at this point in the argument about the church in the world
of today that John Paul's long and varied pastoral experience gives
him sure guidance. He knows that there need be no fundamental
conflict between popular religion, however naïve its mental images,
and the most sophisticated theology, so long as it enshrines Christian truth. Like most priests with much experience, he suspects
that a simple Christian is less likely to fall into serious error than a
scholar anxious to keep up with the latest intellectual fashion. Pride
is the great precursor of anti-truth. It is not a sin to which the poor
and the uneducated are particularly prone. In his experience, too,
the Catholic intelligentsia are by no means immune to the herd
instinct which proved so fatal to the Gadarene swine.

John Paul's analysis of the evangelical task facing the church
seems to run as follows. There are two false roads and a true one.
The first false road is to offer a church of compromise, with enough

relaxation of rigour to keep the indifferent and the lax within the movement of faith, and enough intellectual spice to attract the educated. This would take the church further out into the world, but in his view would lose it in the wilderness of political activism, permissive morality and secularism. The church would cease to be holy and would become primarily a welfare institution, with a decreasingly firm belief in an increasingly nebulous deity.

The second false road is to retreat from the openness of the Council, retire into the fortress and lift up the drawbridge against the modern world again. The church would preserve its truth intact, more fiercely than ever perhaps, but cease to evangelize. This is the route the Jews took. But it is in total conflict with the universalist principle of Catholicism. The attempt to follow it under Pius XII ended in sterility and spiritual drought. John XXIII's decision to call the Council and open up the church was the right one and cannot be reversed. The old fortress church is now a picturesque ruin, good for nostalgia and tourists but no longer serviceable.

Besides, to take the route back into traditionalism would be to ignore the matchless opportunities opening up for Catholic truth. John Paul does not approach the problem, as do advocates of both the false roads, in a defensive or pessimistic spirit. He sometimes has gloomy thoughts about the future of mankind, for he has long experience of the horrific potential of the evil forces loose in the world. He does not flinch, but he fears them with a prudent apprehension. His anxieties, however, do not embrace the church: quite the contrary. The de-Christianizing of Europe, the de-sacralization of institutions and society, are, he believes, at the root of the unprecedented upsurge of violence of which man now seems to be the helpless victim. He thinks that people are beginning to recognize the connection between the two. We have caught our first glimpse of a totally secularized world and it has filled us with terror. We are learning, through bitter experience, that the expulsion of God from our lives denatures man and leads first to barbarism and ultimately to bestiality. The church waves her lamp and beckons us back, and horrified humanity is beginning to heed the light. Thus, in the fifth century AD, did the frightened citizens of a stricken empire turn to Christianity; and St Augustine, in his embattled cathedral, rejoiced that the city of God would be built from the ruins of the city of the world. Today Christian humanism again offers the alternative to disorder.

In these circumstances John Paul believes that Catholicism should assert both its doctrinal rigour and its concern for mass evangelism. The two do not exclude, they complement each other. The note he seeks to strike might be termed enlightened populism. He does not think that the great central clarities of Christianity make uncomfortable bedfellows with the pieties of the masses. Certainly they live easily together in his own breast. So it has always been. Gibbon's celebrated sneer that 'the sublime and simple theology of the primitive Christians ... was degraded by the introduction of a popular mythology which tended to restore the reign of polytheism',[10] poses a false dichotomy in Christianity between a sophisticated élite and the sophisticated masses dragging it back into paganism. In fact the writings of late antiquity show that the cult of the saints, the outstanding characteristic of popular religion, was sponsored by the greatest doctors of the church, such as St Ambrose and St Augustine, and celebrated by its most distinguished poets, such as Paulinus of Nola and Prudentius.[11] It was St Jerome who turned the cult of the holy places in Jerusalem into the pivot of his religion, and it was Gregory the Great who urged his missionaries to appeal to the hearts and imaginations of their converts as well as their heads.

John Paul stands firmly and unapologetically in this warm and honoured tradition. On his first pontifical visit to Latin America, in January 1979, he made directly for the great shrine of the Virgin at Guadalupe, where a cloak is preserved bearing what is believed to be the imprint of her dark, Indian-style features.[12] Some years before, the Bishop of Cuernavaca, a lofty progressive, had opposed the construction of a new basilica at Guadalupe on the grounds that the money would be more sensibly spent on social projects. John Paul preferred the path of divine folly, insisted on visiting the shrine and, to the general satisfaction, placed all the people of Mexico under the Virgin's protection.[13]

John Paul has no fear and no suspicion of *religiosidad popular*, wherever it is to be found. He does not see it as a sociological phenomenon, as an item of living anthropology to be studied and theorized about, but as a message from human hearts, to be heard and heeded. In many of the areas where the number of Catholics is growing, hybrid and syncretistic religious cults are to be found in abundance. There has, for instance, been a rapid growth of Afro-Catholic cults in Brazil.[14] In South, Central and East Africa, the luxuriant profusion of different Zion and healing sects is one of the outstanding features of Christianity. They are much closer to the mainstream of Christian faith than was at first believed.[15] Far from constituting, as progressive Christian observers once confidently asserted, a subdued form of political protest, a reaction to the colour bar or a flaunting of African as opposed to 'colonial' values in religion, they express the yearning of ordinary humanity, in the bewildering new cities, for the consolations of religious belief. That is why they have so much in common, despite geographical and cultural disparity, with the popular religion of Latin America, where a similar convergence of villagers on the cities has produced similar needs. It is a response to alienation. As such, it is not so very different from the devotion of the urbanized former peasants of Poland to their Black Virgin of Czestochowa. It confirms John Paul's confident belief that the answer to modern alienation is not pseudo-Utopian secularity but the re-humanizing process of Christian belief.

The Greeks, said St Paul, search for wisdom, the Jews look for a sign. It is the merit of Christianity to have perceived from its origins that men and women require both. As John Paul's favourite psalm insists, God and his truth are to be found everywhere, in shrines as well as books. So John Paul, in his travels, always seeks out the holy places. He honours the saints. He reveres their authentic relics. Ground hallowed by sanctity or suffering for the faith is sacred to him. Such places as Lourdes, Fatima, Santiago de Compostella, Knock and Loretto, as well as his own beloved Czestochowa, are to him outposts of divinity in the Christian landscape. These celestial manifestations are not exemplars of a dying religious mode but of a continuing, even growing, presence of God in the world, and of the human response to that epiphany. He also sees them as testifying to the power of the Virgin Mary's prayers: the love and the lore of Mary are at the centre of his devotional life. In these respects, as in many others, John Paul is at one with the great majority of ordinary Catholics throughout the world.

John Paul's Christian humanism, then, is a religion of the emotions as well as the mind. Love is its principle of action, the source of being. In his 1976 Lenten sermons in Rome, he included a powerful commentary on the earliest sections of Genesis. Why, he asked, did God create the world? He answered, because love creates the good: 'And God saw everything that he had made, and, behold, it was very good.'[16] 'The motive for creation is love,' John Paul remarked; and he added the remarkable observation: 'Throughout the description of Genesis the heart can be heard beating.'[17]

In accordance with the same principle of love as the source of action, human beings respond to God's creation by sacrifice, with Jesus Christ as their exemplar and the source of the grace which gives them the strength to make it. By sacrifice each man and woman offers an individual atonement for original sin, the concept expressing that radical fault in human nature which, as Pascal says, is the dark side to the stupendous glory of man. Thus humanity is empowered by grace to complete the redemption by love.

Coming from a country where Catholicism has traditionally been seen as the ultimate source of enlightenment and culture, John Paul has always identified true religion with civilization. Christianity is the fountainhead of our values, perhaps more so today than ever before. In his 1976 Lenten series, he quoted some remarks by the great Polish scholar Leszek Kolakowski, originally published in a Polish atheist weekly. Kolakowski listed the five salient European values derived from Christianity as follows: the supplanting of law by love; the ideal of an end to arrogance in human relationships; the truth that man does not live by bread alone; the end of the notion of chosen races with the right to rule over others; and the proposition that the world suffers from an organic imperfection.[18] To which John Paul adds: these values, and others like them, live. They are embodied in a visible, concrete presence in the world today: the holy, Roman, catholic and apostolic church.

In our volatile and violent society the existence of a great international ecclesiastical community, which is committed to the defence of such values, should be a source of comfort. That community has been sick. It is now recovering its health and energy. John Paul has been its skilled and resolute physician. But his task is not over. It may be that the more positive and original portion of it is to come. By restoring the Catholic Church to its old vigour he is performing an important service to humanity. The presence of this genial philosopher-evangelist on St Peter's seat in Rome is a powerful reassurance, to quote the words of Gladstone, that 'the resources of civilization are not exhausted'.

References to Sources

PART ONE *The Making of a Pope*

1 The Forge

1. For a general exposition of Roman Catholicism, see J. L. McKenzie, *The Roman Catholic Church* (London 1969).
2. J. Lécuyer, *Études sur la collégialité épiscopale* (Paris 1964).
3. For Karol Wojtyla's early life see the following: George Blazynski, *John Paul II: a Man from Krakow* (London 1979); Mary Craig, *Man from a Far Country* (London 1979); Mieczyslaw Malinski, *Pope John Paul II: the Life of my Friend Karol Wojtyla* (London 1979); James Oram, *The People's Pope* (Sydney 1979).
4. Craig, *Man*, p. 35.
5. Written for the Italian magazine *Vita e Pensiero*; reprinted as 'Frontiers of Europe', *The Tablet*, 23 June 1979.
6. H. O. Evennett, *The Spirit of the Counter-Reformation* (Cambridge 1968).
7. Blazynski, *John Paul II*, p. 49.
8. *Ibid.*, p. 41.
9. 'Marble Floor' and 'The Quarry' are in *Easter Vigil and Other Poems*, translated by Jerzy Peterkiewicz (London 1979), pp. 48, 25-33.
10. *Ibid.*, pp. 40, 41.
11. Blazynski, *John Paul II*, p. 45: for another view see Malinski, *Pope John Paul II*.
12. Testimony of Joseph L. Lichten, Rome representative of B'nai Brith; Blazynski, *John Paul II*, p. 50.
13. Letter to Madame Pozniakowa, 21 January 1947: quoted in Blazynski, *John Paul II*, p. 57.
14. For a general introduction to the problem, see David E. Roberts, *Existentialism and Religious Belief* (New York 1957).
15. For phenomenology, see H. Spiegelberg, *The Phenomenological Movement*, 2 vols (The Hague 1965).
16. Blazynski, *John Paul II*, p. 65.
17. Professor Pierre David, 'The Church in Poland from its Origins

to 1250' in *Cambridge History of Poland* (Cambridge 1950), I, pp. 61-2.

18. Extracts from early lives of St Stanislas are edited by M. Perlbach in *Monumenta Germaniae Historica*, Scriptores, XXIX (1892), pp. 501-17.

19. David, *The Church in Poland*, p. 84.

20. For Pax, see Lukjan Blit, *The Eastern Pretender: Boleslaw Piasecki, His Life and Times* (London 1965).

21. Peter Raina, *Political Opposition in Poland 1954-77* (London 1978), pp. 406 ff.

22. Vincent C. Chrypinski, 'Polish Catholicism and Social Change', in B. R. Bociurkiw *et al.* (eds), *Religion and Atheism in the USSR and Eastern Europe* (London 1975), pp. 249-51.

23. *Ibid.*, pp. 241 ff.

24. Craig, *Man*, pp. 151-9.

25. For details, see Craig, *Man*, pp. 121-4.

26. Blazynski, *John Paul II*, p. 91.

27. Talk on Vatican Radio, 1963.

28. Speech published in *Osservatore Romano*, 1976.

29. Sermon, July 1978.

30. Sermon, July 1977.

2 The Summons

1. Blazynski, *John Paul II*, p. 106.

2. For example on West German TV, 1976.

3. For text of *Dignitatis Humanae*, see *Acta Apostolicae Sedis*, LVIII (Rome 1966).

4. Text, *ibid.*

5. Text in *Acta Apostolicae Sedis*, LVII (Rome 1965).

6. See Blazynski, *John Paul II*, pp. 107-10; Peter Hebblethwaite, *The Year of the Three Popes* (London 1978), pp. 176-7.

7. W. Daim, *Der Vatikan und der Osten* (Vienna 1967), p. 257.

8. *Ibid.*, p. 278.

9. Blazynski, *John Paul II*, p. 117.

10. Text of *Humanae Vitae* in P. Harris *et al.*, *On Human Life* (London 1968).

11. Published in English translation, London 1979.

12. For a sympathetic portrait of Paul VI, see John G. Clancy, *Apostle for Our Time: Pope John Paul VI* (London 1964).

13. Printed in *Acta Apostolicae Sedis*, LXVII (1975), pp. 609–45.
14. Hebblethwaite, *The Year*, pp. 46 ff.
15. Interview in news magazine *Panorama*, 16 August 1978.
16. For text etc., see London *Times*, 14 August 1978; *Tablet*, 19 August 1978.
17. For this conclave see Giancarlo Zizola, *Quale Papa?* (Rome 1977), pp. 160–72.
18. F. X. Murphy, the pseudonymous author of the series, 'Letters from Vatican City', in *Newsweek*, 11 September 1978.
19. *Il Giorno*, 29 August 1978.
20. *The Five Wounds of the Holy Church*, translated with an introduction by H. P. Liddon (London 1883); C. Leetham, *Life of Rosmini* (London 1957).
21. For the tiara and pallium see J. Braun, *Die liturgische Gewandung im Occident und Orient nach Ursprung und Endwicklung* (Berlin 1907), pp. 498–508, 620–76. See also C. A. Bouman, *Sacring and Crowning* (Groningen 1957).
22. Interview in *Gazzetta del Popolo*, 14 October 1978.
23. For nationalities of all the popes, see Friedrich Gontard, *The Popes*, trans. (London 1964), Appendix I.
24. Malinski, *Pope John Paul II*, p. 53.
25. Hebblethwaite, *The Year*, p. 141.
26. According to Cardinal Confalonieri, *ibid.*, pp. 151–2.
27. *The Pope Teaches*, published by the Catholic Truth Society, London 1979 onwards (continuous series published monthly). Statement on 22 August 1979, p. 374.
28. Hebblethwaite, *The Year*, p. 151.
29. *Annuario Ufficiale della Santa Sede* (Vatican City 1978).

3 The Mission

1. *The Pope Teaches*, 11 March 1979, p. 86.
2. See R. W. and A. J. Carlyle, *A History of Medieval Political Theory in the West* (London 1928), v, pp. 151–234; T. S. R. Boase, *Boniface VIII* (London 1933).
3. B. Tierney, *Foundations of the Conciliar Theory* (Cambridge 1955).
4. Hubert Jedin, *History of the Council of Trent*, trans. (London 1957 ff.); J. A. O'Donohoe, *Tridentine Seminary Legislation* (Louvain 1957); J. C. H. Aveling, *The Jesuits* (London 1981).
5. A. G. Dickens, *The Counter-Reformation* (London 1968).

6. Owen Chadwick, *The Popes and European Revolution* (Oxford 1981).
7. E. R. Y. Hales, *Pio Nono* (London 1954); Dom Cuthbert Butler, *The Vatican Council 1869-70* (London, 2nd ed. 1962).
8. L. P. Wallace, *Leo XIII* (Durham, North Carolina 1966).
9. P. Fernessole, *Pie X*, 2 vols (Paris 1952-3).
10. W. H. Peters, *Benedict XV* (Milwaukee 1959); P. Hughes, *Pius XI* (London 1937); O. Haleki, *Pius XII* (London 1954).
11. For John XXIII and the Council, see E. E. Y. Hales, *Pope John and his Revolution* (London 1965); Paul Johnson, *John XXIII* (London 1975).
12. Aveling, *The Jesuits*, pp. 355-65.
13. Peter Hebblethwaite, *The Papal Year* (London 1981).
14. *The Pope Teaches*, 8 August 1979, p. 369.
15. *Ibid.*, 16 September 1979, p. 382.
16. Figures from the *Annuario Ufficiale*. See Peter Nichols, *The Pope's Divisions: the Roman Catholic Church Today* (London 1981), pp. 22-38.
17. Hebblethwaite, *The Year*, pp. 21 ff.
18. Nichols, *The Pope's Divisions*, pp. 24-5.
19. *Ibid.*, p. 35.
20. Malinski, *Pope John Paul II*, p. 97.

PART TWO *The Five Evils of the Age*

4 The Crucifixion of Man

1. John 3:16.
2. See Mary Wollstonecraft Shelley, *Frankenstein, or the Modern Prometheus* (London 1818).
3. See James Oram, *Pope John Paul II* (London 1979).
4. See for example his encyclical, *Dives in Misericordia* (Catholic Truth Society pamphlet, London 1980), pp. 57-9.
5. See J. M. Bochenski, 'Marxism-Leninism and Religion' in B. R. Bociurkiw *et al.* (eds), *Religion and Atheism in the USSR and Eastern Europe* (London 1975).
6. James Bentley, 'Prometheus versus Christ in the Christian-Marxist Dialogue', *Journal of Theological Studies*, October 1978.
7. Marx, *Grundrisse*, trans. Martin Nicholause (London 1973), p. 110.
8. K. Marx, F. Engels, *Collective Works*, I, p. 30.
9. For example, Roger Garaudy, *Marxism in the 20th Century*, trans.

(The Hague 1970); Ernest Bloch, *Karl Marx*, trans. (Bologna 1972). See Henry Chadwick, *Some Reflections on Conscience: Greek, Jewish and Christian* (London 1968), and for the proper interpretation of the myth, H. Lloyd-Jones, 'Zeus in Aeschylus', *Journal of Hellenic Studies*, LXXVI (1956).

10. Bochenski, *Marxism-Leninism*, p. 8.
11. Lenin's views on religion are typically set out in his letter to Maxim Gorki, 13 January 1913; relevant texts are in V. I. Lenin, *Religion and the Church* (Moscow 1969).
12. T. J. Blakeley, 'Soviet Writings on Atheism and Religion', *Studies in Soviet Thought*, 4 (1964); 5 (1965).
13. Cited in L. Schapiro and P. Reddaway (eds), *Lenin: the Man, the Theorist, the Leader: a Reappraisal* (London 1967).
14. *East Europe*, November 1967; see *ACEN News* (New York), March–April 1967.
15. Peter Prifti, 'Albania: towards an Atheist Society', in Bociurkiw, *Religion and Atheism*, p. 388.
16. Héllène Carrère d'Encausse, *Decline of an Empire: the Soviet Socialist Republics in Revolt* (New York 1979), p. 239.
17. Gerhard Simon, 'The Catholic Church and the Communist State in the Soviet Union and Eastern Europe', in Bociurkiw, *Religion and Atheism.*
18. *Ibid.*, p. 208.
19. *Ibid.*, p. 210. For the 1956 Polish agreement, see H. Stehle, *The Independent Satellite: Society and Politics in Poland since 1945* (London 1965), pp. 309-10.
20. V. Gsovski, *Church and State Behind the Iron Curtain* (New York 1955), pp. 41-2.
21. *The Pope Teaches*, June 1979.
22. *Redemptor Hominis: Encyclical letter on the Redemption of Man* (Catholic Truth Society, London, March 1979).
23. John 8:32.
24. *Acta Apostolicae Sedis*, LVIII (1966).
25. Craig, *Man*, pp. 16-19.
26. John Whale (ed.), *The Pope from Poland: an Assessment* (London 1980), pp. 126-44.
27. *Ibid.*, p. 158.
28. Whale, *The Pope*, pp. 155-6.
29. *The Pope Teaches*, 12 November 1980, p. 326.

30. V. I. Lenin, 'Socialism and Religion' in *Sochineniya* (Collected Works), XII, p. 142.
31. Marx, *Critique of the Hegelian Philosophy of Law*.
32. E.g. the Czech Protestant theologian J. M. Lochman in his *Church in a Marxist Society: a Czechoslovak View*.
33. Blazynski, *John Paul II*, pp. 122, 120.
34. *Ibid.*, pp. 138-9.
35. Sermon in June 1978, *ibid.*, p. 137.
36. *The Pope Teaches*, June 1980, pp. 182-4.
37. John Paul II, *Sign of Contradiction* (London 1979).
38. *Apocrypha*. Wisdom 13:3-4.
39. 1 Corinthians 8:1.
40. *Sign of Contradiction*, pp. 12-15.
41. H. de Lubac, *Athéisme et sense de l'homme* (Paris 1969).
42. Pastoral Letter, 8 May 1977; *The Acting Person*, trans. (London 1979).
43. *Sign of Contradiction*, pp. 140-1.
44. *Dives in Misericordia*, On the Mercy of God (Catholic Truth Society, London 1980).
45. *Ibid.*, pp. 5-6.
46. *Ibid.*, pp. 11-12, 8.
47. *Ibid.*, pp. 30-1.
48. Revelation 21:4.
49. *Dives in Misericordia*, p. 45.
50. *Ibid.*, p. 60.
51. *Hamlet*, Act II, Scene ii.
52. *Dives in Misericordia*, pp. 70-2.
53. Luke 1:51-3.

5 The Temptation of Violence

1. *Sign of Contradiction*, p. 85.
2. For an introduction to the problem, see Edward Norman, *Christianity in the Southern Hemisphere* (Oxford 1981).
3. Ivan Vallier, *Catholicism, Social Control and Modernization in Latin America* (Santa Cruz 1970), and Vallier's essay in Henry Landsberger (ed.), *The Church and Social Change in Latin America* (Notre Dame 1970), pp. 14-27.
4. Norman, *Christianity*, p. 27; R. A. Humphries, *Tradition and Revolt in Latin America* (London 1965); Magnus Morner, *The Political and*

References to Sources

Economic Activities of the Jesuits in the La Plata Region (Stockholm 1953).

5. Norman, *Christianity*, pp. 84–9.
6. For such ideas, see Eduardo Frei Montalva, *Sentido y Forma de una política* (Santiago 1951); F. C. Turner, *Catholicism and Political Development in Latin America* (Chapel Hill 1971).
7. Gerald M. Costello, *Mission to Latin America: the Successes and Failures of a 20th-century Crusade* (Maryknoll, New York 1979).
8. See Peter Hackett, sj, 'Brazilian Awakening: an encounter with the renewed church of the basic Christian communities', *The Month*, October 1979.
9. Nicholas Lash, 'Decomposition or Re-birth? Recent directions in Roman Catholic theology', Part Four, *The Month*, October 1979.
10. 'La Iglesia de América Latina de Medellín a Puebla', *Chile-America*, June–July 1978.
11. *Segunda Conferencia General del Episcopado Latinoamericano, Medellín, Septembre 1968* (6th ed., Buenos Aires 1972), p. 95.
12. *The Month*, February 1979.
13. Gerald MacCarthy, 'What Really Happened at Puebla', *The Month*, March 1979.
14. Pablo Rámos, op: 'New Light on the Pope in Mexico', *The Month*, April 1979.
15. Text in *The Pope Teaches*, January 1979, pp. 32 ff.
16. Printed as Catholic Truth Society pamphlet S 312, London 1978.
17. Catholic Truth Society pamphlet Do 349.
18. *The Pope Teaches*, 29 January 1979, p. 58.
19. *Ibid.*, 25 January 1979, p. 29.
20. *Ibid.*, 30 January 1979, p. 56.
21. Full text in *The Pope Teaches*, 29 September 1979, pp. 392 ff.
22. *Ibid.*, pp. 402, 411, 416.
23. *Ibid.*, 8 December 1979, pp. 528–33.
24. *Ibid.*, 30 June 1980, pp. 195 ff.
25. Hebblethwaite, *The Papal Year*, p. 92.
26. *The Pope Teaches*, July 1980, pp. 203–4.
27. *Ibid.*, pp. 205–6.
28. *Ibid.*, pp. 211–20.
29. *The Guardian*, 18 April 1981.
30. *Laborem Exercens* (Catholic Truth Society pamphlet, London 1981), pp. 41–9.

6 Secularization by Stealth

1. *Dives in Misericordia*, p. 57.
2. *The Pope Teaches*, September 1979, pp. 385, 402, 456.
3. Luke 16:19 ff. *The Pope Teaches*, October 1979, pp. 452-3.
4. *Ibid.*, April 1980, p. 118.
5. Jeremiah 2:20.
6. *Sign of Contradiction*, p. 32 ff.
7. *Dives in Misericordia*, p. 61.
8. *The Pope Teaches*, 7 October 1979, p. 467.
9. *Ibid.*, 13 January 1979, pp. 14-15.
10. Peter Hebblethwaite, *The Papal Year*, p. 34.
11. Blazynski, *John Paul II*, pp. 145-6.
12. J. N. D. Kelly, *Jerome: His Life, Writings and Controversies* (London 1975).
13. Hebblethwaite, *The Papal Year*, p. 22.
14. *The Pope Teaches*, 29 April 1979.
15. Luke 8:2-3.
16. Nichols, *The Pope's Divisions*, pp. 220, 226.
17. Whale, *The Pope*, p. 213.
18. Nichols, *The Pope's Divisions*, p. 229.
19. James Hitchcock, *Pope John Paul II and American Catholicism* (The National Committee of Catholic Laymen, New York 1980).
20. Blazynski, *John Paul II*, p. 88.
21. *The Pope Teaches*, September 1980, pp. 265 ff.
22. Hebblethwaite, *The Papal Year*, p. 72.
23. For official Catholic teaching on marriage, see the Second Vatican Council constitution, *Gaudium et Spes*, Nos 47-52.
24. *The Pope Teaches*, 12 October 1980, p. 299.
25. *Ibid.*, p. 301.
26. *Ibid.*, pp. 313-17.
27. See, for example, *Harper's Magazine*, February 1981.

7 Imperilled Certitudes

1. Quoted in Craig, *Man*.
2. Catholic Truth Society pamphlet Do 507.
3. For the archives, see Owen Chadwick, *Catholicism and History: the Opening of the Vatican Archives* (Cambridge 1978).
4. H. Denzinger and A. Schönmetzer (eds), *Enchiridion Symbolorum*, 34th ed. (Friedburg 1967).

5. There is a translation of *Lumen Gentium* in Appendix II of Xavier Rynne, *The Third Session: the Debates and Decrees of Vatican Council II* (London 1965); see especially pp. 311, 313.
6. *The Pope Teaches*, 15 May 1980, pp. 165-6.
7. Nichols, *The Pope's Divisions*, p. 98.
8. Quoted in Blazynski, *John Paul II*, p. 87.
9. *The Pope Teaches*, 1 June 1980, pp. 117-18.
10. *The Times*, 18 April 1981.
11. For Fr Kolbe, see Craig, *Man*, pp. 127-36.
12. Catholic Truth Society pamphlet Do 507. St Augustine's actual words were 'On your behalf I am a bishop, among you I am a Christian', sermon 340, *Patrologia Latina*, XXXVIII, 1483.
13. Quoted in Whale, *The Pope*, pp. 155-6.
14. *Sign of Contradiction*, p. 129.
15. *The Pope Teaches*, 1 October 1979, p. 420.
16. Matthew 19:12.
17. Catholic Truth Society pamphlet Do 507, pp. 30-4.
18. The Constitution on the Sacred Liturgy, December 1963, is in *Acta Apostolicae Sedis*, LVI (Rome 1964), pp. 95-157.
19. *The Pope Teaches*, 3 May 1980, p. 137.
20. R. McA. Brown, *The Ecumenical Revolution: an Interpretation of the Catholic-Protestant Dialogue* (London 1969).
21. *The Pope Teaches*, 15 May 1980, pp. 166-7.
22. See T. Ware, *The Orthodox Church* (Harmondsworth 1963).
23. J. N. D. Kelly, *Early Christian Creeds* (London 1950), pp. 358-67.

8 The Shadow of Heresy

1. See Nicholas Lash in *The Month*, July-October 1979.
2. Whale, *The Pope*, p. 248.
3. *The Pope Teaches*, 15 November 1980, p. 339.
4. Psalm 139; *Sign of Contradiction*, pp. 8-10.
5. Psalm 111.
6. *The Pope Teaches*, 10 July 1980.
7. *Ibid.*, 1 October 1979, p. 419.
8. *Sign of Contradiction*, pp. 27-36.
9. *Ibid.*, p. 11. See C. H. Tavard, *Transiency and Permanence: the Nature of Theology according to St Bonaventure* (New York 1954).
10. See Gerald Brenan, *St John of the Cross: his Life and Poetry* (Cambridge 1973), pp. 96-7; for St John's life, see Crisógono de Jesús, OCD,

Life of St John of the Cross, trans. (London 1958). His works are translated in Alison Peers, *Works of St John of the Cross*, 3 vols (London 1934-5).

11. Brenan, *St John of the Cross*, pp. 101-37.
12. For this analysis, see P. Lucien-Marie de Saint-Joseph, OCD, 'The Devil in the Writings of St John of the Cross', in Charles Moeller (ed.), *Satan* (London 1951).
13. *The Ascent of Mount Carmel*, I, p. 1; *The Dark Night of the Soul*, II, p. 21.
14. *Ascent*, II, p. 11; II, p. 21.
15. Peers, *Complete Works*, III, p. 224; *Ascent*, III, p. 29; *Dark Night*, II, p. 2.
16. *Ascent*, II, p. 21; *Collected Works*, III, p. 300; III, p. 224.
17. *The Pope Teaches*, 13 September 1980, p. 293.
18. Text in Jacques Maritain, *St Thomas Aquinas, Angel of the School*, trans. (London 1933), Appendix I, pp. 204-6.
19. *The Pope Teaches*, 17 November 1979, pp. 2-3.
20. From *The Essence of Christianity*, translated by George Eliot (London 1954). See E. Kamenka, *The Philosophy of Ludwig Feuerbach* (London 1970).
21. In English translation, *Jesus: an Experiment in Christology* (London 1978).
22. *Ibid.*, pp. 570, 674.
23. Quoted in Whale, *The Pope*, p. 234.
24. For details of Küng's career and bibliography, see Hermann Häring and Karl-Joseph Küschel, *Hans Küng: his Work and his Way*, trans. (London 1979).
25. *Ibid.*, pp. 185-241.
26. *On Being a Christian*, trans. (London 1977), p. 133.
27. *Ibid.*, p. 130.
28. *Christ und Welt*, 5 March 1971.
29. Häring and Küschel, *Hans Küng*, pp. 94, 101, 127, 165, 163.
30. *The Pope Teaches*, 15 May 1980, pp. 162-3.
31. *Ibid.*, 17 May 1979, pp. 333-4.
32. John 14:23-4; *The Pope Teaches*, 14 January 1980, pp. 19-21; 31 January, pp. 42-9.
33. Hebblethwaite, *The Papal Year*, pp. 55-7.

References to Sources

PART THREE *Sources of Authority*

9 Human Instruments

1. *Christus Dominus*, Catholic Truth Society pamphlet Do 356.
2. Nichols, *The Pope's Divisions*, p. 119.
3. Giancarlo Zizola, 'The Pope's Cabinet', *The Tablet*, 23 June 1979.
4. Nichols, *The Pope's Divisions*, p. 161.
5. *The Pope Teaches*, 11 July 1979, p. 353.
6. *Ibid.*, 10 July 1980, p. 221.
7. See, for instance, Corrado Pallenberg, *The Vatican Finances* (London 1971).
8. *Ibid.*, pp. 141–50.
9. *Ibid.*, pp. 173–5.
10. For one unconfirmed account of the Vatican's connection with Sindona, see Charles Levinson, *Vodka-Cola* (London n.d.), pp. 143 ff.
11. For Peter's Pence in England see *Dictionary of English Church History* (London 1912), pp. 457–8.
12. Address to the curia, 28 June 1980.
13. *Osservatore Romano*, 13 June 1980.
14. *The Spectator*, 7 March 1981.
15. See 1 Corinthians 1:27.
16. *The Times*, 8 June 1981.
17. For text see Catholic Truth Society pamphlet Do 511.
18. *The Pope Teaches*, 18 July 1979, pp. 356–7.
19. *Sollicitudo Omnium Ecclesiarum*, published 24 June 1969.
20. Mario Oliveri, *The Representatives: the Real Nature and Function of Papal Legates* (Gerrards Cross 1980).
21. *Ecclesiae Sanctae*, published 6 August 1966.
22. See James Broderick, SJ, *The Origins of the Jesuits; The Progress of the Jesuits* (London 1940, 1946).
23. Aveling, *The Jesuits*, pp. 355–6.
24. *Ibid.*, pp. 369–71.
25. For the use of the 'discipline' by the reformed Carmelites see Crisógono de Jesús, *Life of St John*, pp. 39, 128.
26. See, for example, *The Times*, 12 January 1981.

10 Divine Agency

1. *Provincial Letters* (New York 1941), p. 597.
2. Roberts, *Existentialism*, p. 33.

3. *Pensées*, No. 434.
4. *Ibid.*, No. 430.
5. *Sein und Zeit* (1927), translated into English as *Existence and Being* (1962).
6. *Existentialism* (New York 1947), p. 28.
7. See *L'Être et le néant: essai d'ontologie phénoménologique* (Paris 1943).
8. Karl Rahner, *Foundations of Christian Faith*, trans. (London 1978), pp. 47–8.
9. See Nicholas Lash in *The Month*, September 1979.
10. *Decline and Fall of the Roman Empire* (London 1776–81), Chapter 28.
11. For a recent exposition of this view see Peter Brown, *The Cult of the Saints: its Rise and Function in Latin Christianity* (London 1981).
12. For belief in the Virgin of Guadalupe, see Gregory Reck, *In the Shadow of Tlaloc: Life in a Mexican Village* (London 1978), p. 37.
13. Norman, *Christianity in the Southern Hemisphere*, pp. 60–1.
14. Roger Bastide, *The African Religions of Brazil* (Baltimore 1978).
15. See Bengt G. M. Sundkler, *Bantu Prophets in South Africa* (2nd ed., Oxford 1961), as corrected by his later study *Zulu Zion and Some Swazi Zionists* (Oxford 1976).
16. Genesis 1:31.
17. *Sign of Contradiction*, pp. 21–2.
18. *Ibid.*, pp. 106–7.

Index

A figure 2 in brackets immediately after a page reference indicates that there are two separate references to the subject on that page.

Index

Index

Index

Rhapsody Theatre, 8
Roman Catholic Church, Catholicism,
  3, 124-5, 128-9, 137, 185-6, 194-5;
  and reform, 39; an enormous
  organization, 57; in 'Third World',
  58-9 (*see also* Africa; Latin
  America); and social questions,
  politics, 59-60, 80-1, 83-4, 85, 87,
  88, 97, 102-3 (*see also* freedom;
  human rights); evangelical task,
  60-1, 190-2; in Eastern Europe, 70
  (*see also under* Poland); *see also*
  bishops; Counter-Reformation;
  pope; priests; theology; Vatican
Romano Pontifici Eligendo, 34-5
Rome, 56, 59, 169-70
Rosmini-Serbati, Antonio, 39-40, 51
Rozycki, Fr, 118
Ruether, Rosemary Radford, 115
Runcie, Dr, 140

Sacerdotalis Caelibatus, 135
Sachsenhausen, 8
sacrifice, 194
Sacrorum Antistitum, 147
St John Lateran, 130
St John's Gospel, 72
St Peter's, Rome, 9, 130
Salesian Order, 17
São Paulo, 59
Sapieha, Mgr Adam, 10-11
Sapientia Christiana, 177
Sartre, Jean-Paul, 188
Satan, *see* evil
Schillebeeckx, Fr Edward, 37, 156-7,
  161, 178
science, and Christianity, 149
secularization, materialism, 104, 105-
  9, 122-3
Seper, Cardinal, 159, 162
sex, sexual behaviour, 32, 108-14,
  117, 118-22; *see also* birth-control;
  family; marriage
Silvestrini, Archbishop Achille, 171
Sindona, Michele, 173
Siri, Cardinal Giuseppe, 38, 41, 45
Sixtus V, Pope, 170

Slipyi, Cardinal Josef, 30, 141
social questions, church and, *see under*
  Roman Catholic Church
socialism, Soviet-type, 78; *see also*
  Marxism-Leninism
Solidarity Movement, 76-7, 80
Somolo, Mgr Eduardo Martinez, 172
Soviet Union, 4, 15-16 ('Stalin'),
  30-1, 68-9, 70
Spellman, Cardinal Francis, 173
Stalin, Joseph, 15-16, 68, 151
Stanislas, St, 14, 73, 80-1
Stephen II, Pope, 43
Stroessner, General Alfredo, 88
structuralism, 151
Suenens, Cardinal Léon-Joseph, 38
Syllabus of Errors, 51
synods, general, *see under* bishops

Tang Yiming, Mgr Dominic, 176
Tashkent Moslem Conference (1970),
  70
Teilhard de Chardin, Pierre, 180
Teresa, St, of Avila, 45, 151
Teutonic Knights, 27
theatre, 6-8
'theolibs', 90, 92
theology, 146-65; 'liberation', 37,
  90-3, 96, 181; moral, 54; dogmatic,
  55; 'political', 90; 'engaged', 147;
  German, 154; Dutch school, 156;
  existential, 189
'Third World', 58-9
Tisserant, Cardinal, 44
Torres, Camilio, 88
totalitarian atheism, 65-84, 144-5
Trent, Council of, 49
triumphalism, 49
Trujillo, Archbishop López, 93
Turkey, John Paul II's visit to, 142
Tygodnik, Powszechny, 7, 22, 73(2)
Tyranowski, Jan, 9-10
Tyrrell, George, 147

Ukraine, 15, 16, 70, 141-2
Unam Sanctam, 49
Uniate churches, 15, 16, 70, 141-2